Dice Play and Origin of Chess In Sanskrit Literature

Dice Play and Origin of Chess In Sanskrit Literature

PROF. C. PANDURANGA BHATTA

Motilal Banarsidass Publications

MOTILAL BANARSIDASS
PUBLICATIONS
4741/23, Ansari Road, Daryaganj, New Delhi - 110002 (India)
Email: *mlbd@mlbd.com* | *sales@mlbd.com* | *exports@mlbd.com*
Website: *www.mlbd.com*

Dice Play and Origin of Chess In Sanskrit Literature
by
Prof. C. Panduranga Bhatta

First Edition Published in 2022

Published in India by Motilal Banarsidass Publications

ISBN : 978-93-91759-08-7 (HB)

Printed and bound in India

FOREWORD BY MANFRED A.J. EDER

Once upon a Time...

How many thousand books have been written about CHESS, the Indian Game Caturanga?

All we know: the number is as good as uncountable. And how many books have been written on DICE-PLAY? I would expect easily countable!

This comparison is the more surprising since the History of the Game of Chess goes only 1500 years back, while the History of Dice-Play and Dice-Games is so old that know-body knows!

R.C. Bell summarizes in the introduction to Volume I of his book "Board-and Table-Games from many Civilizations": "*Ninety-one games are described and the oldest was played some five-thousand years ago.*"

Stephan Puille, once archaeologist at the Roemisch-GermanischeZentralmuseunm in Mainz (Germany), delegated in 1994/95 to excavations at Durankulak on the Black See in Bulgaria, discovered four knucklebones (Astragalus) which were dated "*late copper time*", i.e., 3500 BC, the earliest find in Europe, which even out-dates the age of gaming-pieces and dice of the Harappan-Culture, excavated in Mohenjo-Daro and Lothal, witnesses of the earliest Indus civilization. Ulrich Schädler reported of knucklebones used for gaming 5000 BC; and "Boards" (Planograms) are known from 6-7000 BC and even from the Neolithic era.

So – the present re-publication of ***"Dice-Play in Sanskrit Literature"*** expanded by ***"The Origin of Chess in Sanskrit Literature***" in a compilation with several further articles on the subject by Professor Dr. C. Panduranga Bhatta justifies an elementary and principal look through the keyhole into the far distant past to frame his eminent studies.

I) Gaming earlier than Speech? — Some Arguments of Support[1]

The American Anthropologist Ian Tattersall published (2002) his view in "Spektrum der Wissenschaft", a German scientific magazine, that the ability to exchange speech was the essential impact on the evolution and development of the human brain, i.e., to enable mankind to think. His remarkable paper was challenging for the reason that it did not take into account the playing instinct in human beings, i.e., the influence of this instinct on the cognition and growth of consciousness for *Homo Sapiens.* My own assumption discussed with him:

The experience of life instinctively led to discoveries in neighboring surroundings and the environmental stimuli inspired intuition. Observations and imitations were the initial self-generated results which advanced human consciousness and the faculty of understanding. Since the archaic phenomenon of the playing instinct and its manifestation almost certainly predates the invention of speech it does not follow that the ability to exchange speech is the sole significant element in human kinds learning to think.

Tattersall's suggestion (in short translated from German) was to look for a *cultural trigger* in understanding our superior ability to think. Could Gaming have been this catalyst?

The cause for gaming lies in nature. The objects with which human beings played were primeval. Archaic natural articles, "things", caused the discovery of items suitable to be understood as 'toys', meaning something to play with.

---

1 Complete article in German in preparation for printing; complete translation (by M.A.J. Eder & Ajinkya Lele) in "Proceedings" of "Playing with Memories" by InStuCen, Mumbai, 2021

The learning process may have gone via "*assigned objects*" – to serve a certain purpose,to "*designed objects*" – to represent something, which transformed ideas into images. Messages received shape as a visual meaning, turned into dimensional objects.

Gaming = *to play with something*, game-playing = *on a determined territory*, gambling = *requiring calculation and symbolic mental processes* within which later interpretations created realities – for intellectual game-playing eventually ending up, for example,in Dice, Gamesmen, Chess-Figures, and the like.

II) How Game-Playing came about ... – a Probability[2]

Where it happened, how it happened ... who can really tell? But one thing we can be relatively sure of: the history and development of game-playing is closely related to the history of mankind, humanity itself.

Waters flowed and circled, polishing pebbles in the stream, winds moved branches, twigs, leaves. The weather was a working force – and man was there, observing: Noticing how stones got shaped and polished by water, how branches waved to each other in the winds, arranging themselves to geometrical configurations and patterns when a strong blow snapped them off. From there, human's capacity for fantasy and experimentation probably triggered the urge to play. The interplay of light and shadows animated human-made interpretations and reproductions.

The observation of animals while hunting; races, contests, competition, something which we nowadays call sports, the desire to measure one's strength, but also to test one's talents, skill, and luck: these probably were some of the primeval phenomena that were responsible for the transposition of life-experience into a world of play.

From hunting to running races, from races to contests,

2 Translated from the first published version in German in "Schach-Journal" 1/1991

there was some common evolutionary principle at work: as from pebbles buried in the sand or the earth in the game called "Sey", from the cowries later still used in the game of "Pachisi" for example, or from ram's bones used for fortune-telling or as dice - generalizing: from natural objects used for play to objects specially crafted as something to play with, e.g. gaming-pieces.

Firstly, objects became fashioned into geometric shapes, were turned into representatives bearing symbolic character to end up in multiply created toys, figures, eventually picturing humans or animals in their natural and social contexts. Also, rituals and religious practices are to be considered, in which talismans and tokens were used as instruments of magic and bewitchment, and therefore as instruments of power to obtain and maintain powers in force. Which takes us to the ornamental and decorative aspects of gaming-pieces, i.e., their individualization by design.

III) From Gaming Pieces to Chessmen - Which was the Way?[3]

Causative for toys was nature: primeval natural aids caused the invention of objects to play with. Playing was causative for gaming. Gaming was causative – even for the game of chess.

The oldest term for "*gaming-piece*" appears to be the Egyptian hieroglyph "*Dancer*", featuring exactly the abstract shape of a man = human being, consisting of 'head and body'. It was (mostly physical) realities which delivered the images and models for the understanding of toys, i.e., gaming-pieces to serve purpose and idea and concept.

Gods converted into idols; idols transformed into dolls. Animals became things to play with by appearing in gaming-pieces. Fantasy created "dogs" or a "woman's breast" (as

3 Excerpt from the Abstract of the paper presented at the 1st Colloquium "Board Games in Academia" in 1995 at Leiden, The Netherlands

described in the "Nard" – chapter of the Manasollasa) to become constructive design-guides for toys to play with – on gaming-planograms.

This seems to be the most plausible evolutionary development which might also have led from images of war to the creation of figurative interpretations of an (Indian) army to become the toys – for Caturanga in a didactic model to simulate war as the ancestors of gaming-pieces for Chess. Once for chess it was chariots, horse-riders, elephants and foot-soldiers, the king, and his advisor.

IV Dice in Chess?

At the 3rd Conference of Chess Collectors International (CCI) in June 1988 in Munich,Professor Dr. Joachim Petzold, Historian at the Berlin Brandenburgische Akademie derWissenschaften in Berlin presented – as a welcome guest – the essentials of his recently published book "Das Königliche Spiel – Die Kulturgeschichte des Schach".

Core-point was his conclusion regarding the Origin of Chess, which he saw in a "4-handed game", played on the Ashtapada - **with dice**. He shared this view with Dr. Isaak M. Linder, a Russian Historian (and others), who explained his conclusions and conviction already in the first issue of his book "*Chess in Old Russia*" published as early as 1964. For more than 20 years "4-handed Chess" [a terrible term!] was believed to having been the root of the game – and Petzold seemed to have this manifested "forever".

In 1991/92 however, the translation of "*Manasollasa*" by Dr. Andreas Bock-Raming and Dr. Renate Syed, and the Research-Meetings "*Privatissimum Seidenstrase*", 1998 in Berlin, and "*Privatissimum Indien*", 1999 in Munich, made Petzold change his mind and accept the arguments delivered for the priority of "2-handed Chess", played ***without dic***e, supporting the convictions of van der Linde (1874) and Murray (1913),Thieme (1960/62) and Syed

(2001). Renate Syed's book "*Kannauj, die Maukharis und das Caturanga – Der Ursprung des Schachspiels und sein Weg von Indiennach Persien*"[4], expanded all research-results hitherto and confirmed the origin of the game in India on the basis of fundamental sources.

Perhaps the best comment on this FSG-publication was written by Dr. Irving L. Finkel, Curator at the British Museum, London, in 2006 (quotation):

"India is the home of many of the world's most important board games. Chess, the greatest of all, probably grew out of an elaborate teaching device using little warlike figures on a miniature battlefield, that instructed young warriors-to-be in the art of warfare."

Don't we have with this a most remarkable "final point", indicating and summarizing what we envisioned by looking back to "Once upon a Time ..."!?

I fully agree with C Panduranga Bhatta's introduction to his new publication and conclude:

"Dice-Play in Sanskrit Literature" combined with *"The Origin of Chess in Sanskrit Literature"* is a Masterpiece, which many of Games-Researchers, especially younger ones, have been waiting for much too long.

In most of the Games with Dice in Europe and the Western Hemisphere a throw of "6" is the highest and wins. I do wish sincerely, dear Panduranga, that this book will be a "6" i.e., a great success for you – and for our mutual subject!

—Manfred A.J. Eder
President Foerderkreis Schach-Geschichtsforschung e.V.,
a *Charity Trust for Chess-Historic Research* in Germany
Kelkheim/Ts., 23rd October 2021

---

4 "Kannauj, the Maukharis and the Caturanga – The Origin of Chess and its way from India to Persia"

Dedication

This book is dedicated with great love and affection to Mr. Manfred A.J. Eder, the President of FSG - Charity Trust, Chess-Historic Research, Germany.

Manfred has supported me in all my work and conferences related to the Dice play and the Origin of Chess in Sanskrit Literature with great care and enthusiasm!

He is passionate about Research and Scientific Studies of the History of Chess and the Origin and Age of Chessmen, Gaming-Pieces and Dice focusing on Development, Provenance and Spread.

Manfred has founded the "Foerderkreis Schach-Geschichtsforschung e.V." (FSG), a Charity-Trust to support and fund Research-Projects investigating the History of Caturanga = Chess. He has handled many Mile-Stone projects in the last 25 Years related to the history of chess and his immense contribution towards Indian Origin of Chess is praiseworthy and the Indologists and Sanskrit lovers will cherish it forever with great respect.

Big Thanks to You Manfred A.J. Eder!

ACKNOWLEDGEMENT

I thank late Professor Dr. Kunjunni Raja then professor and head of the department of Sanskrit, Madras University who suggested the topic of Dice Play in Sanskrit for my Doctoral thesis and for successfully supervising my thesis which I submitted in 1981.

Mr. Manfred A.J. Eder, who is a friend, philosopher and guide deserves the richest thanks as he supported my research in tracing the roots of chess in Indological sources through various means and methods. The first ever Symposium on Approaching the Roots of Chess fruitfully conducted at the Pondicherry University in 1996 was his brainchild. Even though I was reluctant to conduct any research related to the early history of chess after joining the Indian Institute of Management Calcutta in 1997, it is he who encouraged and supported me all through the 25 years by continuously inspiring me and sharing books and articles related to the history of chess! The idea of producing a book on Dice Play and Origin of Chess in Sanskrit Literature based on my research done so far was again supported by Manfred A.J. Eder who not only highly appreciated the idea but arranged significant financial assistance through the "Foerderkreis Schach-Geschichtsforschung e.V." (FSG), a Chess Charity-Trust for publishing this book. I have no words to thank Mr. Manfred A.J. Eder for writing a very scholarly and updated Foreword to this book. I sincerely acknowledge and thank Mr. Manfred A.J. Eder for allowing me to republish the "Analytical assessment of the contributions for the symposium on Approaching the Roots of Chess," Pondicherry University, 26th-29th November 1996 together with a report on the gaming pieces and chessmen exhibited in the museums of Madras and Hyderabad prepared by Dr. Andreas Bock Raming, in this book. He has also permitted me to reprint the photos of Five Chessmen made in stone and a full-page titled "From Catur-anga-Figures to Chessmen".

I must record my sincere thanks to Mrs. Karin Eder, wife of Mr. Manfred A.J. Eder for assisting me regularly in all my email correspondences with Mr. Eder without fail!

Mr. Egbert Meissenburg must be thanked profusely for encouraging me with financial support in conducting research on the Origin and Genesis of Chess and for publishing the same in 1996 from Seevetal, Germany.

I do acknowledge the good feelings expressed by all Indian and foreign participants of the first ever symposium on Approaching the Roots of Chess conducted in Pondicherry University during 1996 which encouraged me in continuing research related to Origin of Chess in Sanskrit Literature.

I feel sad to notice the passing away of stalwarts connected with the Pondicherry Symposium namely Dr. Andreas Bock Raming, Dr. S.V. Narayanan, Professor M. Narasimhachary, Koichi Masukawa and Dr. R. Vasantha. I pray their souls may rest in peace.

I profusely thank all the members of the "Foerderkreis Schach-Geschichtsforschung e.V." (FSG), a Chess Charity-Trust, Germany for providing significant financial support in an elegant and simple manner towards the publication of this work.

Mr. Rajeev Jain and Mr. Pranav Jain partners of Motilal Banarsidass Publishers must be thanked for publishing this book in an excellent manner from all counts. I also thank

Ms. Poonam and Ms. Manju, copy editors for executing the job neatly with great care and efficiency.

I would like to record my appreciation and thanks to His Excellency Ram Singh Chauhan, Consul for Culture as well as Ms. Mridula Singh, Consul General's Secretary at the Consulate General of India in Frankfurt who helped me in getting some books and research articles needed for this book from Frankfurt through Embassy Channel during tough and difficult pandemic period.

Last but not the least, members of my family must be thanked for supporting me as usual during research and book writing and publishing period. My daughter-in-law, Suman deserves my thanks for computerising the early portion of this book. I thank Abhijit, my elder son for extending his guidance and manuscript editing services despite his busy schedule! My grandson Master Vanyu must be thanked for continuously providing funny entertainment so that I don't become exhausted in my book writing exercise. My dear wife Shobha deserves my sincere thanks as usual for encouraging and putting up with my tedious and time-consuming research work. My younger son Dr. Patanjali and my daughter-in-law Dr. Sahana deserve my sincere thanks for advising me regularly on issues concerning my health.

Dr. C. Panduranga Bhatta
Former Professor,
Indian Institute of Management Calcutta
28/02/2022

ABBREVIATIONS

AB	:	Aitareya Brāhmaṇa
AIOC	:	All-India Oriental Conference
ASK	:	Avanti-Sundarī-Kathāsāra
ALB	:	Adyar Library Bulletin
AP	:	Agni Purāṇa
Āpa. Dha.	:	Āpastamba-Dharmasūtra
Āpa. Gṛh.	:	Āpastamba-Gṛhyasūtra
ASIAR	:	Archaeological Survey of India Annual Report
ASINIS	:	Aarchaeological Survey of India New Imperial Series
ASS	:	Āpastamba-Śrauta-Sūtra
Āśv. Gṛh	:	Āśvalāyana-Gṛhyasūtra
Bau. Dha.	:	Baudhāyana Dharmasūtra
BhāSS	:	Bhāradvāja Śrauta-Sūtra
BORI	:	Bhandarkar Oriental Research Institute
BS	:	Bṛhaspatismṛti
BSS	:	Baudhāyana Śrauta-Sūtra
Ch. Up.	:	Chāndogya Upaniṣad
DKC	:	Daśa-Kumāra-Carita
ERE	:	Encyclopedia of Religion and Ethics
HIL	:	History of Indian Literature
Hir. Gṛh.	:	Hiraṇya Gṛhyasūtra

IHQ	Indian Historical Quarterly
JOR	Journal of Oriental Research, Madras
JRAS	Journal of the Royal Asiatic Society, London
KāSS	Kātyāyana Śrauta-Sūtra
KB	Kauśītakī Brāhmaṇa
KS	Kāṭhaka Saṁhitā
KSS	Kathāsaritsāgara
KSSā.	Kātyāyana Smṛtisāroddhāra
LSS	Lāṭyāyana Śrauta-Sūtra
M.Bh.	Mahābhārata
Mṛcch.	Mṛcchakaṭika
MS	Maitrāyaṇī Saṁhitā
MSS	Mānava Śrauta-Sūtra
NS	Nārada Smṛti
OHRJ	Orissa Historical Research Journal
Paippalāda	Pippalāda Saṁhitā
RV	Ṛg Veda
SA	Sāṅkhāyana Āraṇyaka
SB	Śatapatha Brāhmaṇa
SBE	Sacred Books of the East
TS	Taittīriya Saṁhitā
VIJ	Viśveśvārnanda Indological Journal
VPJ	Vidhura-Paṇḍita Jātaka
VS	Vājasaneyi Saṁhitā
YS	Yājñavalkya Smṛti

CONTENTS

Part I

DICE PLAY IN SANSKRIT LITERATURE

INTRODUCTION

The first part of the book is dedicated to Dice-Play which was one of the popular pastimes of ancient India. In Sanskrit literary works such as the Ṛgveda it is called *akṣakrīḍā* or *vibhītaka.* The Mahābhārata contains numerous references to gambling. The course of events in the great epic might be said to have been set in motion by the game of dice. The arguments and counter arguments of the different characters of the epic throw much light upon the rules and regulations of the game and on the accepted conventions relating to gambling. Besides the Mahābhārata, the Daśakumāracarita and Kathāsartisāgara also reveal to us some of the rules observed in the game of dice and certain practices current among the players.

While there existed some fundamental codes of conduct, the players were normally supposed to stipulate and follow the rules of game from time to time before they commenced the play. Once the concerned parties had agreed upon the method of the game, there was no question of going back on them. Violation of the rules was looked down upon with contempt and appropriate action taken.

In the Ṛgveda one full hymn is devoted to the soliloquy of a penitent dice player whose domestic happiness was destroyed because of his irresistible attraction to dice playing.

The game of dice in ancient India has attracted the attention of scholars and several studies have been made on the various aspects of this interesting game. Distinguished Indologists have already dealt with the various problems related to this game based on references found in Sanskrit literature.

An attempt is made in this book to collect the stories related to the Dice-play from Sanskrit sources and Buddhist literature and to make some general observations related to the nature of the play and some conventions associated with the play as revealed in these stories.

Since Vedic and epic times down to historical periods the dice-play was one of the most alluring pastimes of city-bred youths.

The very nature of the play or game itself remained almost unknown even to specialists. Even eminent Indologists like Luders, De Vreese etc., hold almost diametrically different views regarding the details of the dice-play.

The good and bad aspects of gambling, occasion for playing at dice, technical terms of the dice-play, the rules governing the game, the gambling house and punishment and penalty for defaulter, tax-policy and disputes arising in the play are all presented in detail. Considerable attention has been paid to the practical side of the game, the equipment, and the technique. The book also provides insights into how the game was prohibited, encouraged, curtailed, and tolerated down the centuries.

The relationship between chess, *caturaṅga* and the dice-play also attempted which is of great interest throwing much light on the changes which the dice-play has undergone from time to time.

Several studies have been made on the various aspects of this interesting game. G.A. Grierson's "Guessing the Number of the *vibhīdaka* Seeds",[1] CP. R. Roth's "Vom Baum vibhidaka"[2] K. De Vreese's "The Game of Dice in Ancient India,"[3] A.B. Keith's "The Game of Dice,"[4]

Dr. M.M. Patkar's "The Role of Gambling in Ancient Indian Society"[5] and Lüders's "Das Wurfelspiel im alten Indian" may be mentioned here.

Distinguished Indologists viz. A.A. Macdonell,[6] G.J. Held[7] and Charpentier[8] have already dealt with the various problems raised by the gambling scenes found in 'Sanskrit literature'. The results arrived at by Lüders[9] and the findings of Caland and A.B. Keith have been accepted by scholars in this connection.

Despite insufficient references to this game in Sanskrit literature they were able to draw some conclusions regarding this game. They attempted to reconstruct the methodology of the game with the help of references found in Vedic literature, Buddhist works and the Mahābhārata.

The present attempt is to give a comprehensive and connected account of this game from the Vedic period up to the 8th Century CE and to discuss various aspects connected with the game, such as the rules and regulations of the game, the materials used, the use of board, etc.

Early References to Gambling

The earliest available literary evidence is the Gambler's Hymn in the Ṛgveda.[10] It shows that the game of dice was prevalent during the Vedic period.

The "warning" given by the gambler of the Ṛgveda not to play with dice went unheeded, as is clear from references found in the Yajurveda[11] which accommodates gambling in the rituals named *agnyādheya* and *rājasūya.*

Gamblers could not desist from playing even when they lost everything at the stakes. They continued to haunt the gambling hall (*sabhā*) and stood watching the game played by others. Therefore, they are jocularly called '*sabhā-sthāṇus*' or the pillars of the hall in the Yajurveda.[12] Since it was not possible to prevent people from indulging in gambling, it became necessary to regularise the game.

In Yajurveda[13] itself there is a reference to a superintendent of gambling (*akṣāvāpa*) to assist the king in controlling gambling. Dicing was a royal sport and there must have been a separate department of dicing in the Royal Courts even during the time of Yajurveda.

The Atharvaveda refers to gambling and considers that success could be secured by prayer to Apsarases.[14] Non-payment of debt incurred in gambling required expiation.[15]

Gambling was popular even during the *sūtra* period. Āśvalāyana[16] gives suggestions for building a house in such a way that gamblers can be prevented from occupying it.

Although the institution of gambling is older than the Ṛgveda it does not find mention in the topics of *vyavahāra* in the earliest Dharmaśātras.

Among the writers of religious codes, it is Āpastaṁba[17] who for the first time mentions gambling and allows it under the control of the king.

He directs the king to make a house for playing the game and in his opinion this house must be opened to the Brāhmaṇas too. Manu[18] forbids gambling of all sorts, but his law was not enforced in the land.

Kauṭilya[19] condemns gambling but he allows it under the strict supervision of an officer as a source of revenue. In the Smṛtis of Yājñyavalkya, Bṛhaspati and Nārada we find that gambling had become a public institution regulated by a superintendent appointed by the king to prevent foul play, settle disputes between gamblers and enforce payment of stakes. Pāṇini's *sūtra* "*akṣaśalākāsaṁkhyā pariṇ*"[20] indicates that two types of games viz. *akṣakrīḍā* and *śalṣkakrīḍā* were known in his time.

In Buddhist literature gambling is included among the items of amusements forbidden to the monks. The references found in the Jātakas[21] show that gambling continued to be popular. The sorry plight of the ordinary gamblers who stake and lose is often referred to.

The Mṛcchakaṭikā, a Sanskrit drama composed by Śūdraka reveals to us a very lively picture of gamblers. This drama is important as it contains references to the conventions of rules and regulations which gamblers used to follow in gambling.

There were gambling houses regularly controlled by government officers. The game of dice must have been very popular in the period of Kālidāsa and Bāṇa Bhaṭṭa also.

Gambling as an Art

In the list of 64 fine arts, Vātsyāyana[22] has included "*dyūta-viśeṣa*" and "*ākarṣakrīḍā*". The commentary named Jayamaṅgala on Kāmasūtra cxplains "*dyūtuviśeṣa*" as gambling involving *muṣṭi, kṣullaka*, etc.

In the opinion of Vātsyāyana[23] these games must be played with companions or trusted servants. "*yakṣarātri*" and "*kaumudījāgara*" are the two important festivals mentioned by Vātsyāyana,[24] in which gambling plays a prominent role.

"*Yakṣarātri*" falls on the night of the new moon of *kārttīka*. People freely indulge in gambling during this night. "*dyūta-pratipat*"[25] is the name given to the day which follows "*yakṣarātri*". As Bali the king of the nether world ascended the throne on this day, it is also known as "*balipratipat*[26] and it is the first day of the Indian calendar of the Vikrama era.

The "*kaumudījāgara*" which is also known as "*kojāgara pūrṇimā*" is celebrated on the full-moon night of Āśvina.[27] The goddess Lakṣmī is worshipped on this night, and it is further believed that whoever gambles this night becomes rich.[28] This night which is also called "*dyūtapūrṇimā*" is the clearest moonlit night of the year.

Divine Origin of the Dice-Play

The Sanskrit word for God '*deva*' and the word for play are both derived from the same root '*div*' meaning sport or *krīḍā* ("*divu krīḍāyām*"). Dr. V Raghavan observes on this: "When in play, *krīḍā*, a disinterested, unattached, free play of one's joyous creative spirit, one is in the very image of God in his eternal *līlā* expressing itself in the rhythm of the Universe."[29]

The Atharvaveda[30] recognises Apsarases as the presiding deities of the game of dice and the Gṛhyaūtras[31] contain reference to gambling as part of the expiation for curing a boy attacked by dog-demon and these points indicate that gambling was, connected with religious ceremonies.

Among many stories explaining the significance of the dice-play on Deepāvalī, recorded in the Brahmapurāṇa[32] says that Lord Śiva played dice with Pārvatī on this day.

Held G.J gives some more facts to prove the association of gambling with religion which will be taken up later for analysis.

An astrological work named "Pāśakakevalī"[33] attributed to sage Garga explains the significance of the throws of the dice-play. The discovery of this work makes it clear that gambling as divination method was known to the ancient Indians.

Excavations and Dice-Play

The Indus Valley seals also indicate the existence of some sort of dice-play in that remote past. Cubical dice were found at Brahmanabad in 1854 by Mr. Bellasis.[34]

Figure 9 in Plate XLV of the *stūpa* of *Bharhut* is named "*citu-pāda-śilā*". According to Prof. Alexander Cunningham[35] the scene represented in this sculpture shows two parties of two men playing some game like draughts. Prof. Cunningham is of the opinion that this scene depicts the Jātaka-story of a king named Chetiya, who is saddled with the ill-repute of having told the first lie ever spoken in the world which is given in the Chetiya-Jātaka.

As there is no reference to any game in the Chetiya-Jātaka, Prof. Benimadhab Barua[36] disputes the view of Prof. Cunningham.

The only one birth-story which represents the Bodhisattva as a professional dice-player is the Litta Jātaka. Prof. Barua says that this birth-story explains many details of the scene found on the *stūpa.*

Cave No. 21 discovered in Ellora[37] has a picture in which Śaṅkara and Pārvatī are depicted as playing with dice.

Other Excavations at many historic places also have brought to light several dice and game-boards revealing thereby the popularity of dice-play in different periods.

Excavations at Taxila[38] have disclosed several dice belonging to the Greek and Śaka Parthian periods. Excavations at Kumrahar[39] have also yielded proofs to the existence of this game. Excavations at Nāgārjunakoṇḍa,[40] a famous Buddhist site in Andhra Pradesh, have brought into light several sundry ivory dice with points incised on them in accordance with those known to Vedic India.

A consolidated account of the references found in various texts from Vedic period up to the 8th Century CE and a systematic examination of the details regarding the nature and types of the play are taken up in the following chapters.

Akṣakrīḍā, Aṣṭāpada, Caturaṅga and Chess

The second part of the book deals with the origin of chess based on Sanskrit literature. It is interesting to study the origin and evolution of chess, one of the most intellectual games of the world today, and to see its roots in the dice play which can be traced back to the ancient Indian texts like the Ṛgveda. One of the most outstanding events in the history of Indian games is the introduction of the *caturaṅga* from which developed the modern chess; but that was only by the sixth century CE. There is no record of the existence of board games in the Vedic period. Gambling with lots using the *vibhītaka* nuts was the popular pastime. The *pāśaka* type of dice-play using a board and marked dice is found only in later Vedic literature.

It is certain that the game of chess had its origin in *caturaṅga* which was played on a board having sixty-four squares, called *aṣṭāpada.* There is no specific reference in the Vedic literature to any piece used in dice-play.

The game described in the Mahābhārata resembles the *akṣakrīḍā* of the Vedic period. The story found in the Skānda Purāṇa referring to the dice-play between Lord Śiva and goddess Pārvatī may indicate the antiquity of some play like draught as it refers to a board, twelve squares on the board, fifteen black-coloured pieces and fifteen white-coloured pieces.

It must be noted that no board game existed during the time of Vedas, Rāmāyana, Mahābhārata and Kālidāsa. Based on the references available in these texts, it can be safely said that the four-fold force (*caturaṅga*) supplied the motive for the game.

A study of Sanskrit vocabularies such as *aṣṭāpada, śāra* and *pariṇāya* found in various lexicons, help in deciding the antiquity of certain board games played in India.

It may be argued that the concept of the divinity of the king which is found in Sanskrit literature led to the concept of immortality and inviolability of the king both in war and in the game of chess. The concept of righteous war (*dharmavijaya*) is another unique ancient Indian concept which has exercised considerable influence on the game of chess, in which two opposing parties agree to respect each other's king.

The connection between '*caturaṅga*' and the game of chess can be easily established because both are played as a war game with the king, minister, elephants, horses, chariots, and soldiers.

It may be also said that the symmetrical arrangement of the different pieces in the chess and its advantages have been taken from the ancient Indian war.

The term "*buddhibala*" used to denote chess in Sanskrit is found in Simhāsana-dvātrṁśikā, a work belonging to 1100 CE.

A Historic Moment in Pondicherry

The idea of arranging a congress dealing with the history of chess in the assumed country of the origin of the game (i.e., India) titled Symposium on "Approaching the Roots of Chess" held at Pondicherry in 1996 arose in April 1995 at Leiden, The Netherlands, where Mr. Manfred A J Eder, Irving Finkel and Andreas Bock-Raming met C.

Panduranga Bhatta during the international colloquium on "Board Games in Academia".

A probable conference or symposium talked over a dinner in a Mexican Hotel at Leiden, which at that time did not seem to be more than a dream, was realized most perfectly. Dr. Bhatta organized a symposium on "Approaching the Roots of Chess" From 26th to 29th November 1996, at the Pondicherry Central University located in Pondicherry, India. This was the scene of an event of great importance for the research into chess and related board games.

This first ever International Symposium most efficiently organized by the Pondicherry University, was a successful attempt to convene chess historians and scholars from various disciplines, for the first time in India to discuss and hold lectures on the origin and development of chess. While the largest number of forty participants came from India, Mr. Manfred A J Eder, and Andreas Bock Raming and Mr. Egbert Meissenburg from Germany, Mr. Koichi Masukawa from Japan and Irving Finkel and Micaela Solar from United Kingdom attended this Symposium.

Pondicherry Symposium had 5 very interesting sessions:

(1) Chess in Sanskrit Literature

(2) Approaching the Roots of Chess

(3) Chess and Yoga

(4) Anthropology, Archaeology and Chess

(5) Chess and Regional Literature.

Dr. Andreas Bock-Raming deserves thanks of all lovers of chess history for taking the trouble of giving a brief summary with his own comments on all the papers presented in these five sessions in his article titled Analytical Assessment of the Contributions for the Symposium on "Approaching the Roots of Chess", Pondicherry University,

26th-29th November 1996 together with a report on the gaming pieces and chessmen exhibited in the museums of Madras and Hyderabad, in *Antique Chessmen* published by Mr. Manfred A J Eder and Franz Josef Lang in 1997.

Mr. Eder who was the backbone of this symposium called this as a *Historical Moment* and said, "When such an international event, for the first time ever takes place in INDIA, the assumed country of the Origin of the Game of Chess, I feel entitled to call this 'A Historic Moment'". He appreciated the overall arrangements made for this symposium which included academic sessions, accommodation, food, and local transportation.

This symposium's aim was to seek the final answer as to whether India indeed and truly is the "birth-place" of chess. Mr. Eder mentioned in his speech that the distinctive character and nature of "Chess" was created by the invention and introduction of the concept and rule "no longer kill the king", this would be another historic moment. According to him there can be no doubt, that in a war-game like in war, the stated concept of which is to destroy the enemy, the king becomes inviolable, fidated, this inthronisation of the game of "Chess" is of Indian Origin. This was "The Historic Moment", time back in the past.

Dr. Andreas Bock Raming's comments on Mr. Eder's theory is most important for chess historians: "Mr. Eder's theory has consequence which he did not expressly mention in his lecture: the game which, till now used to call four-handed dice chess does not fall under his definition outlined above and consequently can no longer be called chess because its rules allow any of the four kings to be taken.

Dr. Bhatta's research article "The Origin of Chess in

Relation to War and Peace as Gleaned from Sanskrit Literature" throws more light on the concept of inviolability mentioned by Mr. Eder."

Mr. Eder's untiring effort and enthusiasm which made Pondicherry Symposium a memorable and great success.

Pondicherry Symposium has helped a very successful co-operation between some British and German Chess historians and Indian scholars, representing the faculties of Sanskrit, History and Archaeology focusing on Chess research. The impact of the symposium was significant because it inspired many major international level events and publications.

The 4th Symposium of Initiativ Group Koenigstein

The 4th Symposium of Initiativ Group Koenigstein was held at Wiesbaden in August 1997. Mr. Eder, Founding Member and President of FSG a Charity Trust for Chess-Historic Research arranged the financial support to Indian scholars for attending this Symposium.

Dr. Bhatta and a few Indian scholars doing research on the history of chess attended this Symposium. Right from day one, Mr. Eder was with the participants overlooking all arrangements related to accommodation, food, and transport. He even took the trouble of receiving in person, all the Indian participants at the Frankfort Airport.

Playing with The Past: National Conference on Ancient & Medieval Indian Board Games

This conference was held under the banner of INSTUCEN at Mumbai in India during June 1-2, 2019. Mr. Raamesh Gowri Raghavan organised this conference. This conference was organised to encourage young and amateur researchers to present their work on exploration and documentation of board games, from both living traditions as well as archaeological remains from the prehistoric to the post-colonial periods.

This conference also aimed to draw a comprehensive picture of the role of games in shaping ancient and medieval Indian society, through the following subjects:

1. Archaeological Evidence for Games
2. Games in Indian Literature
3. Field Surveys for Board Games: New Variants or Previously Unreported games
4. Game Revival: Play and Manufacture
5. Mathematical Aspects of Indian Games
6. Board Games in Psychology, Sociology and Religious Studies

The conference was successful as there were more than 13 papers presented in the conference. Some interesting papers presented in the conference are given below for the benefit of Chess historians.

1. History of Chess: Dice or No Dice? -Dr. C. Panduranga Bhatta.
2. Project Kheliya: Mapping India's Heritage Games-Mr. Raamesh Gowri Raghavan.
3. Board Games of Krishnaraja Wodeyar III (who ruled during 1799-1868 C.E).
4. Reviving Ancient Games with Kavade and Attic-Ms. G.S. Sreeranjini.
5. Dating Inscribed Games in the Indian Archaeological Context- Dr. Kurush F. Dalal.
6. Etched in Stone: Game Patterns found in temples and *basadis* in Karnataka-Dr. Dileep K.C.R. Gowda.

7. Board Games found in temples and forts of Andhra Pradesh and Telangana-Dr. Deme Reddy and Ms. Samiksha Deme.

Mission Kannauj 2020

The three main objectives of this meeting were:

1. To exchange knowledge on the early History of Chess,
2. To support the claim that "We must find the Gaming-Pieces – of *Caturanga*", and
3. To encourage the respective authorities for new archaeologic excavations at this historic spot (i.e., Kannauj).

As usual Mr. Manfred A.J. Eder made earnest effort in getting many participants for this meeting and finally following persons agreed to participate in this very important event.

- Prof. (Dr.) C. Panduranga Bhatta, Bengaluru, India
- Mr. Myron Samsin, Canada
- Dr. Elke Rogersdotter, Sweden
- Dr. Jacob Schmidt-Madsen, Denmark
- Prof. Dr. Renate Syed, Munich
- Dr. Leander A. Feiler, Riemerling-Munich
- Mr. Manfred A.J. Eder, Kelkheim/Ts. (Germany)

There was a very fruitful exchange of ideas related to Chess-History under the able guidance of Mr. Manfred A.J. Eder during this Chess Historic Meeting held on February 27-28, 2020.

This meeting resulted in a significant publication brought out by Manfred A.J. Eder titled "Working Papers, Mission

Kannauj 2020." Some of the contributions published in this volume will be taken up for discussion in the 4th chapter of the Part II of this book.

The Story before the 'A Historic Moment' in Pondicherry

Pondicherry 1996 would not be complete without mentioning briefly two books published before this event.

— **Dice-Play in Sanskrit Literature authored by Dr. C. Panduranga Bhatta and published by Amar Prakashan, New Delhi, 1982.**

Professor Ludo Rocher, W. Norman Brown Professor of South Asian Studies, University of Pennsylvania in his Foreword to the book says:

"The principal strength of this book lies in the range of primary sources on which it is based: never have so many textual references to dice-play and gambling generally been made available in one single volume. In addition, the book also displays great familiarity with and critical use of a wide range of secondary literature. The book proceeds logically and systematically, step after step, to cover each aspect of dice-play and gambling in Sanskrit literature. This book gives a comprehensive account of dice-play in ancient India up to the eighth century A.D. based primarily on literary sources-Vedas, Vedāṅgas, Smṛtis, Itihāsas, Epics and Dramas.

The rules and regulations of the game, conventions and practices and the different ways of playing are discussed fully."

Origin and Genesis of Chess authored by Dr. C. Panduranga Bhatta and published by Egbert Meissenburg,

Seevetal, (Germany) in 1994, is also worth mentioning in this context.

This monograph discusses in brief several aspects of the early history of the game of chess from the Vedic period up to the period of Halāyudha (10th century CE). It concludes by saying that it is certain that the game of chess had its origin in '*caturaṅga*' which was played on a board having 64 squares, called '*aṣṭāpada*'. The term '*buddhibala*' used to denote chess in Sanskrit is found in *Siṁhāsana-dvātriṁśikā,* a work belonging to 1100A.D.

This monograph concludes by saying that some works related to chess existed in India and further research should be conducted to trace them as they may provide vital clues to the early existence of chess in India.

REFERENCES TO GAMBLING IN THE VEDAS, BRĀHMAṆAS, ĀRAṆYAKAS AND UPANIṢADS

The Gambler's Hymn

The Ṛgveda, a collection of religious hymns, is the oldest literature in the world. Most of these hymns relate to rituals; but some are, at least apparently, secular in nature. We do not have any direction or ritualistic application in the *anukramaṇis* for some of the hymns, which may therefore be considered as secular.

The gambler's hymn is one such "secular" hymn where there is a clear reference to the game of dice. The gambler's hymn, consisting of fourteen stanzas, occurs in the tenth *manḍala* of the Ṛgveda (Hymn No. 34). The seer of this hymn is Kavaṣa Ailūṣa who is said to have been a gambler himself.[1]

Yāska, the author of Nirukta also says that this hymn is composed by one sage who had lost everything in dice-play: *riṣerakṣaparidyūnasyaitdarṣaṁ vedayante.*[2]

This hymn presents a realistic picture of a repenting gambler, the trials and tribulations faced by him in life. The ulterior motive of this hymn may be self-examination.

The text and English translation of the hymn are given below.

prāvepāmābṛhatomādayanti
pravātejāiriṇevavṛtānāḥ/
somasyeva maujavatasya bhakṣo
vibhīdakojāgṛvirmhyamacchān //1//

These dice nuts, born of a lofty tree in a windy spot, which dance on this gambling ground (*iriṇa*), make me almost mad. The wakeful dice intoxicate me like a draught of Soma from Mount Mūjavant.

namāmimetha na jihṛhīlaaiṣā
śivāsakhibhya uta mahyamāsīt/
akṣasyāhamekaparasya hetor
anuvratāmapajāyāmarodham//2//

Never has she said an angry word to me, nor has she ever scolded me. She has been so pleasing to me and my friends. With all this without any fault of hers I have driven my devoted wife away because of a die exceeding by one (through an unlucky throw).

dveṣṭi śvaśrūrapa jāyā ruṇaddhi
na nāthito vindate marḍitāram/
aśvasyeva jarto vasyanyasya
nāhaṁ vindāmi kitavasya bhogam //3//

My mother-in-law hates me; my wife pushes me away. In his defeat the gambler finds none to pity him. No one has use for the gambler like an aged horse put up for sale.

anyejāyāmparimṛśantyasya
yasyāgṛdhadvedanevajyakṣaḥ/
pitāmātābhrātara enamāhur
najānimonayatābaddhametam //4//

Others start embracing the wife of him whose possessions

are coveted by the grasping die. Even his father, mothers and brothers say of him (When someone comes to arrest the gambler), 'we do not know him; take him away bound'.

yadādīdhyenadaviṣānyebhiḥ
parāyadbhyoavahiyesakhibhyaḥ/
nyuptāśyababhravovāyamakrataṁ
aīmīdeṣāṁniṣktaṁjāriṇīva //5//

Whenever I make a vow to myself that 'I will not gamble in future, I am looked down by my friends, going away' (towards the game). Even the brown dice, thrown down, have raised their voices. And then I go to their place as an adulteress visiting the appointed place.

sabhāmetikitavaḥpṛchhamāno
jeṣyāmītitanvāśśrūśujānāḥ/
akṣāsoasyavitirantikāmaṁ
pratidīvnedadhatuā kṛtāni //6//

The gambler goes to the assembly hall, enquiring from others, with his glowing face and thinking that 'I shall certainly win.' But the dice thwart his desire as they give the lucky throws to his opponent.

akṣāsaideṅkuśinaunitodino
nikṛtvānastapanāstāpayiṣṇavaḥ/
kumāradeṣṇājayataḥpunarhaṇo
madhvāsaṅpṛktāḥkitavasya barhaṇā //7//

The dice are so sharp pointed; they prick me. They are deceitful, hot, and scorching. Unstable are the gifts they grant like those of children. They hit him who wins. Smeared with honey they seize the gambler by force.

tripañcāśaḥkrīḍativrāteṣāṁ
dev ivasavitāsatyadharmā/
ugrasyacinmanyavenānamante
rājācidebhyonamaitkṛṇoti //8//

Their host of three fifties plays like God Savitr whose laws are true. These dice do not become humble or bow before the wrath of a mighty one. Even the king bends low before them or pays his homage to them.

nīyāvartantauparisphurnty-
ahastāsohastavantaṁsahante /
divyāaṅgārāiriṇenyuptāḥ
śītāḥ santo hṛdyaṁnirdahanti //9//

Though the dice are thrown downwards, they spring and dance upwards. Without hands they overcome him who has them. Thrown upon the *iriṇa,* the dice are like pieces of divine coal, which cause the hearts burn, though remaining themselves cold.

jāyātapyate kitavasya hīna
mātāputrasyacartaḥkvasvit /
ṛṇavābibhyaddhanamichhamāno
anyeṣāmastamupanaktameti //10//

The miserable wife of a gambler weeps for her lot; his mother (too) whose son is wandering no one knows where. The gambler thoroughly drenched in the debts as he is, approaches others' homes, towards the nightfall; though he is afraid (of his own people or of the moneylenders) he still wants to get some money (from somewhere).

striyaṁdṛṣṭvāyakitavaṁtatāpā
nyeṣāṁjāyāṁsukṛtaṁ ca yonim /
pūrvāhṇheaśvānyuyuje hibabhrūn
so agnerantevṛṣalaḥpapāda //11//

The gambler feels remorseful, when he sees his own wife on the one hand, and the wives and well-arranged homes of the others, on the other.

Though at dawn he marshalled, the brown dice as though yoking horses, at the day's end he falls near the fire, all spent.

yo vaḥ senānīrmahato gaṇasya
rājā vrātasya prathamo babhūva /
tasmai kṛṇomi na dhanā ruṇadhmi
daśāham prācīstadṛtaṁ vadāmi //12//

I stretch out my ten fingers before the captain of your mighty tribe, before your chief (who rises in the east) and the king. No wealth do I conceal. This is a truth which I declare.

akṣairmādīvyaḥkṛṣimitkṛṣasva
vitte ramasva bahu manyamānaḥ /
tatragāvaḥkitavatatrajāyā
tanme vi caṣṭesavitāyamaryaḥ //13//

Do not play with dice. Cultivate your filed and remain content with whatsoever you gain, thinking that as plenty. Only in this way you will gain the animal, wealth along with the real pleasures of your wife. This has been made clear to me by Lord Savitr himself.

mitraṁkṛṇudhvaṁkhalumṛlatāno
mā no ghoreṇacaratābhidhṛṣṇu/
nivo nu manyurviśatāmarātir
anyobabhrūṇāṁprasitaunvastu //14//

Treat me as a friend. And so be merciful. Do not please overpower us by your magic power. Let your wrath and grudge be appeased! Let another fall in the range of brown ones.

Scholars differ regarding the exact significance of this hymn. According to the Ṛgvidhāna, attributed to Śaunaka, which deals with the mystic and magic efficacy of the recitation of the hymns of the Ṛgveda, the *akṣasūkta* serves as a magic means to become victorious in gambling. The procedure is as follows: The person interested in getting success in gambling must take three dice coming from the '*vibhitaka*' tree and make them fragrant with perfumes. They must then be kept in the open air along with flowers. The first stanza of the *akṣasūkta* must be recited at night holding the dice in his hand. He must do so by standing with his feet kept close. After sunrise, he must go to the gambling-hall and recite the hymn. Constant recitation of the first stanza of this hymn is recommended for sure success in the game. The gambler must also touch the head of the person whom he wants to win and recite the stanza.[3]

The Brāhmaṇas usually give one or two anecdotes to highlight the importance of a particular hymn. But curiously enough no such anecdotes are found in the Brāhmaṇas, highlighting the importance of this hymn.

Stanza 14 of the Gambler's Hymn may be interpreted in support of the view expressed in the Ṛgvidhāna. But the general trend of the hymn is a request made to release the gambler from the grip of the dice. The request is not to bring success in gambling. Otherwise, there is no justification for asking the dice to make some other person as their victim. Again, the advice of the Sun God to the gambler referred to above, viz., that he should till the land, does not suit the context if the entire hymn is intended for getting success in gambling.

Moreover, we have spells in the Atharvaveda which are intended to bring about success in gambling, where the tone is different. In IV.38 Apsarases are considered the presiding deities of the dice and they are praised to get success in gambling. The intention of the speaker is made clear there. He says: "I call hither that Apsaras who makes the winning in the game of dice."

glahekṛtānikṛṇvānāmapsarāṁtāmahihuve/[4]

"When she takes the stakes from the game of dice, when

she desires to win for us, obtain the advantage by (her) magic, may she come to us full of abundance, let them not win this wealth of ours."

yāyaiḥparinṛtyatyādadānākṛtaṁglahāt /
sānaḥkṛtānisīṣatīprahāmānpotumāyayā
sānaḥpayasvatyaitumānojaiṣuridaṁdhanam //[5]

"Oh dice, yield play, profitable as a cow that is rich in milk. Bind me to a streak of gain, as the bow (is bound) with the string."

akṣāphalavatīṁdyuvaṁdattagāṁkṣīriṇīmiva/
saṁmokṛtasyadhārayadhanuhḥsnāvnevanahyata //[6]

"Oh Apsarases, make the rival gambler subject to me."

tā me hastausaṁsṛjantughṛtensapatnaṁ me kitavaṁ randhayantu.[7]

Because of the absence of such prayers in the Gambler's Hymn of the Ṛgveda it is difficult to believe the suggestion made by the Ṛgvidhāna, that this hymn is meant for obtaining victory in gambling.

According to the Bṛhaddevatā which belongs to a period much later after the *sūtras,* the *akṣasūkta* contains a praise of dice.

prāvepāitisūktaṁyattadakṣastutirucyate/
atrākṣāndvādasīstautinavamyādyā ca saptamī//
trayodaśīkṛṣiṁstauti kitvaṁcānuśāsati/
akṣānstuśeṣānindantiabudhraṁvaiśvadevate//[8]

Thus, according to the Bṛhaddevatā stanzas 1, 7, 9 and 12 praise the dice and stanza 13 praises tillage and admonishes the gambler. The Sarvānukramaṇī of Kātyāyana does not provide any details, but says:

akṣa-kṛṣi-praśaṁsacākṣa-kitava-nindā ca/[9]

Thus, only the Ṛgvidhāna and the Bṛhaddevatā explain this hymn to acquire success in gambling.

This hymn has had a tremendous appeal to the modern scholars. Prof. Winternitz says: "The most beautiful amongst the non-religious poems of the Ṛgveda collection is the song of the Gambler."[10] Prof. Macdonell A.A. observes: "The lament of the Gambler strikes a pathetic note. Considering that it is the oldest composition of the kind in existence, we cannot but regard this poem as a most remarkable literary product".[11]

Among the western scholars who made attempts to explain the nature of this hymn, mention may be made of Schroeder L.V., Charpentier, Winternitz and Norman Brown W. To Schroeder L.V., the Gambler's Hymn appears to be a drama in the form of a monologue.[12] This hymn was composed to serve some didactic purposes, says Charpentier.[13]

Prof. Winternitz who traces the origin of Epics to some ballads of the Court bards of the ancient days considers the Gambler's Hymn to be a part of one such ballad.[14] So according to him this must have been a story of some famous gambler like Nala and Yudhiṣṭhira. But since it is not to be recited in any rite either obligatory or non-obligatory its religious nature is very much doubted. According to Prof. Norman Brown W., this hymn is neither a lament nor a prayer.[15]

He has tried to prove this to be an "Act of Truth". The Act of Truth as explained by Prof. Brown is a formal declaration of fact, accompanied by a command or resolution or prayer that the purpose of the agent shall be accomplished. The Act of Truth is generally called *saccakiriya* in Pāli literature. It is like *satyakriyā, satyavacana, satyavākya* etc., in Sanskrit. In the Ṛgveda itself we have its equivalent, *ṛta.*

The Act of Truth becomes effective when the person who declares the Truth performs his duty perfectly in the cosmos.

By this he identifies himself with the cosmos, and his will and the cosmic operation coincide. But the persons who do their duty perfectly are rare and hence the 'Action of Truth' is regarded worthy of comment in the literature.

In this connection Prof. Brown observes: "The hymn can be regarded as the utterance of some with an unconquerable compulsion to gamble, but at the same time with a desire to escape from that compulsion."

To do so he performs an Act of Truth based upon the completeness of his addiction to gambling. Prof. Brown interprets the entire hymn to suit his stand. Stanzas 1-11 clearly show the dominance-of passion to gamble. The Action of Truth (*ṛta*) is performed in the twelfth stanza.

In this stanza the gambler says that he owns nothing but ten fingers, having lost all his wealth in gambling.

> *na dhanā ruṇadhmi*
> *daśāhaṁ prācīstadṛtaṁ vadāmi//*

He addresses the God Savitṛ considering him to be the leader of the dice.

> *yo vaḥ senānīrmahato gaṇasya*
> *rājā vrātasya prathamo babhūva*
> *tasmai kṛṇomi...//*

The Gambler's 'Action of Truth' is successful because the God Savitṛ himself answers and advises him not to play any more after releasing the gambler from his compulsion. It is also stated further that the lost property of the gambler was restored to him by the God Savitr. Prof. Brown has translated the thirteenth stanza as follows:

Play not with dice, cultivate your field! Be content with your possessions, esteeming them plenty. There, O gambler, are your cows, there your wife. Thus does the noble god Savitṛ here instruct me.

The line,

> *tatra gāvaḥ kitava tatra jāyā/*

according to others, is an advice given to the gambler to get wealth through agriculture. And he can get cows and a loving wife through the money got from tillage but not from the wealth made by gambling.

This new interpretation of the hymn and its recitation as an 'Act of Truth' is also favoured by Prof. J. Gonda. He observes:

> The gambler's prayer for deliverance from the power of the dice is perhaps not completely explicit or unambiguous, but from stanza 13 it is apparent that God Savitṛ is willing to release him.[16]

As we have noted, Śaunaka says that this hymn relates to some magic rite which can bring about success in gambling. There is no evidence in favour of the view that it is a dialogue hymn, or some monologue recited or enacted during the intervals of some great sacrifices. But the theory of Prof. Brown who considers this hymn as an "Act of Truth" seems to be acceptable.

Other References in the Ṛgveda

There are some other references to this game in the Ṛgveda.

The word *caturaḥ* in the line

> *caturaściddhadamānādbibhīyādā*
> *nidhātoḥ na duruktāya spṛhayet/*[17]

of the first *maṇḍala* is interpreted by Sāyaṇa as referring to four dice. Indra is described as one who often seizes the foe's riches like a gambler who gathers his winnings.

śvaghnīva yo jigīvālal lakṣamādaduryaḥ
puṣṭāni sa janāsa indraḥ /[18]

We have reference to a father who punished his son for his indulgence in gambling.

pra va eko mimāya bhūryāgo/
yanmā piteva kitavaṁ śaśāsa/[19]

Goddess Dawn is compared to the cunning gambler as she deprives the people of their lives.

śvaghnīva kṛtnurvrija āminānā
martasya devī jarayantyāyuḥ/[20]

Cheating at play was common and we have reference to the same in the Ṛgveda. In one hymn, the Vedic bard requests Varuṇa to pardon him from the cheats he has committed in the play and from the cheats which he may commit in future.

kitavāso yad riripurṇa dīvi
yad vā ghā satyamuta yanna vidma/
sarvā tā visya śithireva devadhā
te syāma varuṇa priyāsaḥ //[21]

Dice along with wine and anger is considered one of the causes which leads men astray.

na sa svo dakṣo varuṇa dhrutiḥ sā/
surā manyurvibhīdako acittiḥ//[22]

Indra selecting a strong person in the battle for killing is compared to a gambler selecting a best throw in a play.

uta prahāmatidīvyā jayāti
kṛtaṁ yacchavagnī vicinoti kāle/[23]

Again, Indra is described as conquering the Sun like a gambler who conquers the stakes by best throws.

kṛtaṁ na śvaghnī vi cinoti devane
saṁvargaṁ yanmaghavā sūryaṁ jayat/[24]

The throwing away of the stars by Indra is compared to the throwing away of the dice at the game.

pīvānaṁ meṣamapacantavīrā
nyuptā akṣā anu dīva āsan/[25]

It is stated that gods give and take wealth like the throws of the game which make one win or lose in a game.

ayā iva pari caranti devā
ye asmabhyaṁ dhanadā udbhidaśca/[26]

We may also note one more passage in the Ṛgveda connected with gambling, the real sense of which is very much doubted.

abhrāteva puṁsa eti pratīcī
gartārugiva sanaye dhanānām /[27]

According to Prof. R.C. Das it implies that sometimes widows visited the dicing hall with a view to making wealth by gambling.[28]

References in the Yajurveda

The Yajurveda mostly deals with the performance of rituals such as *rājasūya, aśvamedha* and other daily rituals. In the Ṛgveda the object of devotion was the deities while the sacrifice was only a means of influencing their will in favour of the offeror; in the Yajurveda the sacrifice itself has become the centre of thought and desire, its correct performance in every detail being all important. The Yajurveda associates gambling with religious rituals.

The Brāhmaṇas and the Śrautasūtras which also speak of the religious significance of gambling mainly draw their source from the Yajurveda.

The Śukla Yajurveda (Vājasaneyī Saṁhitā) contains a reference to dice-play, and it is in connection with the great sacrifice *rājasūya*. In the following passage we have a reference to the priest who hands over five dice to the king as a mark of victory; *abhibhūrasyetāste pañca diśaḥ kalpantām...*[29] Figuratively speaking the five dice represent five quarters, i.e., East, West, South, North and Zenith (*antarikṣa*) and after receiving the five dice the king becomes the conqueror of the five quarters. We have reference to this fact both in the Maitrāyaṇī Saṁhitā[30] and the Taittirīya Saṁhitā of the Yajurveda.[31]

Puruṣamedha (human sacrifice) is a symbolic sacrifice described in book 30 of the Śukla Yajurveda.

It is stated there that as many as 148 persons are to be sacrificed to different deities to please them. This human-sacrifice is interpreted as symbolic in nature. The list of victims as well as of the deities to whom the sacrifice is to be offered makes it clear that it is all figurative and no slaughter of human beings was involved. The list given there contains a gambler, a person who contemplates his adversary's ill-luck, a gamble-manager, a chiefmanager, a person who will not leave the gambling-hall etc. who are to be offered to the dice-king, the dice *kṛta, tretā, dvāpara* and *askanda* respectively.

> *akṣarājāya kitavaṁ kṛtāyādinavadarśaṁ*
> *tretāyai kalpinaṁ dvāparāyādhikalpinama*
> *skandāya sabhāsthāṇum /*[32]

It may be noted that Kitava, Ādinavadarśa, Kalpin, Adhikalpin and Sabhāsthāṇu are the different names of gamblers, and they are to be offered here to different throws and not to deities.

There is a request in another passage made to gods to cast aside a gambler who acquires wealth by unlawful means,

kitavamīryatāyāḍa akitavaṁ /[33]

Gods are also requested to drive away a harlot fond of pastime.

kitavaḥ klīboaśrūdā abrāhmaṇāste prājāpatyāḥ /[34]

In another passage the Aśvin gods are spoken of as assisting in gambling by bringing about success. This is also found in the Ṛgveda.[35]

aptasvatīmaśvinā vācamasme
kṛtaṁ no dasrā vṛṣaṇā manīśām/
adyūtyeavase nihvaye vā vṛdhe
ce no bhavataṁ vājasātau //[36]

"Make ye our speech effectual, O Ye Aśvins, and this our hymn, ye mighty wonderworkers. In luckless game I call on you for succor; strengthen us also on the field of battle."

The commentator Sāyaṅācārya following a different derivation of the word "*adyūta*" used here explains it as in the absence of light, or in the last watch of night when the Aśvins are especially to be worshipped.

The Kāṭhaka and the Maitrāyaṇī Saṁhitās of the Kṛṣṇa Yajurveda contain reference to Akṣāvāpa, the keeper of the gambling hall.[37]

References in the Atharvaveda

In the Atharvaveda we find holy magic for securing wellbeing and spells for getting success in various fields.

We do have expiatory hymns known as *prāyaścittāni* which

being properly employed can remove various sins. The hymns connected with gambling found in this Veda mainly belong to these two kinds.

The Gambler's Hymn of the Ṛgveda, as noted earlier, does not seem to have been used as a magic spell. Both the Śukla and Kṛṣṇa Yajurvedas brought dice-play under *rājasūya* sacrifice. They do not specify any hymn as a magic spell, for bringing about victory in gambling. It is only in the Atharvaveda that we find references to many hymns which are to be used as magic spells to become successful in gambling.

Probably the idea expressed in stanzas 12 and 14 of the Gambler's Hymn of the Ṛgveda in which the gambler offers his salutations to the dice and requests them to release him from their power, would have encouraged the priest of the Atharvaveda to compose hymns praising dice.

In this Veda the Apsarases are praised as the presiding deities of the game. They are described as ever victorious because of their great skill. We have four stanzas addressed to Apsarases in which the seer calls them to make people win in the game of dice.[38] They are described as dancing with dice after taking the stake from the game. They get advantage in the game by their magic power. They are requested to make the opponents lose their stakes. In the last stanza they are described as rejoicing in dice and as carrying grief and wrath of players.

The word Apsaras is used here as Apsarā. According to Sāyaṇācārya the 'Apsarases' are called the presiding deities of the game of dice.[39]

We have also a prayer for success at dice in this Veda. In the following hymn the gambler says that he would beat his opponents in the game as the lightning which strikes the tree.

He praises Agni, Indra and Maruts for success in the play. The gambler grabbing at the stakes is compared to the wolf pouncing upon the sheep. The gambler's desire to overcome poverty by getting cattle is referred to in stanza 7. He says that he would get rid of his hunger by possessing grain. To achieve these things, he is even prepared to adopt cunning devices in the play through which he can win the wealth of his adversary.

The gambler's desire to conquer cattle, horses, wealth, and gold in the play, with gain deposited in his right hand and victory in his left, is beautifully described in the eighth stanza.[40]

There is one more hymn which is to be used to attain success in gambling. Here Agni is requested to carry the ghee for the Apsarases because they should make the rival gambler subject to those who worship them.[41]

The Apsarases are requested to make the opponent a loser and to strike him as a thunderbolt, the tree. It is interesting to note that these hymns of the Atharvaveda, viz., IV.38.1-4; V 11.50 and V.11.109 are specially recommended for getting success in the game. Before reciting these hymns, one must observe certain other ceremonies which are set out in the Kauśikasūtra.

The gambler must dig up a pit under the constellation of Pūrvāṣāḍhā and fill it under Uttarāṣāḍhā. When the place is thus levelled it becomes fit for gambling. The dice must be steeped in honey and curds for three nights and days beginning with the thirteenth day of the month. Now if he throws the dice accompanied by the recitation of these hymns, success in gambling is certain for him.[42 and 43]

We have another hymn in which ill-luck at dice is looked upon as par with death from thirst and hunger.[44]

Varuṇa, establisher of moral codes, is compared to a winning gambler throwing dice and obtaining the stakes in a hymn.[45]

One of the stanzas addressed to a cow request her to be affectionate towards her calf, like a male who always hankers after meat, liquor, gambling-place, and woman.[46] Homage is paid in one of the hymns of this Veda to the dice-loving Apsarases who have the Gandharvas for spouses.[47]

There is another hymn which refers to the removal of the witchcraft made at the gambling hall.[48]

As we have observed already there are expiatory hymns which are to be used to get rid of the sins committed in a game. The Apsarases are requested to forgive the guilt committed in connection with the game of dice. They are requested to see that debts are not demanded from the gamblers which they owe to a game.[49] The gambler approaching people for money has been referred to in a stanza in which he is said to seek the protection of Apsarases.[50] Another person requesting the gods to protect him from losing his wealth in the game is mentioned in a stanza.[51] Some other stanzas refer to the indescribable happiness found in dice, drink, and kine.[52]

People desirous of winning at the game of dice sometimes used to speak untruth and this has been referred to in one of the stanzas of this Veda.[53]

The sixth book of the Atharvaveda contains an interesting hymn which is to be recited by a person who desires the growth of his locks of hair. First, he must rinse his hair with water heated by burning plants that grow upon the earth under trees. Next his head is rinsed off with an effusion (*kvātha*) prepared by heating dice in water. This practice is explained in the Kauśikasūtra.[54] The commentator Keśava makes the idea clear.[55] In another hymn the brilliance of the dice is compared to the effulgence of Varuṇa and the goddess of fortune.[56]

The Paippalādasaṁhitā, another recension of the Atharvaveda, was available in the form of a birchbark manuscript but preserved in a bad condition. Prof. Durgamohan Bhattacharya discovered a palm-leaf manuscript of the same recension. The two versions of the Atharvaveda, the Paippalāda and the Śaunakīya, have a large amount of material in common. It is proved that the texts in the Paippalādasaṁhitā, in many cases, yield better meanings than the mantras of the Śaunakasaṁhitā. Several stanzas of these two recensions of the Atharvaveda refer to gambling. In some of the stanzas of the Śaunakīya version the reading, which is printed as "*ghṛta*" and explained and translated as such by the commentator and translators, occurs as "*kṛta*" (the winning throw) in the Paippalāda manuscripts. Prof. D. Bhattacharya satisfactorily proves that the word "*ghṛta*" must be replaced by the word "*kṛta*". He does so by giving many examples from Atharvaveda as well as from the Ṛgveda where the word *kṛta* occurs.[57]

This will be explained in the fifth chapter. Paippalāda is also important as it has passages belonging to the Atharvaveda quoted by later writers, but which are absent in the Śaunakīya recension.

Another hymn relating to gambling found in the Paippalādasaṁhitā is very close in its sense to hymn 50 of book 7 of the Śauna recension.[58]

The fourth stanza of the same hymn refers to the different throws of the dice-play such as "*kṛta*", "*tretā*", "*dvāpara*" and "*kali*".

> *ā bhadraṁ dvāparaṁ bharamuta tretāṁ parā kalim /*
> *kṛtam me hasta āhitaṁ sa hi saumanaso mahān //*[59]

References in the Brāhmaṇas, the Āraṇyakas and the Upaniṣads

The Brāhmaṇas of the Rgveda and the Yajurveda contain references to the game of dice, The Aitareya Brāhmaṇa belonging to the Ṛgveda refers to the four kinds of throws in the dice-play.

kaliḥ śayāno bhavati saṁjihānastu dvāparaḥ uttiṣṭhanstretā bhavati kṛtaṁ saṁpadyate caraṁścaraiveti iti/ [60]

According to Sāyaṇācārya the words *kali, dvāpara, tretā* and *kṛta* mentioned here refer to the four Ages. Prof. A.B. Keith is of the opinion that the Ages are non-Vedic though they are referred to in the Manusm*ṛ*ti. Despite Prof. Max Muller's agreement with S*ā*ya*ṇ*a Prof. Keith has rejected this idea.

Thus, in his opinion only the names of the throws of the dice-play are referred to here.[61] This will form a topic for discussion in the fifth chapter of this book.

The Taittirīya Brāhmaṇa has some passages where references are made to Akṣāvāpa (Superintendent) of the gambling hall.[62] The king becoming the lord of all the quarters by taking the five dice is mentioned herein.[63] In another passage reference is made to the gamblers who are the victims at the *puruṣamedha* sacrifice. Here, Sabhāvin and Ādinavadarśa are offered to *kṛta* and *tretā* respectively.[64]

As already seen in a passage of the Vājasaneyisaṁhitā, Ādinavadarśa, Kalpin, Adhikalpin and Sabhāsthāṇu are offered to *kṛta, tretā, dvāpara* and *kali* respectively.

The passages of the Śatapatha Brāhmaṇa related to gambling are important for understanding the mode of dice-play as existed during the Vedic period.

An analysis of the technical words found in these passages will be taken for a discussion in the fifth chapter.

The description of the dice-play at the Rājasūya sacrifice given in this Brāhmaṇa is as follows. The Brahman hands over the sacrificial sword to the king saying, Indra's thunderbolt thou art'. After this, he hands over five dice saying, 'this king has overcome the regions'. The charioteer, treasurer and chamberlain are invited by the king using epithets like 'far-famed one', 'most prosperous one', and 'true king'. Then the gaming-ground is made ready with the sacrificial sword by the tribesman and the *pratiprasthātṛ*. After the performance of other minor rites, the *adhvaryu* takes clarified butter in four ladling's and places a piece of gold on the gaming-ground and offers it, saying, 'May ample Agni, the lord of rites, be delighted! May you accept the butter.'

After this the *adhvaryu* throws down the dice, saying, "Hallowed by *svāhā*, strive ye with sun's rays for the middlemost place among brethren."[65]

The significance of this is explained by Sāyaṇa who says that the gaming-ground is the same as 'ample Agni', and those dice are-his coals, thus it is him (Agni) the priest thereby pleases.

According to another reference found in this Brāhmaṇa having brought the "*gavīdhuka*" (seeds) from the houses of the keeper of the dice (*akṣāvāpa*) and the huntsman (*govikartana*) the priest prepares a "*gāvīdhuka*" pap for Rudra at the house of him who is consecrated. It is further stated that he makes that offering because Rudra is hankering after that (cow) which is killed herein this hall. The next passage describes Rudra as Agni, Agni as gaming-board and dice as coals. Rudra is pleased in this way. The keeper of the dice and the huntsman are described as jewels of the king and the king makes them his own faithful followers, The king gives knife and the dice-board as the sacrificial fee for both.[66]

In the Āraṇyakas and the Upaniṣads we see passing references to this game either involving some comparison or just taken up for denouncement.

Among the Āraṇyaka texts the Sāṅkhāyana (or Kauśītaki) Āraṇyaka belonging to the Ṛgveda, refers to the golden dice used in the game. Here we have reference to a person who seeks to attain the splendour of the golden dice, of the cows and horses, of the '*surā*' and of the elephant.[67]

In the Chāndogya Upaniṣad sage Raikva is compared to *kṛta*, a throw of dice. Just as all the lower casts of the dice go over to one, who has won the "*kṛta*", so also whatever good the creatures do, goes over to Raikva; to him who knows what Raikva knows.[68]

The *vibhītaka* fruit or *akṣa* is also referred to in this Upaniṣad in a passage.[69]

The Ṛgvedic references do not provide us much insight into the rules and regulations that governed this game or the technique by which the game was played. The later literature is replete with more detailed references to this game, though the exact significance of some of the technical terms remains vague. It must be pointed out that these terms have been very helpful for later scholars to understand the intricacies of this game. These and allied matters will form the subject of the fifth chapter.

DICE-PLAY IN SŪTRA LITERATURE AND SMṚTIS

Numerous references are found in the Sūtra literature pointing to the popularity of dice-play. The Śrautasūtras prescribe the game of dice at the performance of *agnyādheya* and *rājasūya* sacrifices.[1] Words like *adhidevana, akṣāvāpa, kṛta* etc. connected with gambling are used in this connection. Throwing of the dice, spreading them, and collecting them are also mentioned in some of the passages.

The rites recorded in the Śrautasūtras are summarised here. After pouring out the oblations the Adhvaryu should dig out the place for playing the game of dice between the fireplaces of the *sabhya* and the *āvasathya*. Having arranged the dice there, he must place a piece of gold on the dice.

After spreading the dice, he must collect them and pour a spoonful of clarified butter on them with the following verse:

"Varuna, the controller of ordinances, has sat down in the waters for the sake of overlordship."[2] He must hand over one hundred dice to the sacrifice, and say, 'do you play a cow against paddy; do you cut the joints without injuring'. After this the sacrifice, should win the highest throw in the game, namely, the *kṛta* and get up. The players should play the cow in the hall on that day. The cow should not be immolated. She should be offered to the players. Whatever quantity of paddy he has received in exchange for her, the sacrificer, should accomplish both the rice-portions and feed the Brāhmaṇas with food cooked of that rice.[3]

According to the Mānavaśrautasūtra belonging to the Maitrāyaṇi school of the Yajurveda, the Adhvaryu spreads a new garment on the dicing ground, making its fringes facing the north.[4] The further play described here resembles the play described in other Śrautasūtras.

Among other references found regarding dice, mention must be made of the Gṛhyasūtra of Āpastaṁba belonging to the Kṛṣṇa-Yajurveda. This prescribes a ritual to be performed to cure a boy attacked by dog-demon (i.e., epilepsy).[5] The father or the performer of the ceremony having observed the austerities such as fasting should cover the boy with a net. Then he must cause a bell to be rung and take the boy into the gambling-hall through the opening made in the thatched roof of the hall. Having raised the earth in the middle of the hall he must sprinkle it with water and cast the dice.

Now having placed the boy on his back on the dice, he must sprinkle him with his joined hands with curds and salt in the morning, at noon, and at night.

Hiraṇyakeśiṅs Gṛhyasūtra of the Kṛṣṇa-Yajurveda also treats this rite.[6] This rite is also prescribed to cure another disease called *śaṅkhagraha* in which the patient cries with the sounds resembling a conch (*śaṅkha*).[7] Āvalāyana says that a girl who chooses the lump of earth taken from a gambling-place should not be accepted in marriage. According to him she will be addicted to gambling.[8]

Āpastaṁba in his Dharmasūtra says that a student should not go to assemblies.[9] This is obviously with a view to preventing him from gambling. It is stated in this book that a funeral oblation offered on any day of the latter half of the month gladdens the manes.

But the sacrificer gets different rewards according to the time observed. If he offers on the sixth day, he (sacrificer) will become a great traveller and gambler.[10]

Āpastaṁba also says that the king shall cause to be built a town and a palace, the gates of both looking towards the south.[11] In the midst of the Assembly-hall the superintendent of the house shall raise a place and sprinkle it with water. After this he is to place on it dice in even numbers made of *vibhītaka*, as many as are required for the game.[12]

Prof. Edward W. Hopkins is of the view that this passage found in the Āpastaṁba Dharmasūtra is probably interpolated. According to him the recognition of gambling halls by the state postdates the *sūtra* period.[13] It is to be noted here that gambling is not permitted by other Dharmasūtras.

According to Baudhāyana dicing is the first cause of impurity.[14] Gautama is of the opinion that a student must avoid gambling, serving the low people, taking things not offered and causing injury to animals.[15]

References to Gambling in the Smṛti Literature

The gambling is not treated under the Vyavahāra section in the earliest Dharmasūtras like those of Gautama, Baudhāyana and Vasiṣṭha. As we have seen Āpastaṁba alone allows it under the supervision of the king.[16] But the Viṣṇusmṛti provides for the punishment of persons who play with false dice.[17] This Smṛti also prohibits the king from dice-play along with other vices like wine, women, and hunting.[18] However, gambling finds a place in the Vyavahāra section of the Manusmṛti. Gambling and betting were not allowed by Manu and according to him these two vices cause the destruction of the kingdoms of princes.

Declaring gambling and betting as open theft, Manu advises the king to suppress them. The king is directed to give corporal punishment to all those who either gamble and bet or make others gamble.[19]

According to Manu gamblers are to be banished from the kingdom along with dancers, singers, cruel men, men belonging to a heretical sect, those following forbidden occupations and sellers of spirituous liquor.[20] Manu fears the harassment of the good people by the gamblers if they stay in the realm of a king. He considers them as secret thieves and anti-social elements.[21] Gamblers are branded as concealed rogues by him along with those who take bribes, cheats, and rogues and those who live by teaching the performance of auspicious ceremonies, sanctimonious hypocrites, and fortune-tellers.[22] A gambler is looked down as made from *rajas* (activity) along with drunkards and others.[23]

More serious is the situation when a student takes to gambling. He should never play with dice nor eat lying on a bed, etc.[24] A student is expected to abstain from gambling, quarrelling with people, lying and from gazing and touching women.[25]

A gambler (*kitavaḥ*) should not be entertained at a *śrāddha* ceremony (death anniversary) just as one who has not studied the Vedas, one afflicted with a skin-disease, etc.[26] Even the keeper (*kitavaḥ*) of a gambling-house and a person who always subsists by gambling (*dyūtavṛttiḥ*) also are to be excluded from the *śrāddha* ceremony.[27]

According to Manu a son is not expected to pay the money lost at play by his father.[28]

In the opinion of Manu, the gambling, which is included in the *kāmaja doṣas*, i.e., those which spring from the love of pleasure should not be indulged in by a king because when indulged it deprives him of his wealth and virtue.[29] The vices which spring from the love of pleasure are given in the following verse:

mṛgayākṣo divāsvapnaḥ parivādaḥ striyo madaḥ
tauryatrikaṁ vṛthāṭyā ca kāmajo daśako gaṇaḥ/[30]

Even among the ten vices arising from the love of pleasure drinking, dice, women, and hunting are to be regarded as the four most pernicious in the order in which they are enumerated.[31] Manu says that each preceding vice is more serious than the succeeding one.[32] He says that gambling has caused great enmity in former *kalpa* (Ages) and therefore, according to him it is not desirable for the wise to practise gambling even for amusement.[33]

According to Prof. G. Buhler this warning of Manu regarding the consequences of gambling presupposes a knowledge of the legend of the Kurus and Pāṇḍavas. He observes in this context:

"This statement can only point in the first instance to the match played between Yudhiṣṭira and Duryodhana, which was the immediate cause of the great war. It may also contain, as some commentators think, an allusion to the fate of king Nala, but that can only be a secondary meaning, because war was not the result of gambling." [34]

Prof. Kane P.V., [35] considers this supposition as unnecessary and says that right from the Vedic times[36] the evil effects of gambling were known and even the Mahābhārata[37] contains the same verse.

In the view of Manu, the king must inflict punishment, according to his discretion, on every man who addicts himself to gambling either secretly or openly.[38]

Yājñavalkya allows gambling under the supervision of an officer appointed for the purpose.[39] He prohibits gambling for householders (*snātakas*) along with drinking of water with folded hands, mixing with diseased persons, etc.[40] He also states that the gamblers are to be first examined by the king whenever cases of thefts are referred to him.[41]

In the Bṛhaspati-Smṛti, the section dealing with gambling begins with a statement that gambling has been prohibited by Manu, because it destroys truth, honesty, and wealth. It says that the other lawgivers permit gambling provided the king is allowed a share in every stake.[42]

The Nārada-smṛti speaks of the game of dice involving the use of small slices of leather and little staves of ivory used as dice.[43] Though normally a son is expected to pay the debts of his father, he is exempted from paying the debt incurred by his father through blind-love, intoxication, or gambling.[44] This agrees with the view of Manu.[45] Nārada considers gamblers as open rogues along with those who forge measures and weights, receivers of bribes, robbers, and public prostitutes.[46] The wealth acquired by gambling is considered as black-money along with what is acquired as a bribe from a sick-man, by forgery, robbery or fraud.[47]

Gamblers are considered as incompetent witnesses along with thieves, robbers, and dangerous characters. Nārada says that one cannot expect gamblers to be truthful.[48]

Another important Smṛti-writer Kātyāyana is also not very happy about gambling, and he advises the king to abstain from this vice. Gambling is compared to the poison of a serpent.[49] In this Smṛti also we find the reference to the duties of *sabhika*.

References Found in the Works of Yāska, Pāṇini, Vātsyāyana and Varāhamihira

The Nirukta of Yāska which discusses the meaning of some important words of the Vedas contains references to the game of dice. While explaining the meaning of the Gambler's Hymn he derives the words like *akṣa, kitava,* etc. Dice are called *akṣa* and *Yāska* is of the opinion that this word is derived from the root *aś* (to reach). This is so because the players reach the *akṣas* with their hands or by the *akṣas* players reach the money belonging to their rivals.[50] Dice are said to be wakeful.[51] The commentator Durga explains this since both the winner and the loser keep awake, due to the joy of winning and misery of losing respectively.[52]

Yāska interprets the word *iriṇa* as

> *iriṇaṁ nirṇamṛṇāterapārṇaṁ bhavati/*[53]

The commentator Durga says that the board is called *iriṇa* (i.e., *nirṇa*) because debts incurred on the gambling board, unlike others, are not payable by the descendants of the debtors. *na hi tatra putrapautrānugamṛṇaṁ bhavati/*[54] This view of Durga is in accordance with the statement of Manu and Nārada. Yāska explains the word *kitava* as *vaḥ kṛtavān āśīrnāmakaḥ/*[55] It is so because a gambler may be successful due to the blessings given by his friends. Another definition is *kiṁ tavāstīti*[56] What is thy wager? being the usual question asked by his opponents.

The next word connected with gambling is *śvaghnin* which Yāska tries to explain as follows: *ghnī kitavo bhavati svam hanti/*[57] A professional gambler is traced to *sva+han* literally one who ruins one's fortune.

Yāska is of the opinion that the word *caturaḥ* in the Ṛgvedic passage *cāturaściddhadamānādbibhīyādā nidhātoḥ*[58] refers to four dice. A man should fear him who has all the four dice (in his hand) until they are thrown. Yāska observes:

> *caturoakṣāndhārayataiti/tadyathākitavādbibhīyādevameva duruktāya na saprhayet/*[59]

That is, where two men are playing together, the man who has not the throw of the dice is in anxious apprehension lest it should be against him. In a similar way one should not speak ill-words apprehending bad consequences. Sāyaṇa also explains the meaning of this *sūkta* as explained by Yāksa.

Pāṇini's Aṣṭādhyāyī contains many words related to gambling. One of the rules refers to the two types of dice, namely, *akṣa* and *śalākā.*[60] According to another rule the instrument which accomplishes the action of the verb '*div*' 'to play' is called *karman* (object) as well as *karaṇa.*[61] Thus we get the following usage: *akṣaiḥ dīvyati or akṣān dīvyati* (he plays the dice or with the dice). A rule states that the object of the verb '*div*' is to be placed in the sixth case when it means 'staking' or 'dealing.'[62] Example: *śatasya śataṁ vā pratidīvyati*' (he stakes or deals in hundreds). But if the root '*div*' is preceded by an *upasarga* (pre-position), the above-mentioned rule becomes optional.[63] Example: *śtasya śataṁ vā pratidīvyati* / According to another rule the verb '*div*' in the sense of 'staking' or 'dealing' takes the second case affix, in the Brāhmaṇa literature.[64] This rule debars the genitive case required by the Pāṇinian rule II.3.58. Example may be cited from the Brāhmaṇa literature. *gāmasya tadahaḥ sabhāyāṁ dīvyeyuḥ* /[65]

Next, we have a rule explaining the formation of the word *glaha* (stake).[66] This word is derived from the root '*grah*'. The verb *grah* takes the affix '*ap*' and thus forms '*graha*' and then the '*ra*' is changed to '*la*' when the sense of the root refers to gambling. Example: '*akṣasya glahah*' 'cast of the dice' (i.e., the stake to be delivered on the fall of the dice).

In one rule, reference is made to the throwing of dice with the desire of winning or gaining victory over the opponent.[67]According to this rule the letter '*ta*' is changed into '*na*', after '*div*' when the sense is not that of 'play'. Example: *ādyūnaḥ, paridyūnaḥ.*[68] But we have *dyūtaṁ vartate* because here the play is for gaining victory. Another rule states that the object of the verbs '*vyavahṛ*' and '*paṇ*' is to be placed in the sixth case when they mean dealing in sale or staking in gambling.[69] Example: *śatasya paṇanaṁ* (staking of hundred).

The next rule deals with the formation of words like *akṣaśauṇḍa* (skilled in dice).[70] *akṣeṣu śauṇḍaḥ* becomes *akṣaśauṇḍa* and the compound is *tat-puruṣa.*

Pāṇini explains the formation of the words *ākṣikaḥ* and *ākṣikaṁ. Ākṣika* refers to a person who either plays or conquers with dice.[71] Thus *akṣairdīvyati* or *akṣairjayati* = *ākṣkikaḥ. Ākṣikaṃ* refers to something conquered with dice. One of the rules refers to enmity brought about by dice-play,[72] *ākṣadyūtikaṁ vairaṁ-akṣadyūtena nirvṛttaṁ,* i.e., enmity which was growing but has been completed by gambling. There is one more rule in the Aṣṭādhyāyī which refers to some pieces used in the dice-play.[73] This rule states that the affix '*kha*' comes after the word *ayānaya* in the sense of 'to carry thereto'. The word *ayānaya* refers to a position on the dice-board. *Ayānayīnaḥ śāraḥ* refers to a piece that is taken to that position on the board (i.e., *ayānaya*).

In Vātsyāyana's time the game of dice was a very laudable amusement of the citizens of both sexes. His Kāmasūtra recognises gambling as one of the sixty-four fine arts which a citizen is supposed to know.

Vātsyāyana says that a woman should study the sixty-four arts and practise them in private.[74] Vātsyāyana is of the view that the games and festivities can be relished best in the company of friends of the same status, but not with those that are either above or below one, because permanent good relations and mutual understanding can only be established when each party in a sport seeks to afford pleasure to the other and where each is honoured and respected by the other.[75] In connection with the art of developing attachment and infusing confidence in a young maiden, Vātsyāyana mentions some games among which dice-play is one.

The person interested in securing the love of a girl must indulge in dice-play with her maidservants.[76] Again, it is stated that he must hold her hand under the pretext of a quarrel at dice-play.[77]

Kauṭilya and other Writers on Polity

Kauṭilya in his Arthaśāstra considers gambling as one of the four vices arising from *kāma* (lust). The four vices are hunting, gambling, women, and drink.[78]

While giving the views of his predecessors, Kauṭilya states that according to Piśuna, hunting is worse than gambling for in gambling the winner is always one who is an expert in dice.[79]

Kauṭilya, however, rejects the view of Piśuna and says that gambling means loss for one of the two as is illustrated by Nala and Yudhiṣṭhira. The money won at gambling leads to strained relations between persons.[80]

He further points out the evils of gambling such as uncertainty regarding the existing wealth and obtaining non-existing wealth, loss before a thing is enjoyed, and getting illness due to controlling the calls of nature, hunger, etc. On the other hand, hunting has many advantages such as exercise, getting rid of phlegm, fat, etc.[81]

Another predecessor of Kauṭilya, namely, Kaunapadanta points out that among gambling and women, the vice of gambling is worse. He gives some illustrations to justify his stand in which he says that the gambler keeps on playing his game even at night with a lamp and even when his mother has died. And if questioned about losses, he becomes angry.[82]

Kauṭilya is of the view that of these two (i.e., gambling and women), the addiction to women is more dangerous. But between gambling and wine, gambling is worse, says Kauṭilya. This is so because the success or failure of one side, due to the stakes, leads to strife among the subjects and creates factions. In the case of oligarchies and of royal families having the character of an oligarchy, there are dissensions, caused by gambling, resulting in destruction. Therefore, he says that gambling is the worst evil. It favours evil men and leads to weakness in administration at all levels.[82a] Kauṭilya also, like other lawgivers, allows gambling under the supervision of a superintendent. In his opinion gambling must be conducted in a public place as it helps to find out those who follow a secret profession.[83]

Śukra, a writer on polity, is of the view that too much indulgence in gambling, women and wine produces many disasters; but when within limits, gives rise to wealth, sons, and intelligence.[84] It is stated that Nala and Yudhiṣṭhira were ruined through honest gambling. Śukra says that gambling with dishonesty produces much wealth to those who know it.[85] He has included gambling in the list of things not to be done without the sanction of the State.[86] According to him, hunting, dice-playing, and drinking are condemnable in kings. Dangers from these are illustrated in the case of Pāṇḍu, and Naiṣadha respectively.[87] We have reference to gambling in the work of Kāmandaka, another writer on polity. Of the four vices, namely, women, drink, dice, and hunting, the last two are strictly prohibited for a king as they bring destruction.[88] Kāmandaka prohibits gambling because it results in the expenditure of wealth, collected by working hard for many days.

According to him gambling is associated with vices like untruth, cruelty, anger, greed, violation of dharma, absence of activity, dislike for the company of good men and ambition to be in the company of bad men, etc.[89]

The Bṛhatsaṁhitā of Varāhamihira speaks of people who used to live by gambling. He is of the view that these people (those who live by gambling) will be oppressed under the star *pūrvābhādrapada.*[90] Again, it is stated that the gamblers (*kitavas*) will be oppressed under the star *puṣya.*[91]

Buddhist Literary Works

References to gambling are also found in plenty in the Buddhist literature.

For instance, the Milindapañha compares a person who has left the right path to a gambler who hazards everything at dice, and ultimately fails in life. A weak-minded person fallen into the power of death is again compared to a ruined gamester.[92]

The Dhammapada refers to a gambler, who desirous of winning, cheats others by keeping with him counterfeit dice secretly so that he may use them at an opportune moment. It is further stated here that the people always easily perceive the fault of others, but not their own.

They hide their own faults as the gambler who hides the counterfeit dice.[93]

In Mahāvastu, we have the story of Brahmadatta, who disguised as a Brāhmin plays dice with the king of Kāśi, and, with his wife Padmāvati.[94] Again in the Brahmagālasutta there is a reference to the Brāhmaṇas who were addicts to games and recreations.

In Parābhavasutta, there is a dialogue between a deity and the Buddha regarding things through which a man loses or gains. It is stated by the deity that the man who is addicted to women, strong drinks, and dice, wastes away whatever he has gained.[95]

The Buddhist Jātakas also contain interesting stories connected with gambling.

The Aṇḍabhūta Jātaka has a story in which a king plays dice with his family priest.[96] For luck the king used to sing a song:

> "It is nature's law that rivers wind.
> Trees grow of wood by law of kind;
> And, given opportunity,
> All women work iniquity."[97]

The king always used to win while the priest used to lose. The priest wanted to make the gaming song of the king false and hence he took a new-born baby girl and brought her up without allowing her to see any person, to make her faithful to one man. Thus, when the girl was grown up the priest challenged the king to a game. As the king accepted, the play began.

As usual the king sang his "luck" song while throwing, the dice.

But this time the priest added-"always except my girl". And then luck turned and now the priest won the game.

The Takkāriya Jātaka describes the story of a courtesan named Kālī who had a brother named Tuṇḍila, who was a drunkard and a gambler.[98] Tuṇḍila having got money from his sister lost at play. One day, he returned home when he was beaten up by fellow-gamblers. But Kālī had given command to her serving maids not to give anything to and to take him by the threat and cast him out. When

Tuṇḍila was given that treatment he was saved by a certain merchant's son.

Another Jātaka has a very interesting story of two dicers.[99] During the reign of Brahmadatta, the future Buddha was reborn in a rich family. When he had grown up, he became addicted to dice-play.

Once he met another dicer who was a cheat. During the play, the second dicer used to break the play-ring saying that a die is lost. This he was doing by putting a die into his mouth when he had to meet with failure. The future Buddha desirous of punishing him brought the dice having painted with deadly poison and dried properly. When the play started as usual the second dicer, when he was about to lose, put the die into his mouth. This time seeing him swallowing the die the future Buddha said: "Smeared with the strongest poison was the die the man swallowed but knows it not. Swallow, Oh! Swallow, wicked dicer! Later it will taste bitter to you.''[100] Finally when the second dicer swooned from the effect of the poison the future Buddha made him vomit by giving him a medicine containing herbs and thus saved his life.

The Vidhurapaṇḍita Jātaka has a story in which dice-play takes place between Vidhurapaṇḍita and Yakkapuṇṇaka.[101] This story, it may be noted, corresponds to the story of the Mahābhārata. Yakkapuṇaka who was skilled in dice-play defeated Dhanañjaya Koravya who was not so skilled in the game of dice and seized Vidhurapaṇḍita. We have the description of the play between Yakkapuṇṇaka and Dhanañjaya Koravya. When the play started the king's (Dhanañjaya Koravya's) mother in his last birth who is the guardian deity helped the king to win the play standing close to him. Remembering the goddess, the king used to sing the song of play before throwing the dice into the air. The king due to great skill was able to notice the result even before the dice fell on the ground. If they are to bring loss on him, he was catching them and mixing up even before they fell.

When Yakkapuṇṇaka came to know the reason for the king's success he stared at the goddess as though he were angry with her, and she became frightened took refuge in the Cakkavāla mountain. Afterwards Yakkapuṇṇaka won over the king and shouted three times "I have won".

Gambling has again been referred to in Sussondi Jātaka where king Tamba of Benares plays dice with Bodhisattva disguised as a youth.[102]

In Sūtrakṛtāṅga, a Jain work, we are told that a clever gambler is never defeated as he casts the *kṛta.* He will never cast *kali, tretā* or *dvāpara.*[103]

DICE-PLAY IN THE EPICS AND ANCIENT CLASSICAL LITERATURE

Dice-Play as Referred to in the Epics

References to the game of dice are sparsely found in the Rāmāyaṇa but they do not throw any fresh light on the art of the game or on the state of gamblers in society. But the references made at one or two places unmistakably point to the prevalence of the game during that period.

The game of dice was condemned along with women and drink. In his declaration to Kausalyā, Bharata says that one who is responsible for Rāma's exile must be compared to a person given to wine, women, and gambling.

> *madyaprasavato bhavatu strīsvakṣeṣu ca nityaśaḥ /*
> *kāmakrodhābhibhūtaśca yasyāryonumate gataḥ //*[1]

Vālmīki, the author of the Rāmāyaṇa, compares the lights burning inside lamps of gold to the gamblers in deep contemplation being worsted in gambling by expert gamblers.

> *prādhyāyata ivāpaśyat pradīpāṁstatra kāñcanān/*
> *dhūrtāniva mahādhūrtairdevanena parājitān //*[2]

We have reference to gamblers staking their raiment and ornaments in another stanza. The trees with their tops shorn of leaves, and their blossom and fruit fallen are compared to the gamblers who lost everything in the game.[3]

In contrast to the Rāmāyaṇa, the Mahābhārata contains numerous references to gambling.[4]

The course of events in the great epic might be said to have been set in motion by the game of dice.

The arguments and the counter arguments of the different persons of the epic throw ample light upon the rules and regulations of the game and, also on the accepted conventions relating to gambling. These references will be taken up for a scrutiny in the fifth chapter.

The next important episode wherein figures gambling with dice is that of Nala.[5] Sage Bṛhadaśva narrated it to king Yudhiṣṭhira to demonstrate that he was not the only person who had suffered due to gambling and that hardships can be overcome with fortitude.

The story of Nala gambling under the influence of Kali and losing everything to his brother Puṣkara is quite well-known. It was Puṣkara's suggestion to stake Damayantī that made Nala blaze with rage. Banished by the new king Puṣkara, and disregarded by his own subjects, Nala moved into the forest. Damayantī followed him. Nala confessed to her that his undue passion for dice was responsible for their plight. Another important information got from the story is that Nala served king Ṛtuparṇa who was an expert in the game of dice. Nala learnt that art from Ṛtuparṇa in exchange for his own expertise in chariot driving. Kali quit Nala and he soon got back his kingdom from Puṣkara through the game of dice and lived happily thereafter.

According to Monier-Williams, this episode of Nala belongs to much earlier period.[6]

The prominence given to deities Indra, Agni, Varuṇa and Yama, and the absence of any reference to the great Hindu Triad, connects the narrative more with the Vedic than the Epic and Purāṇic periods. Prof. Brockhaus observes: "The personification of Kali as the demon of the fourth Age, and not of the dice, shows that the modern arranger of the story did not understand this old Vedic term, and is another proof of the earlier existence of the Nala."[7] The game played by Nala with his brother was probably the "*Vibhītaka*"- game referred to in the Vedas.

Another instance where dice-play is referred to is Yudhiṣṭhira's playing the game with king Virāṭa.[8] Yudhiṣṭhira was staying in the court of Virāṭa under the guise of a Brāhmaṇa by name Kaṅka. Once Virāṭa was in a joyous mood that his party won over the Kauravas. Then he invited Kaṅka for a game of dice.

Kaṅka refused saying that it was not proper to play with a person who was in great exaltation.[9]

Many of the characters of the Mahābhārata considered gambling as a vice. Dhṛtarāstra was not in favour of it though out of pressure brought by his son he invited Yudhiṣṭhira for the game.[10] Vidura who unwillingly carried his invitation to Yudhiṣṭhira considered gambling as the root-cause of all maladies and tried to avert the game.[11] Dhṛtarāstra mentions Vidura, Jayadratha, Bhīṣma, Śalya, Bhūriśravas, Purumitra, Jaya, Aśvatthāman, Kṛpa and Droṇa as persons who were against gambling,[12] also tells Duryodhana of the evils of gambling.[13] Kṛṣṇa's talk to Yudhiṣṭhira is like the stand taken by Manu and Kauṭilya.[14] Kṛṣṇa emphasises that gambling is the worst of all evils.[15]

The Harivaṁśa and the Purāṇas

The Harivaṁśa refers to a game of dice that took place between Balarāma, brother of Kṛṣṇa, and Rukmi, brother of Rukmaṇi.[16] The game was arranged by many kings who wanted to bring the defeat of Balarāma. Balarāma betted from ten to a thousand gold coins and was repeatedly defeated by Rukmi. Balarāma then betted one crore gold coins. With great pride Rukmi made the remark that Balarāma lost innumerable gold coins to him, though he (Balarāma) is unconquerable in battle. This remark made all the kings laugh loudly. Balarāma became very angry but somehow controlled himself. He then staked 100 crore gold coins.

Throwing red and copper coloured dice, "take all this", Balarāma said to Rukmi, Balarāma threw the dice bearing four marks and thus defeated Rukmi.[17] But Rukmi said, 'I have won the game'.

Balarāma was enraged at Rukmi's behaviour. Though an invisible voice declared Balarāma as the winner, Rukmi and other kings were prepared to fight with Balarāma. The irate Balarāma killed Rukmi in the encounter.

The story of Balarāma playing dice with Rukmi is repeated in the Bhāgavatapurāṇa.[18]

This story also occurs in the Brahmapurāṇa without much variation.[19] The story given in the Viṣṇupurāṇa is like the version found in the Brahmapurāṇa.[20]

Another interesting story recorded in the Brahmapurāṇa is that of Pramati who an expert in the game of dice was.[21] It is said that Pramati went to Indra and on his suggestion played the game with him. He staked his right hand, whereas Indra staked Ūrvaśī. Indra was defeated and had to surrender Ūrvaśī. Pramati wanted Ūrvaśī to be his servant-maid. Next Indra lost his chariot also. Then Pramati defeated Viśvāvasu a Gandharva, but Viśvāvasu's son Citrasena came forward to play with Pramati. He staked all his wealth, kingdom and his life and won the game defeating Pramati. Then Pramati staked his life and was again defeated. He was bound by the Gandharvas. Citrasena won Ūrvaśī, wealth, army, and kingdom from Pramati. This story was narrated by the sage Madhucchandas to the son of Pramati. After narrating this, he brings out the dangers of gambling.[22] This resembles the Gambler's Hymn of the Ṛgveda.

His advice may be summarised as follows: According to him those who mix with the gamblers and often visit gaming halls suffer a lot committing sins and they must dwell in hell. Even good persons become wicked by joining the company of gamblers. When this is the case of virtuous men then what to talk of gamblers? The wife of a gambler must suffer every day. The gambler also feels sorry after seeing the happy wives of others and realises that there is no greater sinner than himself in the world. Gamblers cannot enjoy any pleasure either here or in the other world. A gambler ultimately feels ashamed of himself for having left the path of virtue and remains in sorrow. One may engage in tilling the land, may tender cows and may even become a merchant but should never play with dice. One who wants to make wealth by cheating others will be deprived of dharma, *artha*, *kāma* and *mokṣa.*

After this the sage told the son of Pramati that as his father took to gambling, nothing could be done to save him. He had to suffer what was ordained for him.

The Brahmapurāṇa quoted in the Caturvargacintāmaṇi records a story to explain the significance of dice-play on Dīpāvalī, according to which Śiva played dice with Pārvatī on that day.[23] In that game Śiva was defeated and became sad while Pārvatī became happy having won the game. Further it is stated that one who wins the game on that day will be happy throughout the year and one who loses will lose wealth in that year.

There is one more story recorded in the Purāṇas related Śiva's dice-play with Pārvatī, which slightly differs from the story recorded in the Brahmapurāṇa.[24]

According to this story, having defeated Śiva in dice-play, Pārvatī played dice with Kumāra and got defeated. Next, Kumāra also lost the game when he played with Gaṇeśa. In order to please the depressed Śiva, Lord Viṣṇu arranged another round of play between the couple on a Dīpāvalī day. In this play Śiva entered the dice by an aspect of His, made them produce the desirable combinations and won the play. Pārvatī became angry but she felt reconciled when she came to know the truth through Viṣṇu. In a happy mood she gave a boon to the people according to which those who gamble on that day (i.e., on Dīpāvalī) will become prosperous throughout the year.

A story is recorded in the Skāndapurāṇa which is related to Śiva playing dice with Pārvatī.[25] Once sage Nārada happened to visit Kailāsa and there he saw Śiva and Pārvatī in a joyous mood.

On his request they started playing dice and Śiva lost the stakes. When Pārvatī demanded the stakes won by her in the game Śiva refused to give them. He argued that it is not possible for anyone to win him. While admitting that Śiva is unconquerable by anyone, Pārvatī argued that he was conquered by her in the game. Nārada and Bhṛṅgī supported Śiva's stand. But being compelled by Pārvatī, Śiva gave all that he possessed and left for penance. Pārvatī was ultimately persuaded to give back those stakes which she got from Śiva and to excuse him for the wrong stand taken by him after being defeated in the game.

There is one more story which describes Śiva playing dice with Pārvatī.[26] According to Agnipurāṇa gambling is a vice and it gives rise to unnecessary quarrels. It robs a person of his possessions and leads him to the grave.[27]

Kāvyas

Kings used to play dice with their sweethearts as a pastime and this is made clear from a reference found in the Raghuvaṁśa of Kālidāsa. During Indumatī's *svayaṁvara,* a certain king sportively cast up the dice to make her know that he was an expert in dice-play.[28] We are also told that some kings used to forget their regal duties when engaged in dice-play. But Daśaratha was not like them. Neither pleasure in hunting, nor gambling, nor wine, nor his beloved diverted him from striving for the prosperity of his kingdom.[29]

In the Kirātārjunīya of Bhāravi dice-play is referred to in one or two places by way of recapitulation of their misfortune by Arjuna and others.

In the first canto the forester informed Yudhiṣṭhira that Duryodhana was taking steps to make the kingdom won in dice-play his own by good administration.[30] Arjuna also felt that their plight was due to his brother's undue passion for dice.[31]

In the Śiśupālavadha of Māgha, there is a reference to gambling connected with watersport, Māgha describes the watersport of ladies with their husbands in which ladies used to be defeated by their husbands as they were unfamiliar with the tricks of gambling. In those games love-sport (*surata*) was the stake.[32]

Prose Works

The game of dice must have been popular in Bāṇabhaṭṭa's days as it has been referred to both in the Kādaṁbarī and the Harṣacarita. In the Kādaṁbarī it is stated that the people of Ujjain knew various arts such as playing at dice, etc.[33] A king was supposed to be familiar with all types of gambling and hence Candrāpīḍa acquired great skill in all the arts of gambling.[34] While describing the Rājakula (palace of king Tārāpīḍa) Bāṇabhaṭṭa says that many princes were playing at dice there at the time of Candrāpīḍā's visit.[35] Bāṇabhaṭṭa also describes Candrāpīḍa as playing dice with the maidens sent by Kādaṁbarī.[36] Śukanāsa considered gambling as a vice and cautioned Candrāpīḍa about rogues who mislead kings by representing gambling as a mere recreation.[37]

Bāṇabhaṭṭa also compares Mahāśvetā to one who is skilled in the art of gambling and has mastered the secret of dice.[38] The Harṣacarita of Bāṇabhaṭṭa refers to two gamblers, viz., Ākhaṇḍala and Bhīmaka who were his friends.[39]

In the Daśakumāracarita of Daṇḍin we have the story of Apahāravarman who once visited a gambling-house and joined the company of the gamesters.[40] It is clear from his narration that the superintendent of the gambling-hall wielded great influence on the gamblers and regularised the payments. The gamblers generally distributed the money they gained in the game. Though a player was supposed to pay 5% or 10% of the money won at gambling, Apahāravarman gave the keeper of the gambling-hall, half of the amount won by him in the play. He did so to please the keeper with his nobility of heart.

In the Daśakumāracarita one Candrapālita, son of a minister, praises gambling in the presence of Vihārabhadra, the king of Vidarbha.[41] According to him gambling reveals several moods of a person when one loses a large amount of money. Even when he loses, he puts forth a sort of detachment. Gambling kindles anger, the only mainspring of manliness. There is scope for the development of one's intellect on account of marking subtle tricks, used in the handling of dice.

It is possible to acquire wonderful power of mental

concentration. Apart from these, gambling also increases one's extreme love for adventures. A gambler becomes a tough person as he has often to face very rough persons.

At another place Daṇḍin says that it is the duty of the mother of a courtesan to train her daughter in games of chance and strife.[42] We have reference to the story of Apahāravarman in the Avantisundarīkathāsāra also.[43]

Popular Tales, Didactic Fables and Poems

In the Kathāsaritsāgara of Somadeva, an abridgement of the Bṛhatkathā of Guṇāḍhya, we have the story of one Bhīmabhaṭṭa who was travelling in search of Śaṅkhadatta.[44] One day he reached the district of Lāṭa where people were leading a diversified and richly coloured life. In a city there he came to a hall of gamblers. He found there several fraudulent dice-players. They were clad in loin-rags and their handsome and well-shaped stout limbs indicated their noble descent.

Bhīmabhaṭṭa was invited for the play by the rogues, who were thinking of winning over him. But contrary to their expectation Bhīmabhaṭṭa defeated them at the dice-play and won all the wealth of the gamblers. As a generous gesture, he gave them back the money. True to their professional rules, the gamblers refused to take the money from Bhīmabhaṭṭa. But one Akṣakṣapaṇaka told others that they must take the wealth offered by Bhīmabhaṭṭa as he treats them as his friends. All the gamblers appreciated the gesture of Bhīmabhaṭṭa and became his friends. They then accepted the money. This Akṣakṣapaṇaka while travelling happened to enter a gambling-hall.[45] There he saw some gamblers and played dice with them. Akṣakṣapaṇaka was surprised to see their nobility and sincerity. He became their slave, being won by their good qualities. Since then, he bore the name Akṣakṣapaṇaka.

We have in the Kathāsaritsāgara, the story of another gambler named Thinṭhākarāla who lived in Ujjain.[46] He lost all his wealth but other gamblers who won in the game were giving him every day a hundred cowries. He was bringing wheat flour and making cakes by kneading it. Baking them in the flame of a funeral pyre in the cemetery, he used to smear them with the grease from the lamp burning before him and eat them in front of Mahākāla. He was sleeping on the bare ground in the temple. One day he saw the images of all the mothers and of the *yakṣas* and other divine beings in the temple of Mahākāla. He then decided to play dice with them. He challenged them to play with him and he thought of himself acting as keeper of the gaming-table. He told them to pay up whenever they lost. But the deities remained silent.

The gambler staked some spotted cowries and threw the dice and as the deities did not raise any objection the gambler thought that they agreed to play with him. Thinṭhākarāla won much gold and demanded the same from the deities and when they did not give, he threatened to cut off their limbs with a saw. As he approached them with a saw in his hand, the deities immediately paid him the gold he had won. Next morning, he went out and lost all the money he got from the deities. In the evening he again demanded more money from the mothers as before. When the gambler made this a habit, a goddess named Cāmuṇḍā told the other deities about the general practice of the gamblers. Thinṭhākarāla baffled by the familiarity of the deities with the rules of the game took refuge in Mahākāla. Through the grace of Lord Mahākāla Thinṭhākarāla accompanied by his wife Kalāvatī went to heaven. When Indra heard from Kalāvatī the artifice of her husband, the gambler, he was delighted. Bṛhaspati, however, said that the gamblers are always tricky.

He narrated the story of another gambler named Kuṭṭinīkapaṭa, known for his dishonesty.[47] This gambler once went to the world of Yama who told him that he will have to live a *kalpa* in hell on account of his crimes, but owing to his single act of charity he was destined to be Indra for one day. When Yama asked about his preference in enjoying these two periods the gambler preferred to enjoy his period as Indra first. Then Yama sent him to heaven and the gods accepted him as their lord for a day. The gambler immediately summoned to heaven the gamblers, his friends, and his female favourites and by virtue of his regal authority, ordered the gods to carry them including himself to all the holy bathing places, in heaven and on earth.

The gods did everything as he had desired and by means of those holy observances his sins were washed away, and he obtained the rank of Indra permanently.

When Citragupta informed Yama about this, Yama was astonished to note that he himself was cheated by the gambler.

Another story given in this book is that of Candrasvāmin, son of Devasvāmin, who was a Brāhmaṇa.[48] Once he lost all his wealth and was unable to pay the dues. The keeper of the gambling house after beating him up heavily asked the fellow gamblers to throw him into some blind well. When the gamblers were carrying his body out of the hall, an old gambler took pity and said, "Candrasvāmin is all but dead and there is no good even if we throw him into a well."

On his advice the other gamblers kept the body on the ground and left the place. After some time, Candrasvāmin rose up and lamented his lot.

We have the story of one Sudarśana who had won all wealth from a dancing teacher in the presence of the teacher's wife Anaṅgaprabhā.[49] After this Anaṅgaprabhā deserted her husband and threw herself into the arms of Sudarśana.

Besides these, Kathāsaritsāgara also contains the stories of Śrīdarśana,[50] Dākineya,[51] Devadatta,[52] and Śaktideva[53] who were all gamblers. The story of Nala found in the Mahābhārata is given in Kathāsaritsāgara also with some variations.[54] According to the story given in the Mahābhārata Kali asked Dvāpara to enter the dice.[55] Here, Dvāpara enters Puṣkara and makes him depart from the true path.[56]

The dice-play between Nala and Puṣkara begins in the Kathāsaritsāgara when Nala sees a beautiful white bull named Dānta in the house of Puṣkara and wants to have the same. It is Puṣkara who tells Nala to take the bull, if he desires, by winning it in the game. Obviously, Somadeva has misunderstood the word *vṛṣa* used in the Mahābhārata. There Nala says: *divyāva vṛṣeṇa.*[57] *Vṛṣa* there means the principal die and not a bull.[58]

In the story found in the Mahābhārata, the birds while flying away with the only garment of Nala address him indignantly. But here Nala hears a voice from heaven which says that those two are the dice in the form of swans, which descended and took off his garment.[59]

In the Kathāsarit-sāgara gambling is stated to be the livelihood of Kali and Dvāpara and is described as a game devoid of law, natural affection and as a cause of misfortunes.[60] Nala's story is again repeated briefly in the Bṛhatkathāmañjarī of Kṣemendra where it is stated that Nala lost everything while playing dice with Puṣkara.[61] And according to this version the birds took away the garment of Nala being ordered to do so by Kali and Dvāpara; this idea is absent both in the Mahābhārata and the Kathā-sarit-sāgara.[62] Almost all the stories of gamblers found in the Kathā-sarit-sāgara are briefly narrated in this work also.[63]

The Śukasaptati of an unknown authorship also contains references to gambling. It is stated that one Madanavinoda was given to passions. He had immense interest in gambling, hunting, and drinking.[64]

In the fifth story of this book, gambling is referred to in the words of Bālapaṇḍitā, daughter of the priest of the king Vikramāditya. She says, "one should not look for purity in a crow, truth in a gambler, forgiveness in a serpent," etc.[65]

Didactic Fables

The Pañcatantra of Viṣṇuśarman says that a wise man should not tender his advice to gambler, one who is defeated and one who is repeatedly upset by obstacles in his undertakings, because these persons get vexed easily and resent the advice given to them.[66]

It is also stated in the same work that one must avoid gambling considering it as a harbinger of Yama.[67]

Didactic Poems

We have some more references to the game of dice in the Anthologies of Subhāṣitas. In many of them gambling is condemned as a vice.[68] The king is also cautioned against employing gamblers and drunkards.[69] Gambling is considered as one of the causes that ruin prosperity.[70] One verse beautifully depicts the position of gamblers in society, by comparing untruth to a tree, the merchants to its roots, the harlots to its branches, the Kāyasthas to its leaves and flowers, and the gamblers to its fruit.[71]

The Subhāṣita-sudhā-nidhi, a collection of Subhāṣitas ascribed to Sāyaṇa, provides a long list of dangers that arise from gambling.[72]

A verse says that lovers played the game of dice with the lower lip (i.e., kiss) as the stake. Now, says the verse, the Cupid must decide as to who is going to win.[73] The following verse portrays the intimate behaviour of another pair, which also had agreed upon kissing as a stake in the gamble.[74]

The Kuṭṭanīmata of Dāmodaragupta refers to dice-play. In one of the verses, it is stated that in the game of dice the players try to intrude into the houses assigned to others.[75] According to another verse the game was played with five dice.[76] We have reference to women playing the game of dice during festival honouring Madana (God of love).[77]

Dramas

The game of dice has been referred to in the dramas of Bhāsa. In the Dūtavākya we have reference to this game in the remarks made by Duryodhana after seeing the pictures of the Pāṇḍavas. The pictures revealed the moods of Yudhiṣṭira and Śakuni at the time of *Draupadī-vastrāpaharaṇa.* In one picture Yudhiṣṭhira, though full of truth and mercy, appeared to be disturbed due to his undue passion for dice.[78] He was depicted as consoling Bhīma. In another picture he was depicted as requesting his brothers to give up their anger and forgive him.[79] In this he was pleading with Nakula and Sahadeva. His words make it clear that the gamblers used to meekly put up with insults and defeats at the game of dice. The next picture was that of Śakuni who an expert in the art of dice.

He was depicted as throwing dice with an arrogant smile of a gambler.[80] In the Dūtaghaṭotkaca, Duryodhana and

Śakuni met Dhṛtarāṣtra after the death of Abhimanyu to offer their salutations. When Śakuni saluted, Dhṛtarāṣtra said that the fire of enmity kindled by Śakuni would not cease without consuming even the children. He obviously refers to the game of dice motivated by Śakuni.[81] The second Act of the Cārudatta refers to the story of Saṁvāhaka who took to gambling for his maintenance.[82]

In the second Act of the Mṛcchakaṭika of Śūdraka we have an interesting scene where Saṁvāhaka, a former employee in Cārudatta's household, runs away from the keeper of the gambling-hall, unable to settle the gambling debt. He had great passion for dice but was not an expert at it. He was defeated, in his own words, by the *gardabhī* and *śakti* dice;[83] he then escaped from the gambling-hall.

He entered a deserted temple walking backwards and stood there as the idol (goddess). The master and the gambler who came there looking for him, noticed his footprints. They were sure of the Saṁvāhaka's presence there; but started playing the game of dice in the temple precincts, to make him come out of his own accord. The sound of dice made Saṁvāhaka impatient. He could no longer resist the temptation.[84] Even though he had taken a decision not to play again the sound of dice as sweet as the song of the cuckoo captivated his heart.[85] Out at once shouting "No, no! It is my turn" and was caught by the master very easily. The master then arrested him in the name of the players' association. When the master was pressing Saṁvāhaka to pay the debt, another gambler named Darduraka came there. Darduraka, who, like Saṁvāhaka, became penniless due to gambling had soft corner for fellow gamblers and wanted to save Saṁvāhaka from the Sabhika.

After many arguments Darduraka picked up a quarrel with the Sabhika and helped Saṁvāhaka escape in the medley.

The speech of Darduraka refers to some technical terms connected with gambling. He says that he lost all his wealth through the *tretā*. His body was parched up by the wrong fall of the *pāvara* and next the path was shown to him by the *nardita*. He was made to fall on the ground (i.e., completely ruined) by the *kaṭa*.[86]

Darduraka represents a confirmed gambler. To him, gambling is a kingdom without a throne.[87] According to him a gambler does not care for defeat from anyone. A gambler always receives and gives away money and because of his immense wealth he is also waited upon by wealthy persons.[88] Darduraka says that he earned wealth, wife, and friends by gambling.[89] Though he lost everything by gambling still he continued to have passion for dice.

In the third Act of this drama it is stated that one cannot turn away a bull who is greedy of corn, a man who is deeply attached to another's wife, and one who is addicted to gambling. It is impossible to cure what is in ones own nature. Cārudatta preferred to lie that he lost the golden ornament given to him by Vasantasenā for safe custody at gambling, instead of saying that it was stolen away.[90] Vasantasenā was happy to hear this.[91]

ANALYSIS OF THE GAME OF DICE

Names for the Game of Dice and the Words Used to Denote Gamblers

The game of dice was called *akṣakrīḍā* or *vibhītaka* in the Ṛgveda. The word *dyūta* is used in the *sūtra* literature but it is left undefined there.[1] Gautama in his Dharmasūtra includes gambling under acts forbidden to a Brahmacārin and he has used the word *dyūta* in this connection.[2] The commentator Haradatta in his Mitākṣarā refers to two kinds of gambling, viz., *prāṇidyūta* and *akṣakrīḍā*.[3]

The Manusmṛti defines *dyūta* as *aprāṇibhiryatkriyate talloke dyūtamucyate/*[4]

It is thus clear that according to Manu when inanimate things are used for staking money on them, the game is called *dyūa* (gambling). The *prāṇidyūta* referred to in the commentary Mitākṣarā on Gautama Dharmasūtra (I-2-23) is called *samāhvaya* by Manu. When animate beings are used for the purpose of gambling, that is to be called *samāhvaya* (betting)[5]

The Nāradasmṛti also defines *dyūta* which is called *devana*, in a similar way. *Dyūta* is defined here as that sport which is carried on with inanimate objects such as dice, pieces of leather, ivory and the like and in which a stake is involved. The sports carried on with living beings such as cocks, pigeons, buffaloes, and rams are called *samāhvaya*.[6]

The word *durodara* used in neuter gender also denotes

gambling and this has been explained as *duṣṭaṁ āsamantāt udaraṁ yasya tat* ("That which has an ignominious stomach").[7]

Words used to Denote Gamblers

There are many words which designate gamblers. In the Vedic period the most popular word used to denote a gambler was *kitava.*[8] In the Saṁhitās of the Yajurveda there are different names used to denote different types of gamblers.[9] They are *Ādinavadarśa, Kalpin, Adhikalpin* and *Sabhāsthāṇu.* They are explained by Mahīdhara in his commentary.[10]

In the Taittirīya Brāhmaṇa some other names such as *sabhāvin* and *bahissada* are given.[11]

The commentator Sāyaṇa explains some of these terms in his commentary.[12] Another word used in the Ṛgveda and the Atharvaveda which denotes a professional gambler is *śvaghnin.*[13] As seen earlier in the ritual called *śvagraha-prāyaścitta* a gambler helps to cure a boy attacked by dog-demon. So, the gambler is one who destroys an evil spirit called *śva* and probably because of this he would have been called *śvaghnin.* The word *durodara,* when used in masculine gender, denotes gambler. *Dyūtakārah* is also used to denote a gambler. According to Pāṇini *ākṣika* and *śalākika* refer to a gambler.[14]

The Type of Dice Used for the Game

The popular term for dice in Sanskrit is *akṣa.* Other terms. used to designate the dice are *vibhītaka, pāśaka, śalākā, bradhna,* etc.

As we have seen Yāska derives the word *akṣa* from the root '*aś*' 'to reach'. The word literally means "possessing eyes" and most probably this refers to the eye-like signs sometimes found on the dice. The actual Indo-European prototype is "*oq*" to "see". It is like the German word "*o'sse*"- "eyes".

Dice are called *vibhītakas* as they were got from the *vibhītaka* trees which grew on mountain slopes. In the Vedas the *vibhītaka* nuts are described as brown (*babhṛu*) in colour.[15] The *vibhītaka* nuts are round with five slightly flattened sides. The size of the *vibhītaka* nut is not very big. One of the Jātakas refers to a gambler, playing false, swallowing a die.

Besides the natural fruit, imitations of wood and even gold seem to have been in use.

Sāyaṇācārya remarks that the dice used in games consisted either of gold cowries (shells) or of gold dice shaped like *vibhītaka* nuts.[16]

Prof. Lüders is of the opinion that the golden dice were used only in the ritual playing of the game.[17] But this view is not supported by Prof. Keith A.B., who says that the golden dice were also used in the secular game based on a reference found in the Śāṅkhāyana Āraṇayaka.[18]

In the ritual game at the *agnyādheya* and the *rājasūya* ceremonies, dice of gold, silver, ivory, and the *vibhītaka* nuts were used on certain occasions, states the Baudhāyana Śrauta Sūtra.[19]

The Mahābhārata also speaks of several types, i.e., those made of gold, ivory and of different colours like black and red.[20] In the Harivaṁśa also we have reference to black and red coloured dice.[21] Golden dice are referred to in some of the Jātakas of the Buddhists.[22] The dice-set which Vasantasenā possessed was bejewelled according to the Mṛcchakaṭika.[23]

The dice discovered in the Indus Valley sites are made of

stones, ivory, and well-baked clay.[24] Excavations at Taxila have disclosed several dice made of ivory, bone, slate, and terracotta.[25]

Besides the *vibhītaka* we have references in the Sanskrit literature to the *pāśaka, śalākā, bradhna* and other types of dice.

A reference is made to *pāśa* in some Jātaka stories.[26] The word *pāśaka* also occurs in the Virāṭaparvan of the Mahābhārata.[27] But many scholars consider this passage to be an interpolation. The Nāradasmṛti refers to the *śalākā* and *bradhna.*[28] The term *śalākā* is explained in the commentary as a four, sided bar made of ivory.[29] The term *bradhna* is explained as a leather-strap.[30] The word *ādi* (etc.) used by Nārada in this connection is taken to designate other objects used in the game of dice. They are explained in the Keśavavaijayantī of Nandapaṇḍita, a commentary on the Viṣṇusmṛti.[31] Both the words *akṣa* and *śalākā* are mentioned by Pāṇini.[32] Kautilya also refers to *śalākā* in his Arthaśāstra.[33]

It is thus clear that many kinds of dice called *vibhītaka, akṣa, śalākā, pāśaka* were used in the game. The word *vibhītaka* refers only to the nuts of vibhītaka tree whereas the word *akṣa* commonly refers to *akṣa, śalākā, pāśaka,* etc. The words *pāśaka* and *śalākā* would have referred to oblong pieces made of gold, ivory, etc. We do not have definite proof to show that the oblong ivory pieces or cubical dice were used during the Vedic age. It seems that only *vibhītaka* nuts were used during that period. The *vibhītaka* nuts used in the game did not bear any marks. The cubical dice and the oblong pieces used to be marked on the sides with points or numbers.

Most of the dice found in Indus Valley are cubical and they vary in their size from 1.2 by 1.2 by 1.2 inches to 1.5

by 1.5 by 1.5 inches. One rectangular die measure 1.6 by 1.4 by 1.1 inches. The sides of these cubical dice are numbered with small ring-marks. The numbers run from one to six and are so arranged that one is opposite two, three opposite four and five opposite six.[34]

This numbering differs from the modern method of marking according to which the sum of each pair of opposite sides is seven. Accordingly in the modern dice the numbers are so arranged that one is opposite six, two opposite five, and three opposite four. The tabular dice are marked with the numbers one, two, and three on three sides and have the remaining side ornamented with longitudinal lines.[35]

The dice found at Brāhmaṇābad are numbered as the present-day dice. Here the sum of each pair of opposite sides is seven.[36] There are many small square pieces which are marked on the top in Plate XLV of the *stupa* of Bhaṛhut named "*chitu-pāda-śilā*".[37] The oblong-shaped dice discovered at Taxila have the numbers 1, 2, 3, and 4 on all four sides by way of concentric circles of simple dots.[38]

The dice found at Nāgārjunakoṇḍa have numbers incised on them in accordance with those known in ancient India. About 20 dice discovered here bear concentric circles while the others are marked out with a simple dot within a circle.[39]

Thus, the Vedic people used to play the game using *vibhītaka* nuts as dice, for which reason the Veda sometimes calls the game itself *vibhītaka*. In the developed form of the game both cubical and rectangular dice came to be used. The rectangular dice were generally called *akṣas* but precisely as *pāśakas* and *śalākās*.

Use of Boards

It seems that boards were used in dice-play only in the later period. The Sanskrit words for the boards are *aṣṭāpada, daśapada, dyūtaphalaka and ākarṣaphalaka.*

The words *iriṇa* and *adhidevana* used in the Vedas and Brāhmaṇās refer to places on which the dice are thrown.[40] The word *iriṇa* is used in the Saṁhitās and Brāhmaṇās in the sense of a cleft in the ground, usually natural (*svakṛta*).[41] At one place the hole is referred to as made by water (*apākṛtam*).[42] Prof. Pischel says that "the dicing board must have been called *iriṇa* because it contained holes into which the dice had to be thrown.[43] Prof. Lüders does not agree with this assumption because in his opinion "the dice were merely thrown on a space dug out, which could be called *iriṇa*, as being a hole in the ground.[44]

Prof. Lüder's suggestion is supported by the commentary of Durga on Yāska's Nirukta in which he says: *iriṇe nirgatarṇe āsphurakasthāne.*[45] Sāyaṇa also explains the word *iriṇa* similarly in his commentary on the Ṛgveda. He says: *iriṇe āsphāre.*[46] Nīlakaṇtha in his commentary on the Mahābhārata explains the word *āsphura* as follows:

> *āsphuramakṣavinyāsapātanādisthānaṁ/*[47]

Yāska explains the word *iriṇa* as follows:

> *iriṇaṁ nirṛṇaṁ-mṛṇāterapārṇaṁ bhavati /*
> *aparatā asmādoṣdhaya iti vā/* [48]

It refers to a place from which herbs have been removed. Another word used in the Ṛgveda in connection with dicing is *devana.*[49] This word like *iriṇa* denotes the place on which the dice are thrown. *Devana* is also called *adhidevana* in some passages.[50]

Durga in his commentary on the Nirukta also explains the word *devana* in the same manner. He says: *devane āstāre.*[51]

We have references to *adhidevana* in the Sūtra literature also. Āpastamba in his Śrauta Sūtra remarks that dice are to be thrown on the *adhidevana* (depression) made for the purpose.

adhidevanamuddhatyāvokṣyākṣānnivapet/
atha sabhāyā madhye-dhidevanamuddhatyāvokṣyākṣānn yupya.[52]

Baudhāyana says:

dakṣiṇato-adhidevanṁ karoti /[53]

The Bhāradvāja Śrauta Sūtra has the following passage:

sabhyāvasaśbhyayormadhye-adhidevanamuddhatya uttareṇāvokṣyādhidevanāya sanstṛṇāti /[54]

In the Āpastaṁba Dharmasūtra, we have the following line:

sabhāyā madhyeadhidevanamuddhatyāvokṣyāī[55]

The commentator Haradatta explains the word *adhidevana* as a place on which gamblers play the game with dice.

yasyopari kitavā ḥakṣaiḥ dīvyanti tatsthānam adhidevanam/[56]

Thus, the references found in the Vedas, Brāhmaṇas and Sūtra literature make it clear that no board was used to throw the dice on. A depression made in the ground alone served the purpose.

One of the earliest references to the board is in the Brahmagālasutta of the Dīghanikāya.[57] Here both *aṣṭāpada*[58] and *daśapada* are referred to. It is stated here that some sages and Brāhmaṇas spend their time in unnecessary pursuits such as the *athapada* and the *dasapada.*

The Sanskrit equivalents of these are *aṣṭāpada* and *daśapada* respectively. Buddha Ghoṣa in his commentary Sumaṅgalavilāsinī on the Dīghanikāya explains the word *aṣṭāpada* as a game on boards with 8 rows having 8 squares in each row.[59]

In the Rāmāyaṇa while describing the town planning of Ayodhyā, the author Vālmīki says that the capital's layout was in the form of an *aṣṭāpada.*

> *citrāmaṣṭāpadākārāṁ varanāṅgaṇāyutām/*
> *sarva-ratnasamākirṇā vimānagṛhaśobhitām//*[60]

The commentator Tilaka explains *aṣtāpada* as *dyūtaphalaka* or diceboard.[61] We have a reference to the word *aṣṭāpada* in the Harivaṁśa. Balarāma is said to have hit Rukmin with the board (*aṣtāpada*) when their play ended in a quarrel.

> *jaghānāmṣṭāpadenaiva pramathya yadunandanaḥ /*
> *aṣṭāpadena balavānrājā vajradharopamaḥ//*[62]

We have references to this fact in the Viṣṇupurāṇa and the Brahmapurāṇa.[63] There is no reference to this word in the Vedic literature. *Daśapada,* as the name itself denotes, is a board with 10 rows having 10 squares in each row. Vidhurapaṇḍita Jātaka refers to a dicing board made of silver.[64] Vātsyāyana refers to *dyūta-phalaka* and *ākarṣa-phalaka.*[65]

In the Indus Valley, a portion of triple-rowed gaming diagram on brick was recovered at a Harappan site.[66] The bas-relief on the Bharhut rails depicting a scene of gambling contains a board which has six times six squares.[67] Traces of game-boards on some of the basement slabs and ghat steps are found both in religious and secular buildings at Nāgārjunakoṇḍa in Andhra Pradesh. Many game-boards have also been discovered at bathing and burning-ghat areas, and at a *maṇḍapa* connected to a four-spoked *stūpa.*

Most of the game-boards discovered here consist of 8 rows having 8 squares in each row. Evidently this is meant for playing *attapada* (*aṣṭāpada*). Other boards incised on the flooring slabs contain rows of two, three and five consisting of some number of squares in each respective row, used in the dice-play.[68]

Board-games seem to have been known to early human civilization. Such boards have been found in tombs at Egypt belonging to the pre-dynastic period of 4000 B.C. Boards have also been found in the pre-historic ruins in Palestine. It may be said that in pre-historic India too board-games were known.[69] Mr. Mackay is of the opinion that the dice discovered in Mohenjodaro were quite possibly used in conjunction with board-games.[70]

Prof. Norman Brown also agrees with the views of Prof. Lüders. He observes: "Board or cloth does not seem to exist in any earlier specimen than those set-in palace courtyards by the emperor Akbar in the second part of the 16th CE.[71] But he does not deny the existence of some simpler forms of gaming boards during that time.

Andreas Bock Raming's observations on Gaming Boards mentioned in Sanskrit texts are worth repeating here. He says that our knowledge of game boards used in Indian board games like chess, *pachisi* and *nard* is based to a large extent on textual evidence contained in the mythological literature like the Rāmāyaṇa, Harivaṁśa, Viṣṇu and Bhāgavatapurāṇas; in grammatical and lexicographical works like those of Pata–jali and Amaru, in various poetical works (e.g., Ratnākara's Haravijaya, Amaracandra's Bālabhārata, Bhartṛhari's Vairāgyaśataka) and in some religious writings of the Buddhist (e.g., the Brahmajālasutta). The investigation of these sources has shown that already in ancient times there existed several terms in India which referred to a game board, namely *aṣṭāpada, daśapada,* (*dyūta*) *phalaka* and *paṭa* (= "cloth").

Most problematic of these terms is *aṣṭāpada* which has often been translated as "chessboard". It occurs in several texts just mentioned above, but in many cases, it is difficult to prove that in these passages it is associated with the game of chess.

For example, the Buddhist scriptures just say that some sinful monks were addicted to such objectionable pleasures like playing on the *aṣāpada* and *daśapada*—this is on a board with eight and ten rows of squares respectively—without giving any information on the type of game thus played, in other texts like the Bālabhārata the *aṣṭāpada* evidently serves as a kind of board whereupon dice are thrown. Only few sources give sufficient evidence that the *aṣṭāpada* was used as a board in chess, e.g., Ratnākara's Haravijaya. As in verse 9 of the 12th chapter of this poem the chess pieces of pawns, knights, chariots, and elephants are mentioned side by side with the *aṣṭāpada*, in this case the latter must have been understood in the sense of a chessboard. Apart from the texts just mentioned above several documents written in the Sanskrit which give a detailed description of the rules for playing chess and other board games, thus belonging to a different literary genre. They are: Someśvara's Mānasollāsa, Raghunandana's Tithitattva; the Nītimayūkha and some others.

A close examination of this material reveals the astonishing fact that these texts never use the term *aṣṭāpada* as a name for the board in chess or any other board games.

With chess, the board is either not designated as such at all or is termed with the same expressions as the board in *nard*, *pachisi* etc.: *paṭa* or *phalaka*. Furthermore, it can be shown that many technical terms relating to the "board" or surface used for playing chess are just the same as those used in connection with the boards in other board games (e.g., the terms for square, corner, file, row, and margin).[71a]

Other Implements of Dice-Play

Cowries (*kapardas*) are as old as the Harappa civilisation, but we do not have any definite idea regarding their use either as money or for gambling. Golden cowries are mentioned in the royal consecration ceremonies. Sāyaṇa refers to golden cowries in his commentary on the Ṛgveda and the Yajurveda.[72-73-74] The Mṛcchakaṭika refers to *kattā*.[75]

According to some scholars this is a technical term for the gambling implements, such as dice or cowries. But others are of the opinion that it refers to a kind of gambling called Nandipura.[76] There is no reference to any box for putting dice before throwing them down. But the word *akṣāvapana* mentioned in the Brāhmaṇas refers to a case for keeping dice.[77] In the *stūpa* at Bhaṛhut is shown a box used probably for keeping the small pieces.

Sometimes dice-board was placed on a table. We have a reference to a table with jewelled dice-board in the Cārudatta drama of Bhāsa.[78] The Mahābhārata refers to dicing-cloth. This used to be spread over the place where dice were thrown. *upastīrṇā sabhā rājan sarve tvayi kṛtakṛṣṇāḥ*[79] The commentator Nīlakaṇṭha explains this as: *āsphurākhyenākṣapātanavāsasā uparistīrṇā* etc.[80]

We have reference to some pieces called *śāras* used in the later form of the dice-play. They are referred to in DKC, ASK, and the Mahābhāśya of Patañjali.[81-82-83]

Both at Mohenjodaro and Harappa several objects have been discovered which are probably pieces used for the type of board-game in which dice are used.[84] This shows that the people of Indus Valley knew some game which required a board and other gamesmen as well. Anyhow, we do not have any reference to *śāras* either in the Vedic literature or in the Mahābhārata.

Technical Terms Related to Dice-Play

Before discussing the exact method in which the game was played in different periods it is necessary to know the meaning of some important words used in connection with dice play.

Kṛta, tretā, dvūpara and *kali* are the technical terms used to denote different throws of the game. The throw named *kṛta* brings total win for the gambler. We see this word frequently used in the sense of a winning throw.

In the Gambler's Hymn of the *Ṛgveda* the word *kṛtāni* stands for lucky throws at dice.[85] The word *kṛta* is used in the sense of "the winning throw" at different places in Vedic literature:

> *sa savyena yamati vrādhataścit*
> *sa dakṣiṇe sangṛbhītā kṛtāni /*

"With the left hand he controls even the increasing wealth, in the right he holds accumulated winnings".[86]

tvayā vayaṁ... bhare kṛtaṁ vi cinuyāma śāśvat /

"We shall gather all the winnings in the context".[87]

> *uta prahāmatidīvyā jayāti /*
> *kṛtaṁ yacchvaghnī vicinoti kāle/*

"He secures wealth as a gambler, wins the lucky throw at play by outplaying the opponent dicer".[88]

Āpastamba and Kātyāyana consider *kṛta* as a winning throw.[89] Bhāradvāja says that the sacrificer should win the highest throw in the game, namely, *kṛta* and get up. In the Chāndogya Upaniṣad, *kṛta* is stated as the winning throw. Reference is made to *kṛta* in the Aṣṭādhyāyī of Pāṇini also.[90]

In the Sabhāparvan of the Mahābhārata Śakuni is described by Vidura as *kṛta-hasta,* i.e., one who takes a winning throw.[91] The commentator Nīlakaṇṭha also says that *kṛta* brings victory to the player.[92] In the Buddhist literature also the word *kṛta* is used in the sense of a winning throw. In VPJ, we have the statement *rājā kaliṁ vijinaṁ aggahesi kaṭaṁ aggahī.*

"The king played the losing throw and Yakka Puṇnaka, the winning throw". In the Bhūridatta Jātaka also the word *kṛta* is used in the sense of gain.[93] Secondarily the word *kṛta* means 'wealth' and booty. In the following passages of the Ṛgveda, *kṛta* is used in its secondary sense.

> *vi cayemā bhare kṛtam /*

"I shall gather booty in battle."[94]

> *īle agniṁ . . . vi cayatkṛtaṭ nah/*

"May (Agni) gather wealth for us".[95]

> *ut sma ... bhare kṛtatṁ vyacedindrasenā /*

"Indrasena acquired wealth in battle".[96]

In the Vedic Index, it is said that the Atharvaveda possibly knew of the *kali* as the winning throw.[97] This view is based on the text *ghṛtena kaliṁ ṣikṣāmi* found in the Śaunaka-recension of the Atharvaveda.[98] It is translated as "with ghee do I aid Kali". Prof. Durgamohan Bhattacarya has shown that the Paippalāda recension of the text contains the term *kṛta* instead of *ghṛta.*[99] Here Agni is addressed for help in securing victory over the opponent at the game of dice. There is no reason to show why one should drop ghee for getting success. It is stated in the commentary of Sāyaṇa that a "win" itself has been called ghee, because it is strength-giving like that fatty substance. *ghṛtavat sārabhūtena jayalalkṣaṇena phalena abhikṣara saṁyojaya* "Unite me with the reward of victory which is as substantial as ghee". But this explanation of the commentator is rather unconvincing. Now the correct line found in the Paippalāda reads: *kṛtena kalilṁ śikṣāmi* (With the aid of *kṛta* (the lucky throw) I gain control over *kali* (the losing throw), i.e., I overwhelm *kali* with *kṛta*).

Prof. Bhattacarya further observes: The authors of the Vedic Index, though aware of the Ṛgvedic evidence pointing to "the use of the *kṛta* as the winning throw, were misled by this incorrect line *ghṛtena kalilṁ śikṣāmi.*"[101] He is of the opinion that when *ghṛtena* occurring in the line is corrected as *kṛtena,* there is no need for such a remark to be made. Further, Apsarases. (Divine nymphs) are said to have special control over *kṛta* (the winnings at dice) (*kṛtāni kṛṇavānām*).[102] Therefore, it is natural that *kṛta* must be carried for them and not *ghṛta.*

In another place also the Paippalāda has *kṛta* instead of *ghṛta: tā me hastau saṁ sṛjantu ghṛtena.*[103] One more passage found in the Paippalāda also contains the term *kṛta: kṛtenāsmā abhikṣara.*[104] Here the gambler requests Apsarases to "plunge him in the winnings". This idea is not at all unusual in the Atharvaveda. The Śaunaka-version itself has an exactly similar idea at another place, where the dice are appealed to for "flooding the gambler" with streams of winning throws.[105]

The throw called *kali* is said to bring complete loss to the player. In the passage found in the Paippalāda (I-49-4), the gambler says that he has avoided *kali.* Now it is proved, as we have seen earlier, that the word *kali* used in the Atharvaveda also refers to a losing throw and not to a winning throw as understood by the authors of the Vedic Index.

Sāyaṇa also while commenting on the Atharvaveda observes: *kaliśabdavācyasyāgamane parājayo bhavati.*[106] From the Śatapatha Brāhmaṇa, it appears that another name for *kali* was *abhibhū.*[107] In the Vājasaneyī Saṁhitā, *kali* is called *āskanda.*[108] Pāṇini refers to the losing throw named *kali* in his Aṣṭādhyāyī.[109] This Sūtra deliberately reads *kala* instead of *kali*, as shown by Kātyāyana Vārttika *halikalayoratvanipātanam.* According to this, there can be no desiderative form in *kalayati* since no one would wish for himself a losing throw. The commentator Nīlakaṇtha on the Mahābhārata says that there is no victory if the throw is *kali*: *kalipāte jayo nāsti.*[110]

Nala lost the game only when he was being possessed by *kali.*[111] We have reference to the word *kali* as a losing throw in the Buddhist literature also.

According to the Dhammapada a deceitful player (*kitava saṭho*) tries to conceal his losing or *kali*-throw. The VPJ says that the king played the losing throw (*rājā kaliṁ vicinam*).

The throw named *tretā* brings success to gambler comparatively lesser than the success brought by *kṛta.* The throw named *dvāpara* brings success to a player in a lesser degree compared to *tretā.* Both *tretā* and *dvāpara* are referred to as favourable throws in the Paippalāda.[112] The Commentator Nīlakaṇṭha observes in this context:

dvāparādipāte uttarottaravṛddhyā jayo-nāsti.[113] In the Mahābhārata we have reference to *dvāpara.*

nākṣān kṣipati gāṇḍvaṁ na kṛtaṁ dvāparaṁ na ca.[114] It is again stated in the same Epic that Śakuni, a notorious gambler, was born out of *dvāpara* and that he rejoined *dvāpara* after his death.[115]

Uvaṭa refers to four throws of the dice-play in his Mantra Bhāṣya on the Vājasaneyī Saṁhitā: *kṛta-tretādvāpara-kalayaścatvāroakṣāḥ.*[116]

Śaṅkarācārya while commenting on the Chāndogya Upaniṣad says that the side of the die marked four is well-known as *kṛta* in the gambling convention.

> *kṛto nāma ayo dyūtasamaye prasiddhascaturāṅkaḥ /*[117]

Ānandagiri, another commentator, explains the meaning of the other terms, viz., *kali, tretā* and *dvāpara*:

> *akṣasya yasminbhāge trayo-ankaḥ sa tretā nāma ayo bhavati/*
> *yatra tu dvāvaṅkau sa dvāparanāmakaḥ/ yatraiko-aṅkaḥ sa kalisaṁjñyā iti vihhāgaḥ/*[118]

The explanations given by Śaṅkara and Ānandagiri apply to the *pāśaka*-type of gambling, which is different from the *vibhītaka*-game in which only the nuts of the *vibhītaka*-tree are used.

Commenting on the Āpastamba Śrautasūtra Rudradatta explains the throws (*ayāḥ*) as follows: "When all dice in a throw are divisible by four, it is termed as *kṛta*; when three dice are left over after division by four, it is *tretā*; when two dice remain over, it is *dvāpara*; and when the remainder is a single die, the throw is called *kali*."[119] In other words, *kṛta* was the name of a die or the side of a die marked with four points or dots. *Tretā* was a throw of a die as well as the side of a die marked with three dots. A die or the side of the die marked with two dots was called *dvāpara* and the die or the side of the die marked with one dot was called *kali*. The St. Petersburg Dictionary also explains these technical terms in a similar way.

While explaining a passage of the Vājasaneyī Saṁhitā Sāyaṇa makes the following observation: "The game is played with five dice, four of which are called *kṛta*, whilst the fifth is called *kali*. If all the dice fall uniformly (*ekarūpa*), i.e., with the marked sides either upwards or downwards then the player wins, and in that case, *kali* is said to overrule the other dice."[120]

Prof. De Vreese is of the opinion that before playing, the dicers predicted the results of their game. If the events agree with the prediction. it is called *kṛta,* i.e., "the prediction is correct", and the game is won. If otherwise, the game is called *kali* and lost.

From this he concludes that the terms *kṛta* and *kali* conveyed not an absolute, but only a relative sense.[121]

Connection Between the Yugas and Dice

It is quite well known that the four Ages of the world are called *kṛta, tretā, dvāpara* and *kali* in Hindu literature. These periods or *yugas* are named after the sides of a die.[122] *Kṛta,* the lucky one, being the side marked with four dots; *tretā,* with three; *dvāpara,* with two and *kali,* the losing one, with one dot. It may be said in general that the proportion of virtue, and the length of each *yuga* conform to the number on the side of a die, after which it is named. According to the tradition virtue (dharma) was fully present in men during the *kṛtayuga* when Dharmadevatā, metaphorically called a cow, is said to stand on her four feet. There was a general decline of virtue in the succeeding periods, when this metaphorical cow is said to stand on three, two and one foot in the *tretā, dvāpara* and *kali-yugas* respectively. Accordingly, the die is named *kṛta, tretā, dvāpara* and *kali* with four, three, two and one dot. Prof. Jacobi observes in this context: "The same proportion holds good about the duration of several Ages. The *kṛtayuga* lasts 4000 years, to which a dawn and a twilight of 400 years each are added. The same items in *tretā* are 3000 and 300; in *dvāpara* 2000 and 200; in Kali 1000 and 100 years."[123] In the Aitareya Brāhmaṇa while describing the merits of exertion, we have reference to the names of kali, *dvāpara, tretā* and *kṛta.* It is said, "A man while lying is the *kali*; moving himself he is *dvāpara*; rising, he is the *tretā,* walking, he becomes the *kṛta.*" The commentator Sāyaṇa points out that this is a reference to the famous four periods of the world.[124]

Prof. Haug is of the opinion that these words refer to dice.[125] Prof. A.B. Keith also is of the view that these words clearly refer to dice and not to the periods as understood by Sāyaṇa. He holds this view because according to him the Ages are not Vedic.[126] Explaining a passage of the Śatapatha Brāhmaṇa Sāyaṇa states that there is relationship between the four periods of the world and the throws of dice-play.[127] Besides these four throws, there existed many other throws to which there are references in the Mṛcchakaṭika and Buddhist works. In the Mṛcchakaṭika references are made to *tretā, dvāpara, nardita* and *kaṭa.*[128] The commentator Pṛthvīdhara says that these are called (in northern India) *tīyā, dūā, nandī* (*nakkī*) and *pūrā* respectively.[129] Probably *tretā, dvāpara* and *kaṭa* would have designated *tretā, dvāpara* and *kṛta* throws of the Vedic period.

We have reference to two more throws, viz., *gardabhī* and *śakti.*[130] It seems that these two throws were considered as unlucky throws.

In VPJ, Yakkapuṇṇaka says that there are 24 throws in playing with dice and they are called *mālika, sāvaṭa, bahula, santi, bhadra,* etc. When he asked the king to choose one of the throws the king chose a throw named *bahula* and Yakkapuṇṇaka chose a throw called *sāvaṭa.*[131] These are not explained in any work.

Durodara and Glaha

The other two important words whose meanings are to be settled are *durodara* and *glaha.* According to the Amarakośa, the word *durodara* means gambling if it is used in neuter gender. When used in masculine gender, it means gambler.[132] This interpretation is supported by the Medinīkośa[133] and the Anekārthasaṁgraha.[134] The commentator of the Mahābhārata, Nīlakaṇṭha also is of the same opinion. That the term *durodara* refers to gambling when used in neuter gender is acceptable to all scholars. But *durodara* used in masculine gender referring to a gambler is not accepted by Prof. De Vreese. In his opinion the masculine gender refers to the stock of dice with which the game is played. According to him the interpretation of *durodara* as *dyūtakāra* is the result of a misunderstanding because the term no less than the game in which it figured was obsolete in the time of Nīlakaṇtha and the lexicographers. Therefore, he says that in those places where *durodara* has been explained as *dyūtakāra*(-*kārin-kṛt*) by Nīlakaṇtha and the lexicographers, the meaning "store or heap of dice" should be substituted for it.[135] According to him this inference is to be made from several passages of the Epic. In the Mahābhārata, Vidura carries the invitation of Dhṛtarāṣṭra to for a game of dice and says: *durodarā vihitā ye tu tatra mahātmanā dhṛtarāṣṭreṇa rājñā/*[136]

Prof. De Vreese is of the opinion that the word durodara here means "heaps of dice" arranged by King Dhṛtarāṣṭra, but Nīlakaṇtha explains *durodarāḥ* as *dyūtakārāḥ.*[137] Again in another place declares that if he had been present at the fatal dicing-match, he would havc rcstraincd Śakuni and would have destroyed the *durodaras* present there.[138] Nīlakaṇtha explains *durodarān* here as *dyūtakārān.* Here also according to Prof. De Vreese *durodara* means the heap of dice. Further examples given by him to justify his stand refer to comparisons made between the battle and the dice-play.

At one place Droṇa compares the army with *durodara* and the arrows with the dice.[139] Nīlakaṇtha as usual explains *durodaram* as *dyūta kāriṇam.* Here the comparison is made between *senā* and *durodara.* It is not two gamblers but two games which are compared with each other. As with the army a battle is fought, so with the *durodara* a game is played and hence *durodara* here should mean the stock of dice. In the same Epic Arjuna compares his bow *gāṇḍīva* with *durodara*, his battle-car with the dicing-place and his arrows with *glahas*.[140] The comparison is clear. As the battle is fought with the bow, which discharges arrows, so the game is played with *durodara* which procures dice. In this place Nīlakaṇṭha, in contrast to his former interpretations, explains *durodara* as *pāśa*.

Thus, Nīlakaṇṭha is not consistent in explaining the word *durodara* used in masculine gender and this encouraged Prof. De Vreese to give a new meaning for that word.

Another word connected with the game is *glaha*. This word denotes the throw at dice and it is a later form of the word *grābha* which occurs in the Atharvaveda.[141] In the Ṛgveda also we have the word *grabha* which designates the throw of dice.[142] In the Yājñavalkya Smṛti[143] there is a reference to this word which has been explained by the commentary called Mitākṣarā as *kitavaparikalpita paṇa*.[144] According to Pāṇini the form *glaha* instead of *graha* is used in connection with the game of dice.[145] As stated in the Amarakośa the word *glaha* refers to stake.[146] In the Sabhāparvan of the Mahābhārata *glaha* invariably means a "wager". Śakuni says that dicing, a noble game, was maligned only because of its association with a stake.[147]

Prof. De Vreese says that *glaha* is that factor in the game which decides, and on which the result of the game is dependent. According to him the purport of the term *glaha* may be deduced from those passages where battle is compared with game. The following passage may be considered in this connection:

> *glahān dhanūṁṣi me viddhi śarān akṣāṅśca bhārata*
> *akṣāṇām hṛdayam me jyāṁ ratham viddhi mamāstaram/*[148]

Nīlakaṇṭha explains the word *glaha* as *paṇa* or stake: *glahān paṇān/pāśādhino glahaḥ paṇo jayaparājayarūpo vyavahāra/*[149] Here the battle-car is compared with the dicing-place, the bow with *glaha*, the bowstring with the skill in dicing, and the arrows with the dice. The bow is compared with the *glaha* because on the bow depends the quality of the shot; the quality of the play also is dependent on the *glaha*. As seen earlier, Arjuna compares the *glahas* with the arrows, *durodara* with the bow, and the dicing-place with the-battle-car. As Arjuna's arrows never miss the mark, so the *glahas* unfailingly kill the opponent in gambling.

At another place the Sindhu king Jayadratha is compared to the *glaha*.[150] Jayadratha being the general of the army, the decision of battle rested on him. At one place Nīlakaṇṭha gives a technical explanation for the word *glaha*. He explains *glahaṁ jagrāha saubalaḥ as pāśaṁ pātitavān*, etc.[151] It appears that in commenting on the terms of gambling Nīlakaṇṭha had in mind the *pāśaka* game. However, this explanation indirectly supports the view of Prof. De Vreese according to whom *glaha* is the grasp made by the gambler from the *durodara* and subsequently thrown down upon the *adhidevana*, to be counted.

Prof. De Vreese further observes: "Linguistically speaking, the word *glaha* belongs to the root *glah* which is identical with the root *grah* to grasp, whence follows that *glaha* is identical with *graha* (a grasp)."[152]

Prof. Caland interprets the word *glaha* as the handful of dice, which one takes up and this view is very close to the one held by Prof. De Vreese.

Prof. Lüders considers the word *glaha* as referring to the dice which one holds in readiness in one's hand, for the throw.[153] This view is disputed by Prof. G.J. Held on the ground that if this interpretation is accepted the word *kali-glaha* becomes unintelligible. According to him one cannot know if the dice one holds in one's hand will produce *kali* or not.[154]

If a player always gets unlucky throws, he may be called *kali-hasta* unlike Śakuni who was called *kṛta-hasta*. In this case it is possible to anticipate the unlucky throws and therefore the term *kali-glaha* becomes meaningful.

The Vibhītaka-Game as Part of Sacrificial Ritual

As seen earlier a dice-play is prescribed both in the *rājasūya* and the *agnyādheya* sacrifices. The description of the dice game in these sacrifices seems to show that no game was played as such. What we have is a reference to the preparation of *adhidevana* (a place where dice are to be thrown) and the collection of *vibhītaka*-nuts or dice covered with gold, silver, etc. But when the king arrives at the place of the game, the priest will hand over five dice saying that those are the dice with which the king had won the game.

The *rājasūya* being the symbolic ceremony to mark the victory of the king, it cannot have any subsidiary ceremony in which a defeat may come to the king. This must have been the reason for the avoidance of an actual game of dice on such occasions. This view is also supported by Sāyaṇa.[155] Scholars like Prof. G.J. Held say that the dice-play described in the rituals is not symbolic in nature.[156] His view is based on the expressions like *akṣān, nyupya* (one throws the *akṣas*), *vyūhya* (divides them), s*amūhya* (brings them together again), etc. used in the Śrautasūtra.[157]

The Secular Vibhītaka-Game

This game was played using the nuts of the *vibhītaka*-tree. These nuts had no numerals marked on them. The shape of these nuts does not allow any side to be on top.

These nuts were used in large number, and we have allusions to this in the Vedic literature. The Gambler's Hymn refers to many nuts used in the game.[158]

Scholars give different interpretations to the word *tripañcāśaḥ* which occurs in the Gamblers Hymn.[159] It is fifteen according to Ludwig, Weber, and Zimmer.[160] Sāyaṇa[161] renders it as 53 which is grammatically correct, and this is accepted by Profs. Roth and Grassmann. Lüders interprets it as one hundred and fifty.[162] The references found in the Śṛautasūtras also point to the large number of dice used. They prescribe more than 100 or 1000 dice for the *rājasūya*, and 104 for *agnyādheya*.[163] The references found in the Mahābhārata also justify the view that many dice were used in the game. One of the passage states that heaps of dice were thrown down by Śakuni in his match against Yudhiṣṭhira.[164]

The commentator Nīlakaṇṭha also explains the word *akṣapūgān* occurring in this passage as *akṣasamūhān* (many dice).[165] Some scholars are of the opinion that this game was played with a few dice.[166] They find support in the following passage of the Ṛgveda which refers to four dice: *caturaściddhamānādbibhīyādā*, etc.

The reference to the priest handing over five dice to the king described in the Brāhmaṇas earlier is also in favour of this view. Based on the available evidence, it may be stated that many *vibhītaka*-nuts were used both in the ritual and secular *vibhītaka* games.

The Method of Playing

The technical terms used in the game such as *durodara*, *adhidevana*, *glaha*, etc. are explained by scholars in different ways to suit their own conception of the method in which the game was played. The verbs used in connection with gambling in the Vedic literature such as *nivapati*, *prakṣipati*, etc., are also helpful in understanding the methodology of the game.

According to Prof. Lüders, one throws a certain number of dice on the place of playing (*adhidevana*) and the other then throws several dice to make up a multiple of four or five.[167] The result is made known in terms of *kṛta*, *tretā*, *dvāpara* and *kali*. If the total number of dice is divisible by four or five it is *kṛta*.

If three dice are left over after the division by four or five it is *tretā* etc. King Ṛtuparṇa according to the Mahābhārata was an expert in dice-play and was known for his power of computation.[168] The theory of Prof. Lüders explains the significance of Nala's learning *akṣahṛdaya* from Ṛtuparṇa and later defeating his brother in the game of dice.

In the opinion of Prof. Caland, a certain number of *vibh taka*-nuts are placed on the *adhidevana*. Each player takes some dice and makes a *glaha* and the game depends on this.[169]

Prof. G.J. Held describes the game as follows: Several *akṣas* were thrown down, and those *akṣas* which fell on a definite side were considered. The dice which were counted were called *glaha*, those not counted, *śeṣaṇa*.[170]

These two words are used in the Atharvaveda in connection with dicing.[171] It may be noted that the *glaha* has been explained by many scholars but the word *śeṣaṇa* was left unexplained.

Both Profs. Caland and Lüders agree that the game depended on quick and accurate counting of the dice. They hold this view based on the great number of dice used in the game.[172] They find support in the fact that King Ṛtuparṇa, who knew the heart of the *akṣas*, was an excellent counter.

According to Prof. De Vreese the *vibhītaka* game was a matter of odd and even. His interpretation of the words *durodara* (stock of *vibhītaka*-nuts) and *glaha* (grasp made by the player) has already been referred to.

In his opinion the *vibhītakas* are thrown down from the *akṣāvapana*, the vessel in which dice are preserved. They can constitute the stock to be played with, i.e., the *durodara.* Now both the dicers take their seats face to face. Arrangements are then made about the number of *glahas*, the stake, etc. according to individual wishes. It is then that the match begins.

Supposing that A is the first to play, two cases are possible; if his *glaha* is right, the game is won and finished, and a fresh game is played. If, however, his *glaha* is wrong, the game continues, and it is the turn of B to make a *glaha* from the *durodara.* If B's *glaha* is correct, the game is over and another game is started. But if his *glaha* proves to be wrong, it is the turn of A again and so on. In the case A is the first to play and wins, and consequently another game is played, it is B who is the first to make a *glaha* and so on.

Accordingly, in the special case a match of one *glaha* only is agreed upon and if A wins, the role of B is of a merely passive nature. The method of playing visualized by Prof. De Vreese is simple. The dicer grasps (i.e., makes a *glaha*) some dice from the stock of *vibhītaka*-nuts (*durodara*) and subsequently throws them down upon the *adhidevana.* If the number of dice grasped proves to be odd or even in agreement with their earlier declaration, the game is won. If not, it is lost. Prof. De Vreese finds support for his theory in some of the passages found both in Sanskrit and Buddhist literature. In many places it is stated that the loss was due to one die. In the Gambler's Hymn we have the statement *akṣasyāhamekaparasya hetoḥ* ("I have driven my devoted wife away in consequence of one *akṣa* having exceeded the agreement").[173]

The Pāyāsisuttānta of the Dīghanikāya describes how a gambler playing false swallowed each *akṣa* which brought about the loss of his game.[174] It is further stated here that by acting thus each lost game was converted into victory. This shows that the difference between the victory and the defeat must have amounted to one die only. Prof. De Vreese also has rejected the views of Professors Lüders and Caland according to whom the *vibhīitaka*-game was a mere matter of counting.

According to him it is humanly impossible to count in a moment the number of dice while making the *glaha.* He observes in this context: "In the most favourable case, given always the same *durodara* a certain routine gained in the course of time might have made it possible to make every time the *glaha* wished for, though in that case it is no longer a matter of counting as meant in the Nalopākhyāna.

Consequently, there remains only the factor of hazard which alone, I think, made the game so attractive to the gambler."[175]

We have some other evidence to prove that the *vibhītaka* game was indeed a game of chance.

In the Mahābhārata Śakuni tells Yudhiṣṭhira that the dice produce numbers by themselves, and they do so, governed by fate.[176]

The commentator Nīlakaṇṭha observes:

> *na tu atra svecchayākapataṁ karttuṁ śakyaṁ daivādhīnatvād akṣapātasyetyarthaḥ/*[177]

As seen earlier according to the Atharvaveda magical powers were active in the game of dice.

The victory in gambling is ascribed to the interference of Apsaras, who is consequently invoked to grant success by her *māyā*. It is stated that Apsaras makes the *kṛta* in the *glaha* (*glahe kṛtāni kṛṇavānām*) and that she grasps the *kṛta* in the *glaha* (*glahe kṛtāni gṛhṇānām*). She is also said to take the *kṛta* away from the *glaha* (*ādadānā kṛtam glahāt*). Prof. De Vreese is of the opinion that the secular *vibhītaka* game is determined by two factors only. viz., *kṛta* and *kali*. The terms *tretā* and *dvāpara*, so well-known from literature both as names of special *glahas* and special *yugas*, are not in place in the secular *vibhītaka* game but belong to the other variety of the game (i.e., ritual *vibhītaka* game).[178]

But his suggestion that the other terms *tretā* and *dvāpara* have no place in the secular *vibhītaka* game, is not fully supported by the evidence available.[179]

The Pāśaka, the Pañcikā and other Forms of Dice-Play

The Pāśaka Game

In the Aṣṭādhyāyī of Pāṇini we have reference to *śalākā*, which has been explained by Patañjali in his Mahabhaṣya.[180] According to Prof. Lüders the game as explained by Patañjali resembles the *pāśaka* game found in one Burmese manuscript of VPJ, in which, instead of *vibhītaka*-nuts, *pāśaka* with four marked sides are used.[181]

Pāśakas are the dice upon the sides of which a certain number of eyes are marked. Symbols have in part been substituted for the concrete *vibhītakas*. According to Prof De Vreese these *pāśakas* are thrown up in a game and after they have fallen, the sides turned upwards are counted. If the number of dice counted agrees with the prediction, the game is *kṛta* and deemed won. If not, it is *kali* and lost.[182] Thus in the *pāṣaka* game, the original large number of dice has been substituted by a small number of marked rectangular dice. Here stress lies on the act of casting whereas in the *vibhītaka* game the act of grasping is important.

The *vibhītaka* game must have existed much earlier than the *pāśaka* game. In Mohenjodaro, the dice excavated resemble the *akṣa* of the *pāśka* game. But this does not affect the conclusion already arrived at, since the culture of Mohenjodaro represents an entirely different stage of civilization.

The Pāñcikā Game

While explaining Pāṇini's rule (II-1-10) Vāmana and Jayāditya in their Kāśikā refer to Pañcikādyūta.[183]

This game was played with five dice or five ivory pieces. When all these five pieces fall with faces turned upward, or all with faces turned down, then the thrower wins the game. But when the fall is, otherwise, he loses it. According to Pāṇini the words *akṣa* (a die), *śalākā* (an ivory piece) and *saṁkhyā* (numeral) are compounded with the word pari, and the compound so formed is called *avyayībhāva.*[184]

According to Patañjali *ekapari* is same as *akṣapari* and *śalākāpari.*[185]

It seems that *ekapari* referred to a throw in which one *akṣa* or *śalākā* was different from the rest. In a similar way if two pieces were different the throw was called *dvipari* and when three pieces differed from the rest it was *tripari.*

Other Types of Dice-Play

Besides the *vibhītaka, pāśaka* and *pañcikā* games there might have existed other forms of game in which dice were used. In DKC we have reference to 25 forms of gambling.[186] Yaśodhara while commenting on the Kāmasūtra of Vātsyāyana notices 20 forms. According to him 15 belong to the *nirjīva* class, wherein the stake is an inanimate object, such as money, and 5 belong to the *sajīva* class, which had a living object such as a cock or a ram as the stake.[187]

The Kāmasūtra of Vātsyāyana refers to what is called *ākarṣakrīḍā.*[188] But the exact connotation of this term is not known. Some scholars are of the opinion that *ākarṣkrīḍā* and *akṣakrīḍā* are identical. But Vātsyāyana mentions two boards named *dyūtaphalaka* and *ākarṣaphalaka.*

Based on this some scholars like Tridibnath Ray consider *ākarṣakrīḍā* to be different from *akṣakrīḍā.* They view that *ākarṣakrīḍā* might have been same as *pāśakakrīḍā.*[189] The Nāradasmṛti refers to the game of dice played in different way. In this game one who produced the same number twice used to be considered as the winner.[190]

Rules Governing the Game of Dice

The M.Bh., the DKC and the KSS reveal to us some rules observed in the game of dice and other practices current among the players.

While there existed some fundamental codes of conduct, the players were normally supposed to stipulate and follow rules of game from time to time before they commenced the play.

Once the concerned parties had agreed upon the modus operandi of the game, there was no question of going back. Violation of the rules was viewed with contempt.

In the M.Bh., Śakuni having invited Yudhiṣṭhira asks him to fix the rules of the game.[191] According to another reference gamblers were not normally allowed to play for others. When Duryodhana told Yudhiṣṭhira that Śakuni would play on his behalf Yudhiṣṭhira said: "Gambling done by a proxy seems contrary to rules."[192] But Yudhiṣṭhira ultimately yielded when his opponents persisted saying that there was nothing wrong in employing a proxy.

Another practice current was that the game in the initial stages consisted of several bets. Thus, for instance, the first match between Yudhiṣṭhira and Śakuni consisted of 20 bets. In special cases, however, there could be only one bet, as in the second dicing-match between them.

Another convention that prevailed was that so long as a player was taking the *kṛta* throw (i.e., was emerging lucky), he could go on repeating his throws. But after the *kali*-throw, the turn went to the other player. According to the accounts found in the Mahābhārata and the VPJ, Śakuni and Yakkapuṇṇaka went on throwing the dice till the end of the game since they won each time with *kṛta*-throws in a series.

According to the KSS if a person invited to gamble declares 'I sit out of this game' he could not be compelled to play. This was the common convention of gamblers.[193] This must have been prevalent during the time of the Mahā bhārata also. Therefore, Duryodhana and Śakuni tried their best and ultimately succeeded in making accept the invitation for gambling.

For, had Yudhiṣṭhira categorically declared that "he would sit out of the game" there could have been no gambling, and the story of the Mahābhārata would have taken a different turn.

Another universal rule current among the gamblers was that if a gambler did not object to the dice being thrown, it was tantamount to his acceptance to play.[194] In the KSS a gambler called Thiṇṭhākarāla compelled the deities to pay what they lost in the game based on such an understanding. The deities did not object when he threw the dice after having invited them to play. References are made to such a practice in the Brahmapurāṇa and the Mahābhārata.

In the play between Rukmin and Balarāma described in the Brahmapurāṇa there arose a dispute related to this matter.[195]

During the play once Balarāma staked ten million *niṣkas* (gold coins). Rukmin threw the dice and was defeated. Rukmin wrongly claimed himself as the winner on the ground that he did not agree to the stake proposed by Balarāma. A heavenly voice declared Balarāma as the winner on the ground that though Rukmin did not accept the pledge in words, he did so by his acts (having cast the dice).[196]

In the Mahābhārata also, a similar dispute arose when Yudhiṣṭhira staked Draupadī. Vikarṇa justifying the stand taken by Draupadī said that he did not consider Draupadī as "lost" in the game as Yudhiṣṭhira staked her only at the instance of Śakuni but not of his own accord.[197]

Karṇa took the opposite stance and contended that though the suggestion to stake Draupadī came from Śakuni, none of the Pāṇḍavas objected to it.[198] Further, Yudhiṣṭhira kept silent while Śakuni was casting the dice which showed his willingness to play the game. According to another convention what was won in gambling was not to be returned. This has been alluded to in the story of Akṣakṣapaṇaka found in the ASS.[199]

The M.Bh. refers to another convention according to which in a fair play, a person skilled at dice was not supposed to play with an unskilled person. Draupadī voices this when she came to know about the defeat of Yudhiṣṭhira at the hands of Śakuni. When Bhīṣma said that Yudhiṣṭhira had voluntarily staked with Śakuni, Draupadī pointed out that Yudhiṣṭhira, with no skill in dice play, was forced to play with skilful, wicked, deceitful, and desperate gamblers.[200] Sātyaki also held such a view.[201] According to him the Kauravas violated the vow of a Kṣatriya. A Kṣatriya was not supposed to decline when invited either to a battle or a game. Yudhiṣṭhira himself refers to this vow at a few places:

āhūto-ahaṁ na nivarte kadācit/
tadāhitṁ śāśvataṁ vai vrataṁ me//[201a]

The expression "*āhitaṁ śāśvataṁ vrataṁ*" (an eternally enjoined vow) makes it clear that such a practice was normally binding on all well-bred *kṣatriyas.* When Bhīma was angry with Yudhiṣṭhira for having staked Draupadī, Arjuna pacifies him stating that Yudhiṣṭhira acted in the true spirit of a Kṣatriya.[202] But this is a strange remark made by Arjuna because gambling has not been mentioned in the list of duties prescribed for the *kṣatriyas.*

Gambling is considered as a vice and cannot be taken to be capable of increasing one's fame.

Prof. Kane P.V., observes in this context, "conceding for the sake of argument that indulgence in gambling even on the part of such a virtuous noble and philosophic warrior as Yudhiṣṭhira was justified or at least excusable, there is nothing to show that the code of *kṣatriya* chivalry permitted him to gamble away his own spirit, devoted and virtuous queen and his four valiant brothers."[203] Balarāma's views in this context are interesting.[204] According to him the fault lay with Yudhiṣṭhira. First, Yudhiṣṭhira's passion for dice was so high that he did not pay heed to the advice tendered by his well-wishers. Secondly, he could have opted to play with others rather than with Śakuni who was a noted gambler.

Thirdly, when the dice went against him, he could have stopped playing further. As such no blame could be apportioned to Śakuni.

According to one reference found in the Mṛcchakaṭika gamblers used to form a sort of association for which they had very high regard. When Saṁvāhaka did not pay the debt which he owed to his opponent, the keeper of the gambling house drew a circle round him and said that

Saṁvāhaka was bound by the gamblers ring.[205] Such a circle drawn round the defaulted players is also referred to in some of the Jātakas of the Buddha.[206] According to the convention the defaulters could not go out of the ring until the debts were settled. This is somewhat like the views expressed in the Nāradasmṛti according to which the gamblers should not enter another gambling house before paying their debts.[207]

The Nature of Stake and Eligibility to Stake

As regards the nature of the stake and the eligibility to stake we have some interesting observations both in the M.Bh. and the KSS. According to the M.Bh. one that has no money himself cannot stake the money belonging to others.[208] In the Ṛgveda also we have reference to men staking their personal freedom in games.[209] After losing all wealth, men used to stake their dependents besides staking their own selves. According to the Epic, Yudhiṣṭhira staked and lost Nakula, Sahadeva, Arjuna and Bhīma one by one. When nothing was left to stake, Yudhiṣṭhira then staked himself and lost; thereafter, at the suggestion of Śakuni, he staked Draupadī and lost her too. The points raised by different characters of the Epic regarding the propriety of such a stake may be considered in this connection.

The very fact that different persons view at it differently makes it clear that there was no final opinion on the issue. Each one had his own interpretation, making the things worst confounded.

According to Vidura people who lost personal freedom did not have any right over their dependents. He contended that Draupadī could not become Duryodhana's property as she was staked by the king who lost himself first in the game.[210] To think that Yudhiṣṭhira had a right to stake her was as absurd as claiming money gained in a dream.[211]

When Draupadī was informed by Prātikāmin about Yudhiṣṭhira losing her in the game she did not believe it at first.[212] This indicates that kings' staking their wives in games was not a common practice. Draupadī further said that Yudhiṣṭhira's action only revealed his undue passion for dice.[213]

The points raised by Draupadī regarding the propriety of her husband staking her indicate the considerable freedom of speech which women had those days. They could voice their concern against any disastrous steps taken by their husbands although it cannot be said that such attempts always met with general approval and success, as in the case of Draupadī herself. Draupadī contended that Yudhiṣṭhira had lost all right to stake her, having first lost his own independence.[214] In her opinion the play was null and void. Bhīṣma found the issue too complicated for him to decide. He was of the view that, Yudhiṣṭhira voluntarily staked and he himself did not consider Śakuni as having adopted deceitful means in the play.[215] Bhīma while taking strong exception to Yudhiṣṭhira's act referred to certain norms of behaviour among the gamblers of those days.

According to him a gambler never staked even a woman of loose character much less one's own wife of avowed character.[216] Yudhiṣṭhira was exceptional in that he staked not only his kingdom and himself, but also his brothers and finally his wife.[217] The speech made by, Vikarṇa in support of Draupadī also reveals how public looked upon gambling those days. According to him hunting, drinking, gambling and indulgence in women are the four vices of kings. One addicted to these leads an ignoble life. The words of such a person do not arouse conviction or a sense of authority in others. Yudhiṣṭhira was deeply engaged in one of these vices, viz., gambling, and as such his acts carry no authority or approbation.[218] Therefore, Vikarṇa did not consider Draupadī as "lost" in the game of dice. Moreover, Draupadī was the common wife of all the sons of Pāṇḍu and Yudhiṣṭhira did not have exclusive right over her.[219]

Opposing the stand taken by Vikarṇa, Karṇa observed that Draupadī was one of the "possessions" of Yudhiṣṭhira and as such, there was no point in Vikarṇa's argument.[220] Karṇa personally felt that Draupadī, by virtue of marrying five men, had gone against the divine rule which ordains only one husband for one woman.[221] But still, the question of Yudhiṣṭhira's right to stake his wife remained unanswered in the Epic. A person losing his right over his wife after losing his own personal freedom in the game is hinted at in the Gambler's Hymn of the Ṛgveda also. As we know, at last Dhṛtarāṣṭra intervened. Much to the chagrin of Duryodhana he granted Draupadī's request, and gave the Pāṇḍavas their lost property.

The story of Nala, as already observed, belongs to much earlier period of history even though it is found in the Mahābhārata.

Nala's behaviour towards his wedded wife Damayantī is nobler compared to that of Yudhiṣṭhira towards Draupadī. Like Śakuni in the Epic, here also Nala's brother Puṣkara suggested to stake Damayantī when Nala had nothing else to stake. But the words of Puṣkara made Nala blaze with fire. He immediately left that country.[222] This fact can be taken to suggest the high regard women enjoyed in society during the period in which Nala lived. In the KSS the story of Akṣakṣapaṇaka speaks of people staking their personal freedom in games. Akṣakṣapaṇaka himself had gambled with another person on the mutual understanding that whoever was defeated had to become the slave of the victor. When he defeated his opponents, they all became his slaves.[223]

Another point concerning gambling which has drawn the attention of scholars is regarding the question whether the defeated gamblers had to give up their clothes also. We do not have any reference to this practice in the Vedic literature. According to the M.Bh. when Draupadī was arguing about the genuineness of Yudhiṣṭhira's action in staking her, Karṇa ordered Du*śśā*sana to remove the garments of the Pāṇḍavas as well as of Draupadī.[224] Hearing his words the Pāṇḍava brothers took off their upper garments.[225] When Du*śśā*sana started stripping Draupadī's garments they were miraculously replaced by Lord Sri Kṛṣṇa.[226] Profs. Franklin Edgerton and G.H. Bhatt consider that the portion of the M.Bh. referring to Draupadī's *vastrāpaharaṇa* (Sabhā,68,40-50) is interpolated.

Prof. Edgerton considers Draupadī's celebrated prayer to Lord Sri Kṛṣṇa as interpolated.[227] According to him it is apparently implied (though not stated) that cosmic justice automatically or magically prevented the chaste and noble Draupad from being stripped in public.

Prof. Bhatt G.H., considers the entire episode of Draupadī*vastrāpaharaṇa* as an interpolation.[228] His theory is based on two arguments. One is the omission of this from several other contexts in the Epic where recapitulations of the things done by Dhṛtarāṣṭra is given. Second argument is the unlikelihood of such a depraved act being committed even by Duśśāsana. In his opinion this portion has been added later on with the object of depicting the Kauravas in the worst light possible for satisfying the readers whose sympathies always went with the Pāṇḍavas.

Dr. Raghavan V., however, observes: "The *vastrāpaharaṇa* is not a special insult offered to Draupadī, but it is part and parcel of a customary disgrace that has to be there as an *aṅga* of *dyūta*."[229] He is of the view that there is no game of dice without the forcible snatching away of the clothes of the defeated or the defeated themselves casting off their *uttarīyas* as an act of submission. This is necessary to make them deprived of everything in their possession. He refers to the episode of Nala where Nala, after complete defeat, leaves with a single garment and later, the dice come again as birds and deprive him of even the remaining part of his garment.[230] The address made by the dice in this context is significant.[231]

We have references to gamblers losing their clothes in some stories of the KSS.

One gambler named Devadatta having lost his clothes could not return to his father's house. So, he entered a dilapidated temple.[232] Reference is also made to one Candrasvāmin and Śrīdarśana who too had a similar plight. One gambler called Tuṇḍila, whose story is found in one of the Jātakas of the Buddha, also lost clothes on his person and came to his sister's house wrapping him with rag of loin cloth.

Based on these references, however, it is difficult to state that the forceful removal of clothes of a defeated person was a part and parcel of the game. The episode of Draupadī *vastrāpaharaṇa* is a solitary instance. Yudhiṣṭhira's right to stake Draupadī itself is not settled in the Epic. Even in the KSS no reference is made to the forcible removal of the clothes of the defeated persons.

Further, though the society described in the Mṛcchakaṭika and the DKC does not show any high standard of morality, we have no reference to a defeated person being forcibly disrobed. Perhaps the loser giving up his second cloth (*uttarīya*) might have been a general practice, though its literal application in the case of Draupadī, trying to disrobe her in public, could never have been in vogue.

GAMBLING HOUSES—RULES AND REGULATIONS AND THEIR IMPLEMENTATION

House of Gambling

During the Ṛgvedic period people used to play the game of dice in an assembly hall called *sabhā*.[1] In the Yajurveda we have the word *sabhāsthāṇu* given to a dicer because of his constant presence in the *sabhā* [2] The Atharvaveda also refers to *sabhā* as a place of gambling.[3] The Sūtra literature also has references to the gambling hall called *sabhā*. The existence of gambling-hall during the time of Āśvalāyana is proved by the reference found in his Gṛhyasūtra. According to some of his predecessors the assembly hall inclined to the south will be free from gambling. But others feel that such an assembly hall was occupied by young men for the purpose of gambling. Āśvalāyana himself subscribes to the views of the latter and says that if the assembly hall is built on a spot which is inclined towards the south, men in such an assembly hall become gamblers, quarrelsome and short-lived.

To prevent this, he suggests that the assembly hall be built on a spot where the water flows off easily in all directions. Such a spot would prove lucky and there would be no gambling in it.[4]

Āpastamba says that a king must provide a hall for gambling and that it must be open to truthful and pure Āryas. It seems that during the times of Āpastamba the game of dice had to be played in the hall meant for that purpose. Commentator Haradatta says that persons who play elsewhere are liable to fine.[5]

The Yājñavalkyasmṛti refers to two kinds of gambling halls, one presided over by an officer appointed by the king and the other a secret one with no control by the State.[6] According to Nārada people may gamble even in an open place outside the gambling hall provided they pay the kings share in the stake. If they do so they are not liable for punishment.[7]

In the opinion of Kātyāyana the assembly hall meant for gambling must have a special arch-like structure near the door so that it would not be mistaken by respectable people.

There are many references to gambling halls in the Mahābhārata, the Purāṇas and the classical literature.

According to the Mahābhārata the assembly hall caused to be built by Dhṛtarāṣṭra had a thousand pillars and hundred doors made out of gold and studded with diamonds. The hall was named *toraṇasphāṭikā.* There were many golden seats and costly beds in it. The hall was very large, one *krośa* in length and one *krośa* in width, according to the great Epic.[8]

The Harivaṁśa[8a] refers to a game of dice arranged between Rukmin and Balarāma in a beautiful hall with golden pillars. Its floor was covered with flowers and the entire hall was sprinkled with sandal water.

The Kathāsaritsāgara speaks of a gamblers' hostel caused to be built by King Śrīsena of Mālava who, in his youth, suffered because of his passion for gambling. But when he became king, he provided a glorious asylum for gamblers and looked after their comforts as a generous gesture.[9] Public and private gaming halls in big cities are alluded to in the plays of Bhāsa.[10] Kautilya also refers to gambling houses.[11]

In the Daśakumāracarita gambling houses (*dyūtasabhās*) in big cities are alluded to. These houses were recognised by the government and were strictly supervised by the officers known as *sabhikas* or *dyūtādhyakṣas.*[12] Daṇḍin also describes the atmosphere that prevailed in those gambling-houses. He refers to the tumultuous din and clamours raised by gamblers at intervals mostly consisting of indecent and vulgar talk.[13] Though we have references to men visiting gambling houses, we do not have references to show that either during Vedic times or in later periods ladies visited such houses. However, Prof. R.C. Das is of the view that a hymn of the Ṛgveda shows that sometimes widows visited the dicing hall with a view to gaining wealth by gambling.[14]

He further observes: "Such conduct on their part was, of course, not approved, as the conduct of a brother-less young woman who sought the company of young men met with public disapprobation."[15] The commentator Veṅkaṭamādhava also holds the same view.[16] During the time of the Mahābhārata ladies do not appear to have visited gambling halls. This point is suggested by the words of Draupadī when she was dragged into the gambling hall where Yudhiṣṭhira gambled with Duryodhana. She says that she was neither brought before any assembly nor exposed to the gaze of the public.[17] It also appears that the ladies born of high families had the privilege of not being compelled to enter the public halls. Draupadī says that nothing could be more distressing than her being dragged to a public hall though she was high-born.[18] It also appears that in ancient times, kings did not take their wedded wives into the public halls.[19]

Prof. Edward W. Hopkins observes in this context: "This indignity even more than the forcible disrobing, seems to fire the indignation of the helpless heroes."[20]

The Purāṇas and the classical literary works also do not refer to ladies playing the game of dice in a gambling hall. However, this evidence of the Mahābhārata does not prevent us from guessing the entry of common women into the gambling halls.

The Officers in Charge of Gambling Houses

Right from the Vedic period it appears that gambling houses were under the custody of some important persons. According to Sāyaṇa the word of *sabhāvin* found in the Taittirīya Brāhmaṇa denotes the keeper of a gambling hall.[21]

Akṣāvāpa is another word which probably refers to a professional dicer who plays with the king or watches his play. It is also possible that this word would have referred to a public person who oversaw gambling halls of the state and collected the tax money due to the king.[22]

It also appears that in the Vedic period there were some persons in the royal entourage called *ratnins*, in whose houses a special fire-ritual called *ratnahavis* used to be performed, as part of the *rājasūya* ceremony. *Akṣāvāpa* was one of the *ratnins* (receivers of gifts).[23] *Akṣāvāpa* has been referred to in the Saṁhitās and the Brāhmaṇas of the Yajurveda.

In the *sūtra* literature we do not have any specific reference to an officer in charge of a gambling hall. Haradatta while explaining a passage of the Āpastamba Dharmasūtra says that the players used to pay some money to the keeper of the gambling hall as agreed beforehand. According to him, that officer in turn pays to the state a regular sum for the privilege of keeping the gambling hall. He may pay the tax for the total receipts every day or once in a month or once a year.[24]

Among the Smṛti-writers Yājñyavalkya is the first to make a specific reference to the officer in charge of gambling and his duties. The officer was called *sabhika.*[25]

The commentary Mitākṣarā explains that *sabhika* was the keeper of the gambling house. To him belonged the house where the gamesters stay.

Sabhāpati was the name given to an officer who was supposed to provide the necessary instruments of gambling such as dice and receive some money. This officer used to maintain himself on the income derived therefrom.[26]

According to Yājñavalkya the *sabhika* being well protected must pay a a fixed portion of his income to the king. The *sabhika* must also recover the amount of the wager and pay to the winner. Being ever patient, he must make correct decisions in disputes related to gambling.[27] According to Yājñavalkya as interpreted by the commentator Mitramiśra the *sabhika* was to receive 5% when the stake was 100 *paṇas* or more, and 10% when the stake was less than 100 *paṇas.*[28] Another commentator Aparārka explains that the *sabhika* was to receive as his fee 5% from the victorious gambler and 10% from the losing gambler.[29]

Bṛhaspati says that gambling must be conducted under the superintendence of keepers of gambling houses, as it serves the purpose of discovering thieves.[30] According to Nārada, it is the duty of the *sabhika* to arrange for the game in a hall.[31] He says that the gamblers must also obey the master of the gambling house and must pay of their own accord what they owe to him.[32] He prescribes a flat rate of 10% of the stake as the fee of the *sabhika.*[33]

According to Kauṭilya the cowrie-shells and dice must be provided by the *sabhika* for which he could collect rent. Drinking water may also be provided and charged for. The *sabhika* could also take 5% from the gains of the winners for the upkeep of the gambling house. He shall also look after the pledging and sale of articles. For not prohibiting certain offences concerning the game such as dexterous manoeuvres of the hand, the master (*sabhika*) himself shall be fined double the usual amount.[34]

In the opinion of Kātyāyana if the losing gambler has no money to pay to the winner, the *sabhika* may pay the winner the prize money from his own resources and may recover the amount from the loser within three fortnights or at once if there is fear of losing the money.[35]

According to Yājñavalkya if the *sabhika* is unable to make the defeated gambler pay the money to the victor, the king shall make the former pay to the latter provided the game took place openly in the presence of the *sabhika* and other gamblers. The money due to the state exchequer must also have been paid by the *sabhika.* Only then the king would interfere in the matter.[36] Kātyāyana adds that the *sabhika* should force the defeated gambler to pay his dues in the gambling hall itself and not elsewhere. The exact procedure to be followed in matters relating to gambling was stipulated by the *sabhika* only.[36a] The duties and powers of the *sabhika* given in the Agnipurāṇa are nearly the same as those given by Yājñavalkya.[37]

The Mṛcchakaṭika throws sufficient light on the office of a *sabhika,* A *sabhika* named Māthura maintained a gambling score or record-book (*lekhaka*) in which the earnings and losses were entered.[38] The players had to square up these accounts before they entered another gambling house. It seems that the *sabhika* was also reporting important matters to the king.[39] The remark of Māthura after receiving the bracelet from Madanikā (as the money to be paid by Saṁvāhaka) shows that a *sabhika* used to cordially invite even a defeated gambler for another round of play provided he had come with money, although he might have persecuted him a minute before for his dues.[40] Māthura's forcefully extracting the money from Saṁvāhaka on behalf of the winning gambler clearly shows that collection of arrears was the chief duty of a *sabhika*, as stated in the Smṛtis. The dialogue of Saṁvāhaka and Māthura found in the Mṛcchakaṭika makes this clear. We have also a reference to the punishment meted out to the losing gamblers by the *sabhika*. As revealed in this drama the *sabhika* was a very powerful man in society and his words were, as it were, law to the gamblers.

The words of a gambler who played dice with Saṁvāhaka may be noted in this context: (given in simple translation)

"Even if you now go to the nether regions, or seek the protection of Indra himself, nobody, not even Śiva, would be able to save you, excepting the keeper of the gambling house alone"[41].

The running away of the defaulting gamblers at the sight of the *sabhika* was quite common.[42]

In Daśakumāracarita also we have reference to gambling houses controlled by *sabhikas* (*dyūtādhyakṣas*) whose permission was necessary for a stranger to participate in a game in which other members were already taking a part.[43] The *sabhikas* used to be friendly with gamblers and we have a reference to a *sabhika* who arranged a dinner in his house for a victorious gambler.[44]

The Kathāsaritsāgara refers to a *sabhika* who beat a gambler with sticks for not having paid the debts. When the gambler fainted, the angry *sabhika* asked other gamblers to throw him into some blind well. The *sabhika* however assured the winning gamblers that he himself would pay the amount due to them.[45] This is in conformity with the statement found in the Kātyāyana Smṛti.

Disputes Arising during Gambling

In general people used to consider the gamblers to be rogues and dishonest people and therefore the task of settling disputes between them was entrusted to persons who were familiar with the fraudulent practices of the gamblers. According to Yājñavalkya and Nārada the gamblers themselves must be the judges for settling the cases of gamblers. The gamesters themselves must act as witnesses too.[46]

Mitākṣarā on Yājñavalkya says that here exemption is given to the general injunction that gamblers could neither be witnesses in lawsuits nor sit in an assembly as assessors. The gamblers are to be appointed by the king as judges and the usual rule that a judge shall be accomplished in learning, etc. is not applicable when deciding disputes concerning gambling.[47] Kātyāyana also makes a similar observation.[48] According to Bṛhaspati the *sabhika* assisted by three other gamblers may also act as witness in a dispute and if the gamblers are alleged to be inimical to the disputants, the king may himself decide the matter.[49]

According to Kātyāyana an honest *sabhika* is the final authority in settling disputes concerning victory, money due to the winner and the employment of false dice.[50] Bṛhaspati advocates the release of persons defeated in the game if they are ignorant of the rules. Moreover, even those who are well acquainted with the game must be released if they are defeated by false dice or by deceit.

Again, Bṛhaspati says that if a person loses all his wealth in the game, he should not be compelled to give up the whole of it.[51] Kātyāyana too says that if a gambler is defeated because of his ignorance of the game, he can be released.[52]

In the Arthaśāstra of Kauṭilya there are references to suits involving gambling. Gamblers who cannot settle their disputes will naturally prefer a suit in the court of the king. According to earlier authorities the winner of the game, as decided in the suit, must be punished with the lowest fine and the loser must be punished heavily evidently because of his wrong claim. Kauṭilya does not agree with his predecessors on this point and says that if the loser is punished with a double fine, no one will approach the king for justice.

Even if anybody wins by cheating the other man, the loser may not seek justice from the court, being afraid of the heavy fine which he may have to pay in case of losing the suit also.

Again, it is said that gamblers are generally fraudulent people and therefore there cannot be any distinction between the winner and the loser. Moreover, if a gambler who wins by cheating and wins the suit as well is let off with a lighter fine, this would encourage further cheating. With this view in mind Kauṭilya objects to variation in fines for gamble-suitors. If' both the parties had played without license, both must be punished. If the winner is decided by a court, there should not be any fine for either.[53]

Crime and Punishment Related to Gambling

Cheating at play was one of the most frequent crimes. One poet says that it is a sin against the ordinances of Varuṇa.[54] The words *kitava* and *dhūrta* used as names for a gamester in the Ṛgveda later came to mean a cheat and a rogue respectively in classical Sanskrit.[55] There are references to cheating at play in the Ṛgveda and the Atharvaveda.[56]

According to the Mahābhārata Yudhṣṭhira was not in favour of dice-play because of the element of cheat involved in it.[57]

Most of the characters of the great epic knew that Śakuni won the game by deceit. However, there is no reference to the exact mode of cheating adopted by Śakuni to win the game. A Buddhist story refers to a gambler winning the game by swallowing the unwanted die. Another story refers to a king who with his magical power could prevent unwanted throws by holding the die in the middle.

Kauṭilya and some Smṛti writers have noted some of the fraudulent practices of gamblers and prescribed punishments. The commentator Nandapaṇḍita on the Viṣṇuṣmṛti explains some practices followed by gamblers to win the game.[58]

To minimize the fraudulent practices Āpastamba, Yājñavalkya and Kauṭilya state that gambling must be carried out in houses recognised by the state.

According to Yājñavalkya and Nārada if gambling is carried on secretly and without the king's permission the gamblers and the *sabhika* would not be able to gain their object (i.e., recovering bets won or the fee) and would be liable to punishment.[59] Bṛhaspati also states that the game should be conducted in public, and the false gamblers should be banished.[60] The Viṣṇusmṛti states that those who use false dice in gambling shall have their hands lopped off. Those who resort to fraudulent practices in gaming shall lose the forefinger and the thumb.[61] The Yājñavalkyasmṛti states that those who play with false dice or use other deceitful tricks shall be punished by branding on the head (with dog's foot and the like) and banished from the land.[62] According to Nārada the banished gamblers would have wreaths of dice tied round their necks.[63] According to Bṛhaspati, those who use false dice in a game or cheat by making false computations, and others who deprive the king of his due share must be punished.[64] Kauṭilya says that those who play in places not recognised by the state must be punished with 12 *paṇas.*[65]

He fixes the fine at the rate of 12 *paṇas* for substituting cowrie-shells or dice. The winnings of those who play falsely must be confiscated and the cheats must also be punished alike.[66] Gamblers used to be punished severely for non-payment of outstanding debts. In the Mṛcchakaṭika the *Saṁvāhaka* ran for his life, did all possible tricks to throw dust into the eyes of the *sabhika* but was finally punished.[67] The defaulters were physically assaulted, to the extent of bleeding through nostrils, by the keepers of the gambling houses.[68] The players were sometimes made to sell off even their parents to pay off their debts incurred in gambling.[69] There are also references to other tortures to which the defaulters were subjected. For instance, they were suspended (by their legs) with head hanging down for a whole day; at times they were dragged on rough roads so that their backs were bruised by clods of earth and stones. Sometimes hounds were let loose on them who nibbled at the flesh on the thighs.[70]

Some of the stories recorded in the Kathā-sarit-sāgara also describe the punishments meted out to the defaulters. One gambler named Thiṇṭhākarāla tells the deities that he would adopt with them the same course as is usually adopted with a defaulting gambler, who makes himself as silent as a stone. Then he was about to saw their limbs with a saw.[71] Another gambler named Candrasvāmin made himself motionless as a stone and appeared dead-stiff when he was beaten up by the sabhika.[72] One more gambler called Dākineya was bound by his fellow-gamblers. They did so to obtain from him the borrowed money which also he had lost in the game. As he had nothing with him, they tortured him with sticks and other instruments. He made himself motionless like a stone and seemed as stiff as a corpse. Then all the gamblers took him away and threw him into a large dark well, fearing that, if he lived, he might take vengeance on them.

Indus Valley Dice

Vibhītaka Nuts

Dice discovered at Indus Valley

Part II

ORIGIN OF CHESS IN SANSKRIT LITERATURE

INTRODUCTION BY EGBERT MEISSENBURG

Egbert Meissenburg's Introduction to the Monograph "Origin and Genesis of Chess" prepared by Professor C. Panduranga Bhatta

The present study has its story. It begins with the first symposium of chess historians, privately held in Königstein/Taunus, near Frankfurt am Main, Germany, in August 1991. The plenum decided i.e., to draw the attention of Indologists to chess themes. Two approaches were prepared, both originating from Germany; Dr. Joachim Petzold from Berlin wrote many letters to German Universities Indologic seminaries.

He had welcome success: Dr. Andreas Bock-Raming from the University of Freiburg/Breisgau, Germany, could become interested in the game and his contribution was a very important one: the translation and thorough interpretation of the chess part in the Mānasollāsa [MS] of Someśvara[1 and 2].

Egbert Meissenburg contacted Dr. C. Panduranga Bhatta of the University of Pondicherry, India. Dr. Bhatta's interest in the origin and development of chess[3] lead to his joining the INITIATIV-GRUPPE KÖNIGSTEIN and to writing some lines on the development of the game of chess in the publication "Chess Historical Research" privately published in Seevetal 1991 and 1992. Dr. Bhatta has been requested for a comprehensive study of the early history of chess in India. Letters went from Pondicherry to Seevetal, and from Seevetal to Pondicherry. The result of Dr. Bhatta's logical and systematic research which has been finished in October 1993 is now in the hands of the reader.

Before leaving the reader to make a thorough study of Dr. Bhatta's thesis it seems useful to provide some information and interpretations of the present state of research into the early history of chess. Arabic chess is well documented in the thesis of Reinhard Wieber "Das Schachspiel in der arabischen Literatur von den Anfängen bis zur zweiten Hälfte des 16. Jahrhunderts" (University of Bonn 1972 and published by a commercial publisher, VfO, 1972).

Unfortunately, it is not possible to make the same statement for chess in India, the homeland of our game. No systematic research has been done to find out and examine the literary sources of the game in Sanskrit literature; the archeological finds in India are not well documented. This deficiency is not (!) a matter of the nonexistence, of such material but - only? - a matter of not (yet) discovering it. The Indologists who treated the subject were no chess historians, while the chess historians who wrote on early chess in India were no Indologists. Chess historians disputed and argued on the priority of the two-handed or four-handed game, and whether it was an invention or had gone through a period of evolution.

This is my opinion: This debate was and is completely idle and useless to a certain degree, blocking the way to more literary and archeological material. It is like writing a thesis before taking any lessons. The better way seems, first, to look over the shelves of a well-preserved Indological library of university rank, to examine the bibliographies, dictionaries and all the other books and periodicals for references to chess and other board games.

I am sure that we need not years to find a lot of material unknown to us, but years of examining and publishing it in a scientific manner. Concerning early Indian chess and its literature we need more facts and less fantasy. Ad fontes!!

One of the most valuable texts for the early (Indian) chess history is the chess part in the MS (first half of the 12th century).

We have a special kind of rediscovery, as the MS was known for more than 100 years to chess historians and Indologists as "chessic." Please, see the following. Georg Bühler was the first to draw the attention of chess researchers to this text (notice from Allahabad March 26, 1874; published in "Monatsberichte der Königlichen Preussischen Akademie der Wissenschaften zu Berlin aus dem Jahre 874", p. 283). Following Bühler, Antonius van der Linde (1833-1897) who believed the MS was a text from the 11th century though it has been attributed to the Indian king Someśvara wrote in his "Geschichte und Litteratur des Schachspiels" [=G&L], Berlin 1874, volume II, page 463: "Der Mānasollāsa des Cālukya-Fūrsten Someśvara beschzeibt alle Vergnūgungen der indiscien Fürsten, darunter auch das Schachspiel. Someśvara I., genannt Ahavamalla, und Someśvara II. herrschten im XI. Jht. in Kalyānakata im Dekhan." He tried to get more details about the MS.

The famous Berlin Indologist Albrecht Weber (1825-1901) visited the 1874 London congress of orientalists and promised a "sofortige vorläufige Nachricht". Weber examined the London libraries: "Proh dolor, der Sanskrittext ist nicht in London!"- this was the reaction of the productive Dutch chess historian. He published part of the letter of Albrecht Weber [written from London to Arnhem] page X of the preface of G&L II: "Der Mānasollāsa des Someśvara ist leider nicht hier; ich habe aber an Bühler geschrieben, und baldigste Zuserdung der Abschrift gebeten" (the preface of G&L II dates 'Arnheim am Tage der Sedanfeier 1874'). Anyone who is fluent in German should read in G&L II 464 Van der Linde's "encipherment" of Weber's recension of G&L I in "Li terarisches Centralblatt", 1874 (Sp. 1053): ... "Ich wette auf Zweischach!" Albrecht Weber wrote to A. van der Linde from Berlin dated October 28, 1874 (i.e., after the publication of "Geschichte und Litteratur"): ... Von Bühler, und dem Mānasollāsa, habe ich noch keine Nachricht ('De Schaakwereld', Wijk bij Duurstede [NL] 1875, p. 327 "uit mijne wetenschappelijke schaakkorrespondencie"). No further details of the MS came to the attention of Van der Linde: his "Quellenstudien" (1881) have no mention of the MS. H.J.R. Murray [20:56] read the note of Bühler and Van der Linde respectively without attempting to examine the matter. The chess text of the MS has been edited no earlier than 1961[T3].

V. Raghavan wrote in his "Festivals, Sports and Pastimes in India" (Ahmedabad 1979) after discussing the other recreations in the MS: "Someśvara gives a detailed description of the game [= chess] and a variety of its playing is called *sarvatobhadra.*" in his thesis of 1985 Dr. Bhatta made good use of the MS for the purpose of his subject. S.Y. Wakankar wrote in 1986.[4]

"In the Krīḍāviṁśati, verses 560-633, he [=Someśvara] has extensively described the game as it was current and known to him at that time."

The first study of Andreas Bock-Raming[5] was already ready for the printer in May 1992 as we have an only privately distributed comment by Joachim Petzold from this date.

My aim is not merely to claim that we need more facts concerning Indian chess. I can give two references to textual editions concerning the game of chess in India which seem to have not yet come to the knowledge of the chess historians:

[1] A text with the heading "Caturaṅgam has been edited and translated by Mahamahopadhyaya Haraprasad Shastri in: Journal of the Bihar and Orissa Research Society, Patna, vol. VII, part I, March 1922, pp. 60-77. This edition of the *caturaṅga*-section of Tithitattva arises some problems which cannot be discussed in this short introduction.

[2] In 1950, published in Madras, S.R. Ramanatha Sastri critically edited and introduced the Hariharacaturaṅgam of Godavara Miśra (=Madras Government Oriental Series XVII). The last chapter, the 8th, of this work on politics and military science is devoted to chess.

Before concluding my introduction let me give a rough outline of the development of chess research concerning proto chess (Urschach) during the last 80 years.

It is my opinion expressed already in 1991 that chess is a "reali tats-orientierte Transponierung der Glieder des indischen Heeres auf das Ashtapada" [see 30: 127] a kind of strategic exercise for war. The Spanish chess historian Ricardo Calvo disagrees,[6] proto chess is a pure game of numbers ("reines Zahlenspiel"). This game lead via a logical sequence to the creation of moves of the 6 different figures (men) of then an intellectual game round about the middle of the 6th century in Persia. Hans Holländer[7] renders impossible the derivation of chess from racing games; the combination of a hunting game and of a strategic game seems more likely to him.

Discussing the bibliographical matters, we must pay attention to two articles.

The first was written by Chintaharan Chakravarti[8] in 1938, the second by S.Y. Wakankar[9] in 1986. The latter collected a wealth of material mainly preserved (or no more preserved!!) in Indian libraries with good descriptions of the manuscripts when and where they were available and with comments to the printed editions. From the thirties of this century, we have two textual editions: M. Ghosh edited the Caturaṅgadīpikā of Śūlapāṇi [T1], a 15th century author who describes the four-handed chess. M. Ghosh gave valuable references to other early texts with chess terminology or to texts which could be of some value to chess historians. G.R. Kulkarni Haldikar edited Vilāsamaṇimañjarī of Trivengadacarya in Marathi a 19th century text parts of which already had been edited in 1814.

In 1913, Murray H.J.R.,[10] was not able to add to our knowledge of the early history of chess in India much beyond what he had from the famous Albrecht Weber, from Antonius van der Linde and from Macdonell A.A.[11] In 1936, Murray claims from three considerations, that the invention of chess took place round about 570 CE.[12] I leave now without any discussion the opinions of Ferdinand Bork [1935, 1951], of Paul Seyferth [1937] and of Heinrich Fuhrmann [1941]. Starting with the year 1951, new ideas arise from the Macedonian philosopher and chess master Pavle Bidev[13] (1912-1988) the greatest authority on the history of early chess. His papers, mostly written and published in German, though not his mother tongue, are at the highest intellectual and academic level.

In my opinion Pavle Bidev will never be surpass/ed for the brilliance of his ideas, though some of them are without any proof while others need detailed examination. Hellmut Rosenfeld (1907-1993), a researcher par excellence into the early history of playing cards,[14] already published in 1958 ("Archiv für Geschichte des Buchwesens", p.122) a hypothesis of the evolution of the "Tschaturangaspiel" into the "kriegerisch-strategisches Denkspiel" His paper of 1960[15], vs. W. Lauterbach[16]; maintained[17] claims the "Ursprünglichkeit des Würfelvierschachs." The "alte Würfelvierschach" (the 'old' chess played by four persons with dice) grew up out of the Old Indian "Fürstenspiegel" as "aristokratisches Kriegsspiel." Pavle Bidev never resolved of his arguments against the priority of the game of chess with four persons in his discussion with Hellmut Rosenfeld and Joachim Petzold.[18&19]

The opinion of H. Rosenfeld was supported by J. Petzold.[20] The paper of the world-famous Indologist Paul Thieme (University Tübingen) published in 1962[21] influenced the discussion to a lesser degree than it deserves (Richard Eales [1985]: "not convincing") though his arguments were ingenious in the same way as the Sanskrit texts he analysed.

Görschen F.C., stated in 1980[22] that the "inventor" realized chess during the reign of Kumaragupta (414-455 CE). The 1991 article of the Italian chess historian Franco Pratesi[23] summarized various opinions concerning "Urschach." It was the Munich Indologist Dieter Schlingloff[24] who made an end to the apparently endless discussion concerning the Stupa of Bharhut by identifying the four persons shown on this relief as two players and two onlookers. His pupil Renate Syed published a preliminary translation of the Manuscript in 1994.[25] In her opinion there is no proof of *caturaṅga* before the 7th century (giving a reminder to the famous statement of Daniel Willard Fiske as the summary of the findings of Van der Linde and Von der Lasa [1905]); she says on the other hand that *caturaṅga* developed in India in the first centuries of Christian era.

The analysis of the chess text of the Manuscript must be credited in first place to Andreas Bock-Raming who presented two papers in 1993[26] and 1994[27] respectively (with one more extensive work ready for the printer since more than one year).

There was a lively dispute "India or China?" started by Joseph Needham in 1962[28] and followed by Pavle Bidev not before 1972. The latest development in this part of proto-chess discussion is that of Rainer Schmidt:[29] A game called "Bo" early reached India and Persia finding an "ausbaufähigere und flexiblere Verwirklichung" on the *aṣṭāpada* board. New ideas came from Franco Pratesi in 1994.[30] Furthermore we must pay attention to the hypothesis of Jurij Averbakh[31] whose idea is the appearance of a race-game *aṣṭāpada* with dice on a board of 8 x 8 cells, a game which changed to a wargame for two persons without dice under Greek influence, especially that of petteia.

The opinion of Gerhard Josten[32&33] that chess came from Mesopotamia seems to lack actual proof; yet his starting point of examining board games from civilisations other than the Indian is very useful.

Analysing the discussion of "Urschach", I could state that we have a less dogmatic manner in research and discussion than five to ten years ago (see 'Meinungsbericht' by M. Eder.[34]

We have old ideas in modern settings (see Mānasollāsa; the idea of derivation of chess from a race-game (Pachisi!?] already has been discussed by Stewart Culin in 1898) and many completely new ideas.

We have a vast and hard to follow-up literature on "Urschach." Our task: Who solves the 'riddle'? If the invention of chess was not beyond the power of a single genius[35] why it is not beyond the power of a single ingenious researcher in the kind of a modern Buzurgmihr to solve the riddle of its...invention!? ... or ... evolution!?

This researcher should cut away the dissents from "China", "Greece" and "Persia" and should conclude. If there is no 'single genius' in chess research: why no organizing a team of Indologists, Sinologists, Iranists, Orientalists, Historians and Linguists to solve the problem?

India gave chess to the world. We expect that a researcher of Indological science or the team of researchers will find the means and ways to prove this assumption with full evidence. I am sure that the study of Dr. Bhatta is a good step on this way.

Finally: A hearty "THANK YOU" not only to Dr. Bhatta but also to two other personages for their valuable cooperation: To Mr. Kenneth Whyld from Caistor [GB] who polished up my English in the first draft of this introduction and in parts of its final version; to Herrn Dr. Bock-Raming from Freiburg/Breisgau [D] who read the proofs of the text.

ORIGIN AND GENESIS OF CHESS IN SANSKRIT

An attempt has been made in this chapter to scrutinize the views, discussions and conclusions arrived at by various scholars in the light of the references to chess found in the Sanskrit literature.

From the Vedas till Halāyudha (10th century CE), all the references to *aṣṭāpada, caturaṅga* and *buddhibala* are studied in a comparative and critical manner. Special emphasis is given to the aspect connecting chess with ancient Indian battle.

Murray. H.J.R., Paul Thieme and Richard Eales, Prof. Dr. Renate Syed, Manfred A.J. Eder, Andreas Bock Raming, Egbert Meissenburg, and many others believe that chess originated in India, and it was played on a board of sixty-four squares by two persons. A few works related to chess hitherto not consulted by chess historians are also included in this chapter.

A few Photographs of sculptures and drawings bearing relevance on the topic are also included.

Sir William Jones[1] has quoted in translation thirty-five verses from the Tithitattva of Raghunandana in his article on the Indian game of chess. This passage occurs in the Śabdakalpadruma, a recent work on lexicography under the *caturaṅga.* These verses are found at the beginning of the Caturaṅgadīpikā of Śūlapāṇi, a work devoted to the description of the game called *caturaṇga.*[2] As Śūlapāṇi, a Bengal writer on Smṛti flourished in the fifteenth century

CE it may be said that Raghunandana has quoted those verses from the work of Śūlapāṇi.

Sir William Jones[3] argued that '*caturaṅga*' was introduced into Persia in the sixth century CE and thence, as *shatranj* into the Arab land. Murray. H.J. R.,[4] also concluded that chess is a descendant of an Indian game transmitted to the west in the shape it had assumed in the seventh century CE.

Richard Eales[5] expresses the opinion that the four-handed game was more probably an offshoot of the two-handed game rather than the other way round. His conclusion is since there are no references to the four handed game earlier than the 11th century CE. Pandit. V.D.,[6] says that '*caturaṅga*' was in vogue in India some 4,500 years ago and the *caturaṅga* pieces discovered during the excavations at Lothal are dated 2,500 B. C. with the help of carbon tests. Bob Meadley[7] and Hugh Myers[8] have discussed the views expressed by Pandit V.D. and concluded that chess of the 6th century CE was *caturaṅga* and that prior to that time there was no such thing as *caturaṅga* except for the non-chessic use of the word. Paul Thieme,[9] rejects the assumption of Macdonell. A.A.,[10] that a "primitive form of chess" "an applied form of the ancient game of dice" can have developed into "the highly intellectual game of double chess" only in later times. He supposes that this game was the result of a prolonged evolution which is difficult to trace.

He observes: "Surely, a civilisation that gave birth to the grammar of Pāṇini can easily be trusted to have also produced a game that was above the grasp of children and could be played for the sheer joy in puzzling out intricate problems of an abstract nature.[11]

There are many evidences to support the theory of Tylor

E.B., according to whom the game of chess was the invention of some Hindu who devised a game of war with the *aṣṭāpada* board as his field of battle.

It seems that there existed many works dealing with the game of *caturaṅga.* Caturaṅgadīpikā[12] refers to Vyāsa, Yama, Pitāmaha, Gautama, Bhṛgu, Manu, Ṛṣyaśṛṅga, Agastya, Jābāla, Yājnavalkya and Gurucaraṇa as the authorities on the game. Sulapāṇi[13] also mentions Caturaṅga Paddhati, Divyamālikā (or Mālikā), Yāmala and Bharata as the works referring to the game. Unfortunately, these works have not come to posterity. Only Caturaṅga-taraṅgiṇī[14] is available. The Hindi commentator on Krīḍākauśalya[15] mentions the following books

(1) Caturaṅgadīpikā of Gadādhara Śāstri written in śaka 1621(1699 CE) in Sanskrit.

(2) Shataranj Tasnif of Nabob Khankhana in Hijri 977 (1556 CE) in Urdū.

(3) Vinodaśataka by Devadatta.

Harikṛṣṇa, son of Venkatarāman, who lived in Aurangabad in the Maharāstra state of India composed an encyclopedic work called Bṛhajjyotiṣārṇava in six parts. Krīḍākauśalya is the twentieth chapter in the sixth part of this voluminous work. He gives an account of the game called '*buddhibala*' (chess), a trial for the intellect.[16] He quotes some verses as those of Kālidāsa and Nīlakaṇṭha. Two verses are quoted as from Kālidāsa. They are given below in translation.[17]

(1) O Lotus-eyed lady! In this game there are two kings, two ministers, four each of elephants, horses, and camels and sixteen footmen at all.

    I shall tell you the position of all these [powers], their movements in the sixty-four squares, and how they fight and kill the opponent in the battlefield [i.e., the chessboard].

(2) O Beautiful lady! The elephant stands at the four comers, in the next adjacent squares the horses, and camels and in the two central squares the minister and king; in front of these in the adjacent row stand the footmen [pawns] [eight on either side].

Then Harikṛṣṇa quotes the rules relating to the game of chess given by one Nīlakaṇṭha, son of Śaṅkara. It is given below in translation.[18]

On a board or a cloth or on the ground itself nine lines should be drawn from top of bottom [with equal spacing] and similarly another nine lines from left to right. It will thus become a square figure with sixty-four small squares.

The four corner squares, the two in the middle in each of the first columns on all four sides, and the four central ones [in all 16 squares] should be marked off with cross lines in the form of the feet of a swan. Then the powers of the two fighting armies should be arranged in two columns at top and bottom.

In the two central squares in the bottom and top columns should be placed the king and the minister; in the squares adjacent to both, the two camels; in the squares adjacent to them the two horses and adjacent to the horses [in the corners] the two elephants. In the next columns [both at bottom and top] should be placed the eight footmen [pawns] of both sides. The two fighting sides should be arranged in this manner.[19]

According to Nīlakaṇṭha , the game is of two kinds:

(1) *anāvṛtti* in which a power when it moves forward does not think of retracing its step

(2) *parāvṛtti* in which a power while moving forward keeps in view its retracing position.

But we do not have any further explanation on these two methods.

Harikṛṣṇa's quotations from Kālidāsa and Nīlakaṇṭha unmistakably point out the existence of some other works dealing with the game of chess. But the author keeps us in dark about exact source from which he quotes. Two verses quoted as from Kālidāsa are not found in any of the known works of the famous Sanskrit poet Kālidāsa, the author of the Abhijñanaśākuntala.[20]

Towards the end of his work Harikṛṣṇa says that the camel was substituted for the elephant by people living in desert areas and nearby places where camels are common, and elephants cannot survive.[21] Interestingly in the verses quoted as from Kālidāsa and Nīlakaṇṭha the camel is mentioned in the place of chariots. This evidently proves that both Kālidāsa and Nīlakaṇṭha whom Harikṛṣṇa quotes belong to later times.

Caturaṅga probably originated on the analogy of the four parts of a king's army in ancient days in India which consisted of elephants, horses, chariots, and footmen. Camel never constituted the part of an Ancient Indian army. Harikṛṣṇa figuratively considers *caturaṅga* as a kingdom and describes it as follows:

In one and the same city brave kings, always running on foot in the battlefield followed by their ministers and army which consists of elephants, horses, camels, and footmen, fight each other, lo! Without any weapons. It is really a wonder of wonders; for not only the kings do not die but even the dead army (elephants, horses etc.) comes back to live.[22]

It is signiicant that in this description also we have the camel instead of chariot. Thus, it may be pointed out that in the descriptions of the game given by Kālidāsa, Nīlakaṇṭha and Harikṛṣṇa camel has replaced the traditional chariot which was one of the important constituents of the game.

In India from the earliest times down to the end of the epoch of the epics and several centuries after, chariots played a very prominent part in warfare. There are many references to chariots in the Vedas and in the Brāhmaṇas.[23] The large number of references to chariots in the Aitareya Brāhmaṇa would seem to indicate that the chariot was an important instrument of war in those days. The importance and value of chariots in warfare can be seen also in the epics.[24] In the fourth century BCE two fighting men are seen in each chariot besides the charioteer. This is testified by the fragments of Megasthenes.[25] Gradually the use of chariots in war declined, and we have no mention of it in Bāṇabhaṭṭa's Harṣacarita (7th century CE) in his description of Harṣa's army.[26] It is not seen in the army of Pulakeśin II (641 CE).[27] In the Kuram Pallava grant about 650 CE which describes the battle of Peruvala Nallur, only elephants, horses and footmen are mentioned and not chariots.[28] Even in the history of the Chola kings of South India, during the succeeding centuries mention is only made of the other three divisions of the army.

From these instances it becomes clear that the chariots must have become obsolete in later times.

In Burmese 'Sittuyin' (chess) boat occurs in the place of chariot. In Siamese chess also boat occurs in the place of chariot. This indicates that probably the game found in Siam was derived from the Bengal-Bihar region where we see *caturaṅga* having 'boat' in the place of 'chariot.'

In Malayan *chator* (chess) also boat (rook) has replaced the traditional chariot. The name *'ter'* for boat may relate to Sanskrit '*tari*.' Javanese chess also has the boat (*prahu*) in the place of chariot. It is possible to conclude that those countries which have 'boat' in the place of 'chariot' have received the game from north-eastern India.

The tradition enshrined in the Shāhnāma of Firdausī and in Chatrang namāk that chess was introduced from India to Persia in the reign of Khusrau Nushirwan (531-579 CE) is accepted by the chess historians as a plausible hypothesis.[29] According to these books an envoy from the king of India came to the court of Shah and informed him about the invention of a game which resembled a battlefield.

The envoy while giving the details of the game said that they must be able to identify the foot soldier, the elephant, and the rest of the army, such as the chariot and the horse etc.[30]

It is worth noting here that when chess was first introduced to Persia it consisted of chariots as one of its constituents and not the camel. These references help us to conclude that Kālidāsa and Nīlakaṇṭha quoted by Harikṛṣṇa belong to late period in the history and they need not be mistaken as ancient authorities on chess.

There are many myths attributing chess to the wife of Rāvaṇa or to the wife of Pāṇḍavas, averring that either of these ladies invented the game to while away time in imitation of the battle which their husbands were fighting.[31] Pandit. V.D., heavily depends on the myth according to which Maṇḍodarī, the Queen of King Rāvaṇa of Laṅkā invented chess to amuse her warring husband. He has used this myth to prove the early existence of chess.

According to another myth current in South India the game of chess was invented by Draupadī, the wife of the Pāṇḍavas who played it with her friends in the harem, imitating the actual war being waged by her husbands with the Kauravas.[32] But it is interesting to observe here that Vātsyāyana in his Kāmasūtra[33] says that a woman should study the sixty-four arts and practice them in private. He includes dice-play in the sixty-four arts. Harikṛṣṇa[33a] also says that the game of chess is mostly intended for women and hence it has no live units of any such as elephants, horses etc.

It is worth noting here that even though Maṇodarī and Draupadī are credited with the invention of this highly intellectual game neither the Rāmāyaṇa nor the Mahābhārata makes any mention of chess. Moreover for a serious researcher who mainly depends on reliable data furnished by literature and archaeology the value of such myths is negligible.

Firdausī also mentions myth in his Shāhnāma which describes the earlier invention of the game in India.[34]

According to this the game was invented for a queen following a civil war between her two sons Gau and Talkhand, in which Talkhand had been killed. It was meant to serve as an explanation of his death, in that only one *shah* could come off victorious. Arabic chess writers[35] mention several reasons for the invention of the game such as to educate a prince, to replace a war, or to occupy the time of a king who, like Alexander, had defeated all his enemies within reach and, was at a loss for something destructive to do. Harikṛṣṇa says [36] that one Vrajalāla, son of Śaśinātha who a Brahmin was highly learned and intelligent, invented chess for the pleasure of his king and queen. Further details of Vrajalāla are not available and hence nothing could be said about the genuineness of Harikṛṣṇa's statement.[37]

Caturaṅgasārasarvasva is attributed to Kṛṣṇarāja Wodeyar III of Mysore (1794-1868 CE).[38] But this work is yet to be traced. However, Harikṛṣṇa has quoted in his work a few verses as from Kṛṣṇarāja Wodeyar. These verses are related to the ways of horse movement mentioned by the king of Karnāṭaka, Śrī Kṛṣṇadevaraya Wodeyar.

Caturaṅgikā-camatkṛta-cakra-mañjarī is also attributed to Kṛṣṇarāja.[39] Śrītattvanidhi[40] is a marvellous specimen of painting produced by the artists under the patronage of Mummudi Kṛṣṇarāja Wodeyar III during the year 1800 CE. It contains more than 1500 colour paintings on papers under nine chapters. Incidentally the artist has also painted different kinds of dice-play. This confirms the fact that the Kṛṣṇarāja was an expert in chess.

A relation of the four-fold division of the army with the game of chess is often pointed out. Ramachandra Dikshitar V.R., states that references to the game of chess are common in the literature but the term *caturaṅga* is met with only in the epics and hence he concludes that 'the principle of chess supplied ideas to the progressive development of the modes and constituents of the army'.[41] But his contention is difficult to prove. His statement that the use of the word '*aṣṭāpada*' is believed to indicate familiarity with chess cannot be accepted. It may be shown that the word *aṣṭāpada* found in the Rāmāyaṇa cannot be associated with the game of chess.

There is no doubt about the fact that ancient India possessed the classical four-fold force of chariots, elephants, horsemen, and infantry, collectively known as *caturaṅgabala.*[42]

Chess is also a game of war, and in each game, there are a king, a councillor, two elephants, two horses, two chariots, and eight foot-soldiers. According to Tylor, Edward B., the game of chess was the invention of some Hindu who devised a game of war with the *aṣṭāpada* board as his field of battle.[43]

The relative values of the chess pieces were analogues to of identical with the relative values of different arms as laid by Kauṭilya, Śukra, and Vaiśaṃpāyana. By this

Ramachandra Dikshitar V.R., again concludes that the value of different kinds of forces (made arbitrarily) were borrowed from chess.[44] According to him the organisation of the Indian army which came to be known as *caturaṅga* both in epic, Sanskrit and Pali literature was based on the ancient game.[45]

He is of the opinion that the two methods of winning in early chess were the checkmate and the barring of the opponent's king. An exact reproduction of these methods is seen in ancient warfare, the prime object of which was the vanquishing of the enemy forces, secured by the capture or death of the opponent or by the devastation of his army. He also adds that a symmetrical arrangement of the different forces and its advantages must have been taken from chess.[46] Finally, he says that we meet with the term *caturaṅga*, a four-fold force, only in epic literature and not in the earlier Vedic literature. According to him the Vedic works are full of references to the game of chess. Therefore, he concludes that the principles of chess supplied ideas to the progressive development of the modes and constituents of the army and not vice versa.[47] However, it can be argued that it is the four-fold force that supplied the motive for the game and not vice versa.

The Vedic references do not provide us much insight into the rules and regulations that governed the game or the technique by which the game was played.

There is no specific reference in the Vedic literature to any piece used in dice-play. The *adhidevana* found in the Vedas and the Brāhmaṇas is to be interpreted as referring to the place on which the dice used to be thrown.[48] The Gambler's Hymn refers to some numbers of dice used in the game. Some scholars are of the view that these may refer to *śāris,* i.e., men or pieces on the dice-board.[49] But other evidences found in the Vedas, the Brahmaṇas and the Sūtras do not seen to favour such interpretations.[50]

The two most important words related to the game of chess, namely *aṣṭāpada* and *caturaṅga* are not at all used in the epics in the sense of chess. In the Rāmāyaṇa, while describing the town planning of Ayodhyā, author Vālmīki says that the capital's layout was in the form of an, *aṣṭāpada.*[51] The commentator Tilaka[52] explains *aṣṭāpada* as *dyūtaphalaka* or gameboard. But another commentator namely Mādhavayogi (1700 CE) in his commentary called Amṛtakaṭaka explains *aṣṭāpada* as gold. According to him the capital was decorated with golden ornaments.[53]

The contradiction existing between these commentators is remarkable because the word *aṣṭāpada* occurs only once in the epic. We have reference to the word *aṣṭāpada* only in the Harivaṁśa which is a supplement to the Mahābhārata.[54] It is rather surprising that the voluminous epic Mahābhārata has no reference to this very significant word in its body proper. The term *aṣṭāpada* occurs in the Hīnayāna Buddhist scriptures (500 BCE) like Brahmajāla sutta and Vinayapiṭaka.[55] Though Rhys David quotes the view of the Sinhalese commentator (c. 1000 CE) that "game of *aṣṭāpada* was played with dice and pieces such as kings and so on" he denies that *aṣṭāpada* may mean chess.[56]

The Mahābhārata[56a] refers to dicing cloth. This was used to be spread over the place where dice were thrown.

upastīrṇā sabhā rājan sarve tvayi kṛtakṣaṇāḥ

The commentary of Nīlakaṇṭtha explains this as:

āsphurākhyenākṣapātanavāsasā uparistīrṇā etc.

The Sanskrit drama, Mṛcchakaṭika (4.27,37) of Śūdraka refers to dicing board (*pāśapīṭha*) while describing Vasantasenā's apartments. The *pīṭha* is one of the synonyms for the board on which the dice are thrown. The term *nardita* occurs in Mṛcchakaṭika (Act 2, verse 9).

It is a name of the unluckiest throw (*kali*) in dicing.[57] It is not used here as a name of a game and hence cannot be a Sanskritization of the Persian *nard* backgammon.[58] It is significant to note that the story found in the Chatrang nāmak attributes the invention of *nard* to Buzurgmihr. It also says that he sent that as a challenge to the Indian King, whose Brāhman courtiers were of course unable to discover its rules.[59]

The word *caturaṅga* literally means having four members. Later it came to denote an army consisting of elephants, chariots, cavalry, and infantry. Amarakoṣa defines the four parts of the army as *hasyaśvarathapadātaṃ seāgaṁ syāccatuṣṭayam.*[60]

Even though the word *caturaṅga* is found both in the Ṛgveda and the Śatapatha Brāhmaṇa, it is only used there in the sense of 'one having four limbs or parts' and it does not refer to any game.[61] The *caturaṅga* is used in the Rāmāyaṇa in the sense of an army consisting of four parts. King Daśaratha is said to have ordered to make ready the army with its four parts to follow him to Mithilā.[62] In another context we have Hanumān giving a detailed description of Laṅkā and the army of Rāvaṇa which consisted of four parts.[63] The term *caturaṅga-bala* and allusions to the chariots, the elephants, the horses, and the foot soldiers as constituting the army are profusely available in the Rāmāyaṇa. In the Rāmāyaṇa the princes and the demons are described as having strong and large units of infantry, cavalry, elephantry and the chariot-corps.[64] The Vānara army, however, was constituted only of infantry.

The game described in the Mahābhārata resembles the *akṣakrīḍā* of the Vedic period. The story of Nala further strengthens this assumption as it refers to the *vibhītaka*-tree.[65]

The quickness with which Śakuni was winning the game clearly points out that the game played was *akṣakrīḍā* and not *caturaṅga*. The declaration of victory seems to take some more time in the game of draughts and *caturaṅga*, as it depends on the clear movement of pieces on the board in accordance with the fall of dice. But the commentator Nīlakaṇṭha at certain places explains the terms found in the Great Epic as connected with some game like draughts. While explaining a verse of the Virāṭaparva he says that the word *phala* used there refers to container for rattling the dice. According to him the dice are to be rattled in a vessel before throwing them down and the pieces (*śāris*) are to be moved on the board according to the fall of dice.[66] But his interpretation is not supported by other evidences found in the same Epic. The game of dice is compared with a battle at many places in the Mahābhārata. But no reference is made either to *śāris* (pieces) or to *aṣṭāpada* (board). The following passage may be considered in this connection.

glahān dhanūṁśi me viddhi śarān akṣāṁśca bhārata.[67]

Here the battle-car is compared with the dicing-place, the bow with *glaha*, the bowstring with the skill in dicing, and the arrows with the dice. At another place Droṇa compares the army with *durodara* and the arrow with dice.[68] Here, the comparison is made between *senā* and *durodara*. As with the army a battle is fought, so with the *durodara* a game is played. Arjuna at another place compares his bow Gāṇḍīva with *durodara*, his battle-car with the dicing-place and his arrows with *glahas*.[69] In all these instances no reference is made either to *caturaṅga* or *aṣṭāpada* even though *caturaṅga* is also a war game.

It would be interesting to consider the disposition of the army or order of battle, called *vyūha* in Sanskrit literature in this connection.[70] This belongs to the province of tactics, while the plan of war is strategy. Arthaśāstra of Kauṭilya mentions *sama, viśama, hasti, rathi, aśva* and *patti vyūhas.*[71] The different dispositions of army under the *maṇḍala* classification are *sarvatomukha* (capable of turning in all directions) *savotabhadra* (auspicious) etc.

One aspect of the *caturaṅga* which may vouch for its antiquity is its primitive *maṇḍala* which has four conquerors (*vijigīṣu*) one ally (*mitra*), one enemy (*ari*) and one enemy's ally (*arimitra*). Arthaśāstra and other works on polity mention various types of *maṇḍalas* consisting of kings whose number is 4, 6, 8, 12 or more.[72] It may be said that *maṇḍalas* of 12 or more kings have evolved from the primitive *maṇḍala* of four kings which is found in the *caturaṅga.* This would place the game long before Kauṭilya.[73]

The application of these arrays is practically illustrated in the great Mahābhārata battle. Seeing himself numerically inferior but backed by the superior strategy and experience, Yudhiṣṭhira advises Arjuna to form a pin-like array as it was decisive in battles where a few had to fight against many.[74] We have a reference to the *sarvatobhadra* array of Bhīṣma's army.[75] In times of necessity, armies used to have various formations like *sarvatobhadra, cakrabandha* and *murajabandha.*[76] Kauṭilya refers to the mixed formation of forces consisting of horse units, elephants and chariots.

The different arrays in a formation could attack the enemy forces in a variety of ways. The four basic types are: a straight line, a snake, a circle or dispersed. In the straight line or 'truncheon', the centre, flanks, and wings advanced evenly, in the snake, unevenly in a sinuous manner, in the circle, radiating outwards and in the dispersed, independently of each other.[77]

The story in Chatrang namāk (pre 800 CE)[77a] is important

because it gives such details as the names of the pieces. It is significant to note that chariot has not been replaced here either by boat or camel. It also supports the theory that chess of that period was indeed a game for two players, played on a board of sixty-four squares. It is recorded there that Buzurgmihr[77b] who succeeded in identifying the game said that the sage has invented a battlefield, amid which the king takes up his station. To left and right of him the army is dispersed, the foot-soldiers occupying the rank in front. At the king's side stands his minister and in two directions the elephants are posted and beyond them are stationed the war-horses, etc. This also confirms the theory that originally chess was played as a war game.

In the Campūrāmāyaṇa of Bhoja, Hanumān, when he was about to kill Akṣa, the son of Rāvaṇa is compared to one ready to play dice (*akṣakrīḍā*). Naturally, the poet has used the word *akṣa* to advantage. He compares the demons to pieces and the earth to the board.[78] Even the later texts dealing with chess often refer to its connection with battle. Harikṛṣṇa's text refers to two arrangements in chess that are successful in warding the opponent's attacks just like the wheel-like arrangement (*cakravyūha*) in actual battle:

vyūhadvayamidaṃ cakravyūhavat paramāraṇam[79]

cakravyūha is an arrangement of the army in the form of a wheel with the king or general at the centre, so that it is difficult for the enemy to get to the centre. At another place he refers to the movement of the king as follows: The king adopts straight forward and crooked methods according to the situation. He is brave, intelligent, and daring; always caring for the safety of his subjects; and emulates the Gods by his fame.[80] The idea is that just like an actual king he behaves in this game as well.

In 1977, Soviet archaeologists excavated seven ivory figurines in Afrasiab (Samarkand) which can be identified as king, rook, queen (?)/knight, bishop, knight and 2 pawns. It is interesting to note here that the foot-soldier is holding a shield in his left hand and a short sword in his right. On his left side there is a scabbard, while a quiver for arrows is on his back. The bishop (pil) is an elephant, and its body is covered with a coat or mail and on its head sits a warrior in full battle garb, with a sword in his left hand.

The king (*shah*) is also depicted as a warrior mounted on horses.[81] These figurines of the Afrasiab excavation like the account found in Chatrang namāk confirm that chess arose as a game reflecting warfare.

It may be pointed out here that Mahābhārata does not contain any direct evidence about *caturaṅga.* What we learn from this work about any board-game is about the *akṣa* or *akṣadyūta* or the so-called dice. This *akṣa* often translated was then considered a knightly recreation.[82] Yudhiṣṭhira says that on being challenged for a game of dice he cannot turn his back on it.[83] Dice-play as a knightly recreation seems to suggest that it was a war-game associated with dice. According to tradition Yudhiṣṭhira played the game of *caturaṅga* which symbolized a fight between kings.[84] According to the epic Mahābhārata a *kṣatriya* was not supposed to decline when invited either to a battle or a game. Yudhiṣṭhira himself refers to this vow at a few places:

> *āhūtoham na nivarte kadācit/*
> *tadāhitaṁ śāśvataṁ vai vrataṁ me//*[85]

The expression *āhitaṁ śāśvataṁ vrataṁ* an eternally enjoined makes it clear that such a practice was normally binding on all well-bred *kṣatriyas.*

When Bhīma was angry with Yudhiṣṭhira for having staked Draupadī, Arjuna pacifies him stating that Yudhiṣṭhira acted in true spirit of Kṣatriya.[86]

The *bandhas* or the astonishing feats of verbal jugglery seem to have originated from the art of arraying armies in different forms in the battlefield. As seen earlier Arthaśastra of Kauṭilya describes in detail the various arrays into which the army used to be formed.[87]

Daṇḍin is the first Sanskrit critic who recognised these arrays as being used for poetry. He mentions the *gomūtrikā, ardhabhramaka* and their characteristics in his Kāvyādarśa.[88] The *bandha* called *sarvatobhadra* consists of sixty-four squares, in eight rows of eight squares each. In the first horizontal rows, four lines of a stanza are to be written, one letter in each square. Then, in the next four rows, all the four lines are to be written serially in a reverse order, i.e., fourth line first etc. Then the first horizontal row from all the four sides shall contain the first line, the second the third and so on.[89]

Ardhabhramaka is like *sarvatobhadra,* the only difference being that half the line, instead of the full one, is repeated. Rudraṭa (900 CE) in his Kāvyālaṅkāra describes some more acrostics (*citra-kāvyas*) which are also a sort of metrical puzzle. They are to be read in accordance with the moves of pieces.[89] Hermann Jacobi has discussed the reference found in Rudraṭa's work and says that this refers to modern chess. The movement of the chariot given by Rudraṭa is not available from any such text on *caturaṅga.* But it has some affinity to the movement of boat in modern (Bengali) game of chess. It may be assumed that by Rudraṭa's time itself the game returned to India from Persia with some changes.[90] *Sārayantrabandha* also must be understood in the light of the movement of chess steps. The four feet of the verse are written out in four lines but we gradually get all these four feet again. For the first two feet, the movement will be downwards and for the last two upwards. For every successive letter in all the feet, we must move out into the other feet, otherwise, for every alternative letter, we must come to the foot undertaken. Bhoja gives *sārayantrabandha* in his Sarasvatīkaṇṭhābharaṇa.[91]

The Kāmasūtra of Vātsyāyana refers to what is called *ākarṣakrīḍā* (I.3.14). But the exact connotation of this term is not known. Some scholars are of the opinion that *ākarṣakrīḍā* and *akṣakrīḍā* are identical. But Vātsyāyana mentions boards named *dyūtaphalaka* and *ākarṣaphaaka* based on this Tridibnath Ray considers *ākarṣakrīḍā* to be different from *akṣakrīḍā.*[92]

It is of some interest to note here that Kāmasūtra (IV.12) refers to Yakṣarātri and Kaumudījāgara festivals. The terms Yakṣarātri and Kaumudījāgara refer to the night of the full moon in the month of Kārtīka and Āśvina respectively. According to the Tithitattva the night of the full moon in the month of Āśvina is to be spent in playing the game of *caturaṅga.*

Pāṇini, the great Sanskrit grammarian was aware of the word *aṣṭāpada* being used in the technical sense: *aṣṭanaḥ saṁjñayām*[93]

Pāṇini's explicit statement that in his Grammar *aṣṭa* appears in ordinary *bahuvrīīhi* adjectives, but *aṣṭa* in a name (*saṃjñāyām*) which means in inherited terms that were formed at a time when was still the norm helps us to conclude that *aṣṭāpada* is older than Pāṇini's grammar. Another Pāṇinian rule (5.2.9) teaches the formation of a nominal stem *ayānayīna* in the sense of 'what is to be led to the *ayānaya*'.

Scholars have expressed different opinions about the game referred to here. Agrawala. V.S.,[94] says that the word *ayānayīna* refers to a gamesman fit to be moved to a square of safety. In his opinion this refers to Chaupur,[95] a game played on a board. On each side of the board used for this game there will be such chequered squares in which rival gamesmen may rest without being attacked. According to another Pāṇinian rule[96] the affix *ghan* comes after the root *nī* (to lead), when the preposition *pari* is in composition with it, and when the word so formed means 'a game'. According to another rule (1-3-10) the verb *pari+ni* takes *ghan* when it means 'gambling', e.g., *pariṇayena śarān hanti* (He kills (or takes) many pieces by moving a piece).[97]

This example is given by Patañjali in his Mahābhaṣya.[98] Paul Thieme says that the qualification of the movement Patañjali does give is not characteristic for backgammon.[99] According to Patañjali *aṣṭāpada* is formed in the same manner as *saptaparṇa* a plant that has seven leaves at each joint (*parvan*) of its stalks: *paṅktau paṅktau aṣṭau padānīti. aṣṭāpada* is called a board that has eight fields in each row. Paul Thieme states that this kind of board can be meaningfully used only in chess or something like it, certainly not in backgammon or in simple gambling with dice.[100]

In Subandhu's Vāsavadattā (about 600 CE) the following passage occurs:

...pītaharitaiḥ kṛṣṇa-kedārikā-koṣṭiṣu samutptadbhir jātuṣa durodairiva daruraśiśukaiḥ nayadyūtairiva cikrīḍa ... ghanakālaḥ[101]

"The time of the rains played its game with frogs for chessmen, which, yellow and green in colour as if mottled with lac, leapt upon the black field squares." Paul Thieme does not quote this as a reference to the game of chess.[102]

Gray, L., translates *durodara* found in this passage as 'chessmen'. This does not seem to be satisfactory. According to Amarakoṣa, the word *durodara* means gambling if it is used in neuter gender. When used in masculine gender, it means gambler.[103] But *durodara* used in masculine gender, referring to a gambler is not accepted by de Vreese. K. In his opinion the masculine gender refers to the stock of dice with which the game is played. According to him the interpretation of *durodara* as *dyūtakara* is the result of a misunderstanding because the term no less than the game in which it figured was obsolete in time of Nīlakaṇṭha and the lexicographers.[104] Thomas considered the *nayadyūta* appearing in the passage of Subandhu as *catutaṅga.*[105] Medinīkośa mentions *naya* as a kind of gambling *nayo nītidyūtaviśeśaḥ.*[106]

Besides the Vibhītaka, Pāśaka and the Pañcika games there might have been existed other forms of games in which dice were used.

In Daśakumāracarita of Daṇḍin we have reference to 25 forms of gambling:

> *teṣāṃ ca pañcaviṃśati-prakārāsu sarvāsu dyūtāśrayāsu kalāsu kauśalyam.*[107]

Yaśodhara while commenting on the Kāmasūtra of Vātsyāyana notices 20 forms. According to him 15 belong to the *nirjīva* class, wherein the stake in an inanimate object, such as money, and five belong to the *sajīva* class which had a living object such as cock or a ram as the stake.[108] Under *nirjīva* class he refers to one type called *nayajñānam.* According to Murray the passage found in Subandhu refers to chess.[109]

Bāṇabhaṭṭa's Harṣacarita refers to *aṣṭāpada* in the context of describing the forehead of sage Dūrvasas. Dūrvasas knit eyebrow into a terrific curve whereby his broad forehead was contracted into winkles. These winkles looked like the lines on a chess board. P.V. Kane expresses the opinion that *aṣṭāpada* mentioned in the above passage is a reference to a chess board rather than a draughts board.[110]

Chessmen were grouped into black and white or red to mark the opposing sides and Bāṇabhaṭṭa knew it.

Ratnākara's Haravijaya[111] has a reference to *aṣṭāpada.* Hermann Jacobi who discussed this passage said that *aṣṭāpada* in the passage refers to modern chess and later Macdonell. A. A., also expressed the same view.[112]

Halāyudha is a writer of a famous lexicon known after his name, besides Kavirahasya and Mṛtasañjīvinī. The former is really a *dhātu-paṭha* or a list of verbs with meanings, written in verse. It explains the conjugational peculiarities of roots having the same form, and its preface mentions expressly the patronage given to him by Kṛṣṇa III (939-966 CE) the last Rāṣṭrakūṭa King. In his commentary Mṛtasañjīvinī Halāyudha refers to *caturaṅga* and a game-board with 64 squares.[112a]

Franklin Edgerton edited the Siṃhāsana Dvātriṃśika or 32 tales of the Vikrama cycle which came into existence in four different recensions between 1500 CE and 1100 CE. The twenty seventh story has a reference to various games such as *caturaṅga*, chess *dyūtakrīḍa* etc.

> *ahaṁ durodare cātra divyāmyakṣairahrniśam/*
> *gatāgataṁ ca jānāmi glahādānapaṇḍitaḥ//*
> *hastyaśva mantri śakaṭa vyūha durbheda varmaṇaḥ/*
> *jāne buddhibalaṁ cāpi caturaṅgasya devane//*
> *nipuṇo'ham dhanādāna balino'pi parājitaḥ//*

"In gambling I shall always (literally: day and night) play with dice. I know (to manipulate) the movements (of pieces) and am skilled in winning (*ādāna*) of stakes.

I know the (special game of) *buddhibala* included in the game of *caturaṅga* class, which possesses unassailable armours such as elephants, horses, chariots, and pawns. I am skilled in winning money and even the powerful are vanquished by me".[113] This passage is significant because the word *buddhibala* in the sense of chess is found used here for the first time.

There is no reference to *aṣṭāpada* in the Vedic literature. In pre-historic India board-games were known. Mckay. E.J.H., is of the opinion that the dice discovered in Mohenjodaro were quite possibly used in conjunction with board-games.[114] It is difficult to say whether the board games which appear to have been played by the Mohenjodaro people were in any way connected with the game of *caturaṅga*.[115]

But it is worth noting that the dice discovered in the Indus valley is cube-sized and has on it marks of 1, 2, 3, 4, 5 and 6. These marks are made not by numerals but by small ring-mark.

In dice connected with *caturaṅga* too similar marks are used for indicating 1, 2, 3, 4, 5 and 6. Traces of game-boards on some of the basement slabs and ghat steps are found both in religious and secular buildings at Nāgārjunakoṇḍa in Āndhrapradesh. Many game-boards have also been discovered at bathing and burning ghat areas, and at a *maṇḍapa* connected to a four-spoked *stūpa.* Most of the game-boards discovered here consist of eight rows having eight squares in each row. Evidently this is meant for playing *aṭṭapada* (*aṣṭāpada*).[116]

Figure nine in plate XLV of the *stūpa* of Bhārhut is named *chitupādaśilā.* Hultzsch translates the title as *citrā utpātā yatra sā śilā,* the rock where miraculous portents happen.[117] Scholars consider this as picture of a board of 36 squares, along with what appear to be seven dice or coins.[118] According to Alexander Cunningham the scene represented in this sculpture shows the parties of two men playing some game like draughts.[119] This scene is significant as it throws some light on the number of players involved in the game.[120] According to Basham A.L., primitive chess was a four handed game.[121]

There is no clue preserved in the structure of the game to betray whether original chess was played with dice or not. Andreas Bock-Raming in his scholarly article "The Gambling Scenes of Bhārhut and Bodhgaya: A Critical Assessment of Their Previous Interpretations and Some New Suggestions" makes his final conclusions as given below:

1. on account of the arrangement of the figures the game depicted is not four-handed dice-chess.
2. the game is shown at its end or at the end of it present round with the second figure from the left being the winner and the right figure in the front the loser.
3. it was played for money, the coins in the upper left of the picture being the stake won by the left player in the previous rounds. Furthermore.
4. from the inscription it can be concluded that something supernatural, a king of magic is involved.

According to recent investigations, this game of dice was played by two players surrounded by curious onlookers.

Andreas further observes: "Summing up, it may be said that on both the reliefs, that of Bhārhut as well as that of Bodhgaya, a game is represented in which a board was used. For the reasons adduced above it is, however, rather improbable that the depictions refer to the board game 'chess' as there is also no real evidence that they have something to do with divination or mathematics."[122]

The objects among the Indus valley finds suspected by Macky E.J.H.,[123] to be chessmen might be real chessmen associated with a kind of dice-chess or they might be pieces used in ordinary dice. From these it may be presumed that dice connected with *caturaṅga* probably goes back to the time of the Indus valley civilization. A. van der Linde supposes that the combination of chess with dicing is younger than simple chess.[124]

Murry H.J.R., states that chess must have been originally exported from India as a game for two players and have survived in that form alone over virtually the whole of Asia and beyond.[125]

Richard Eales says that from India varieties of chess spread not only West to Persia and to Europe, but also North to Tibet and Central Asia, South to Malaya, and East to Burma and Indochina. In all these places chess survives as a game for two players, which is also the dominant form of the traditional game in India itself.[126]

God Śiva is described as playing dice with his consort Pārvatī in some Purāṇas and classical literary works. The Matsyapurāṇa (154-520) refers to such an event. In one of the references found in Mahābhārata, Śiva is represented as playing dice with his spouse being seated on a mountain.[127]

Clear references to a kind of draughts game are found in Bhartṛhari's Vairāgya Śataka and Skāndapurāṇa. Bhartṛhari describes a symbolic dice play between God of death and his wife.[128] The principle of destruction is personified as male and female (i.e., *kāla* and *kālī*). The earth is described as the board, the mortals as pieces (*śāras*) and the day and night as two dice.

In the Skāndapurāṇa,[129] we have a beautiful imagery of the game said to have been played by Śiva and Pārvatī. In it, earth is described as the board, the 12 months as the squares on the board, the 15 days of the dark fortnight as black-coloured pieces and the 15 days of the bright fortnight as white-coloured pieces. It is stated that the two *ayanas* (*uttarāyaṇa* and *dakśiṇāyana*) served as *akṣas* (dice).

In both the descriptions there are references to board, two dice and pieces.

Ellora is situated near Aurangabad in Mahārāṣṭra state of India, and it has many cave temples. The world famous Kailāsa temple at Ellora was constructed by the Rāṣṭrakūṭa king Kṛṣṇa I (756-774 CE). The caves excavated in the sides of the hills round the temple contain extensive halls decorated with finely wrought images of Hindu Gods. Cave number 14 is known as Rāvaṇa-ka-Khai. On the southern wall there are Śaiva sculptures. They include Śiva and Pārvatī playing a board game (Chaupur?).

It may be said that those sculptures are influenced by the descriptions of Śiva's play with Pārvatī found in the Purāṇas and other works. In the sculpture found in the cave number 16 Śiva and Pārvatī are depicted as engaged in an argument as to who play next. In another sculpture found in the cave number 21 Śiva is persuading a reluctant Pārvatī to play one more game. Cave numbers 14 and 16 have sculptures depicting Śiva and Pārvatī playing with dice.[130]

Conclusions

Having discussed in brief several aspects of the early history of the game of chess from the Vedic period up to the period of Halāyudha (10th century CE) it is necessary to draw the different lines of arguments to a finale.

It is certain that the game of chess had its origin in *caturaṅga* which was played on a board having 64 squares, called *aṣṭāpada*. The connection between *caturaṅga* and the game of chess can be easily established because both are played as a war game with a king, minister, elephants,

Shiva and Parvati Playing Dice at Ellora Caves

horses, chariots, and soldiers. The replacement of the traditional chariot by camel and boat is important from the point of view of the early history of the game of chess. References to two handed board games are available in plenty in literature and sculptures. Hence it is apt to conclude that the two-handed chess precedes the four-handed chess as rightly believed by many chess historians. It is Śūlapāṇi who gives an account of *caturaṅga* for the first time and not Raghunandana as believed by Sir William Jones and others. It also becomes necessary to state that Edward B. Tylor's statement that 'the game of chess was the invention of some Hindu who devised a game of war with the *aṣṭāpada* board as his field of battle deserves serious attention as the history of the chess pieces and the plan of the game may be successfully traced to the Ancient Indian War.

It may be said that the symmetrical arrangement of the different pieces in the chess and its advantages have been taken from the Ancient Indian War.

The four-fold force supplied the motive for the game and not vice-versa as argued by Ramachandra Dikshitar V.R., The *bandhas* or metrical puzzles mentioned by Rudraṭa seem to have originated from the art of arranging armies in different forms in the battlefield. Some *bandhas* like *sarvatobhadra* are mentioned in Kauṭilya in the Arthaśāstra and its application is practically illustrated in the great Mahābhārata battle. Hence it may be argued that the puzzles go back to very ancient period.

Halāyudha's reference to *caturaṅga* occurs in his commentary on Piṅgala's work. As Piṅgala is placed in the 2nd century BCE it may be said that the game existed long before Piṅgala. It is shown here that the term *buddhibala* used to denote chess in Sanskrit is found in Siṁhāsanadvātriṁśikā, a work belonging to 1100 CE.

Since some verses attributed to Kālidāsa and Nīlakaṇṭha are found in the work Bṛhajjyotiṣārṇava it may be concluded that some more works related to chess existed in India and research should be conducted to trace them because they may provide vital clues to the early existence of chess in India.

Different formations suggested by Kautilya by combining chariots, elephants and horses are given below:

1. Chariot units in the centre, horses on the flanks, elephant unit at the extremities

Elephant		Elephant
Chariot		
Horses		Horses

2. Elephant units in the centre, chariot units on the flanks, horses on the wings.

Horses		Horses
	Elephants	
Chariot		Chariot

3. Horses in the centre, elephant units in the flanks, chariot units in the wing

Chariot		Chariot
	Horses	
Elephant		Elephant

4. When the formation also includes infantry, the placement shall be:
   Infantry on the wing, horses at the flanks, elephants in the front and chariots in the rear

Infantry		Infantry
	Elephants	
Horses		Horses
	Chariots	

5. The four forces can also be arranged in three arms.

Infantry			Infantry
Chariot	Elephant	Chariot	
Infantry			Infantry

6. Another arrangement is

Infantry Infantry

Chariot

Elephant Elephant

Horses

7. In the immovable array infantry, horses, chariots, and elephants are stationed one behind the other.

Infantry

Horses

Chariots

Elephants

References

1. Arthaśāstra of Kauṭilya, X.5.31,
2. Ibid., X.5.32.
3. Ibid., X.5.33.
4. Ibid., X.5.38-40.
5. Ibid.
6. Ibid., X.6.20 23, 32,43.
7. Ibid., X.6.39-41.

ANALYTICAL ASSESSMENT OF THE CONTRIBUTIONS FOR THE SYMPOSIUM ON "APPROACHING THE ROOTS OF CHESS", PONDICHERRY UNIVERSITY, 26TH-29TH NOVEMBER 1996 TOGETHER WITH A REPORT ON THE GAMING PIECES AND CHESSMEN EXHIBITED IN THE MUSEUMS OF MADRAS AND HYDERABAD PREPARED BY ANDREAS BOCK RAMING, FREIBURG GERMANY.

Introduction

From 26th - 29th November 1996, the University of Pondicherry was the scene of an event of great importance for the research into chess and related board games: The international symposium "Approaching the Roots of Chess", which had been, most efficiently, organized by Dr. C. Panduranga Bhatta, reader at the Department of Sanskrit there, was a successful attempt to convene chess historians and scholars from various disciplines for the first time in India to discuss and hold lectures on the origin and development of chess.

While the largest number of the forty or so participants were from India, a few others came from Japan (represented by Mr. Koichi Masukawa), Germany (represented by Mr. Manfred Eder, Mr. Egbert Meissenburg and I) and the United Kingdom (represented by Dr. Irving Finkel and Dr. Micaela Soar).

The idea to arrange a congress dealing with the history of chess in the (assumed) country of the origin of the game arose in April 1995 at Leiden, The Netherlands, where Mr. Eder, Dr. Finkel and I met Dr. Bhatta during the international colloquium "Board Games in Academia". Thanks to Dr. Bhatta's untiring enthusiasm and the dedication of his colleagues, the project planned at Leiden, which at that time did not seem to be more than a dream, was realized most perfectly.

The present paper is intended to give a summary of the main results of the contributions for this conference, supplemented by additional and sometimes critical remarks of my own which are meant to stimulate further scholarly discussion of important problems.

The study is divided into two main parts called A and B,

the former of which falls, corresponding to the different sessions of the symposium, into 7 chapters.

It is based on the following sources:

1. The *Abstracts (of the) International Symposium on Approaching the Roots of Chess.* Sponsored by Pondicherry University, International Council for Indian Studies, *Centre for Tourism Studies*, Pondicherry 1996. This booklet will henceforth be referred to as Abstracts Pondicherry.
2. *Approaching the Roots of Chess. Abstracts and Papers dedicated and presented to the Organizers and Participants of the Symposium at Pondicherry University, Pondicherry (India). November 26th through 29th, 1996.* Edited by Egbert Meissenburg on behalf of Initiative-Gruppe Konigstein" and "Forderkreis Schach-Geschichichtsforschung e.V", Seevetal 1996.

   This brochure which also contains the papers of those European contributors who were not able to come to Pondicherry, will henceforth be referred to as *Abstracts and Papers.*
3. Notes and information gathered by the German participants during the symposium and on their visits to the museums at Madras and Hyderabad.

The Ceremonial

The symposium was inaugurated by Ms. Yogacharini Meenakshi Devi Bhavanani (Director of the International Centre of Yoga Education and Research, Pondicherry), who in her speech referred to the relationship between chess and yoga. Further addresses were delivered by Prof. M Narasimhachary (Head of the Department of Vaishnavism of Madras University), Dr. S.V. Narayanan (Director of the Centre for Tourism Studies, Pondicherry University) as well as by Dr. Bhatta and Mr. Meissenburg.

Mr. Eder who presided over the inaugural ceremony called the symposium in his "Homage to Pondicherry" a historic moment.

A. The Programme

1. Chess in Sanskrit Literature

Altogether 5 papers were read in this session, the first being Dr. Siddharth Y. Wakankar's paper on "Chaturanga, Buddhibala and Their Literary Descriptions" (Abstracts Pondicherry, pp. 4-5) which mainly concentrated on the opposition of the two terms *caturaṅga* and *buddhibala.*

According to Dr. Wakankar, these expressions are identical with what European chess historians are used to call four-handed dice chess and two-handed chess as a game of intellect played without dice. Dr. Wakankar pointed out that in addition to the (non-)use of dice there is another important difference between *caturaṅga* and *buddhibala*: while the former was played with four kings two of which were considered as allies and each of which was liable to capture, in the latter there were only two kings which were immune from being taken. From Dr. Wakankar's observation that "the *Ratha* or *Nauka* in the *Caturaṅga* is replaced by *Uṣṭra* or Camel (Bishop) in *buddhibala*" (Abstracts Pondicherry, p. 5) it becomes evident that he implicitly considers *buddhibala,* the two-handed game, to have developed from *caturaṅga,* the four-handed dice chess.

Thus, he strongly favours the position of scholars and chess historians like J. Averbach,[1] J Petzold[2] and others.

Comment:

As far as the expression *buddhibala* is concerned, I agree with Dr. Wakankar that it is evidently not a very old term for "chess". If one goes through the known Sanskrit literature dealing with the rules of chess, one finds that *buddhibala* as a term for the two-handed form of chess seems to be restricted to rather late texts.

One example is verse 1 of Nīlakaṇṭha's Nītimayūkha (1600 or 1700 CE.): *...vadati krīḍāṃ buddhibalāśritām.*[3]

I am not convinced, however, that the term *caturaṅga* always signified the four-handed dice chess. As the Mānasollāsa from the 12th CE. with its description of the rules of chess clearly shows, this expression was also used for the two-handed game of intellect.[4]

Terminological considerations were also in the fore ground of my own article on "The Game Board in Indian Chess and Other Board Games" (Abstracts Pondicherry, pp.6-7; Abstracts and Papers, p.7). Investigating the history and development of the various terms for "gaming board" such as *aṣṭāpada, phalaka* and *paṭa* = "cloth" in the relevant Sanskrit literature and trying to give a tentative dating of the contexts in which these terms occur, one obtains the following results:

1. The earliest literary evidence for the use of a "board" - i.e., any surface for performing a game - is provided by a couple of Sanskrit terms all of which mean "cloth" (e.g., *vāsas*).
2. The term *aṣṭāpada* seems to have come out of use, with one or two exceptions, around the 9th -10th CE.

   Instead, later authors preferred other terms like *phalaka* and *paṭa* which is confirmed by several texts on the rules for playing chess and other board games like the Mānasollāsa, the Hariharacaturaṅga etc., which were composed between the 12th and 19th centuries.

   One reason why *aṣṭāpada* obviously became obsolete is possibly its ambiguity as it may also stand for a kind of board game - the character of which, however, remains unclear from the descriptions in the relevant texts - and beyond that may be used as an expression for gold.

3. In non-mythological texts like the Mānasollāsa etc. there are no specific terms that are exclusively applied to a particular board: *paṭa*, e.g., is used for the chessboard as well as for the boards of running and hunting games like Pachisi and its variants.
4. This result is paralleled to a certain extent by observations relating to the terminology used to describe the details of a board. Evidently, some of the names of these details - e.g., the terms for "row" and "file" (*paṅkti, rekhā*) or for "square" (koṣṭha; gṛha) - were not restricted to the board of a particular game but were used for the board in chess as well as in other games.

The paper presented by Dr. C. S. Radhakrishnan on "Dice Play in Sanskrit Poesy" (*Abstracts Pondicherry*, p. 8) showed that terminological investigations are not only useful in the field of chess but can be also meaningfully applied to other board games played with and without dice.

Dr. Radhakrishnan stated that the constituents of such games - the board, the gaming pieces etc. - have never ceased to inspire the imagination of Sanskrit poets.

One example is the famous Bhartṛhari (around 600 CE.) who in verse 42 of his Vairāgyaśataka says that the god of time is playing with the second as his partner by rhythmically moving to and from in his hand day and night like two dice, using the living beings as gaming pieces on the earth which is identified as a gaming board (*bhuvanaphalaka*).

As Dr. Radhakrishnan rightly pointed out, such poetic

images are not only important because of their literary and aesthetic value, but also on account of "the significance of the words used which thereby reveal the very concept of the game as understood by the Sanskrit poets" (*Abstracts Pondicherry*, p. 8).

Comment:

It may be added that the metaphor of the earth as a gaming board occurs not only in the verse of the Vairāgyaśataka quoted by Dr. Radhakrishnan but is also used in the Ṛṣabhapañcāśikā composed by Dhanapāla (around 973 CE.) and in the Campūrāmāyaṇa (1st half of the 11th CE.).

Chess as reflected in the Sanskrit poetical literature was also the subject of Dr. C. Rajendran's paper: "A Note on Caturaṅgāṣṭaka of Melputtur Narayāṇa Bhattatiri" (*Abstracts Pondicherry*, p. 9).

According to the information given by Dr. Rajendran, Melputtur Narāyaṇa Bhattatiri was an erudite poet of Kerala who about 400 years ago wrote eight verses in Sanskrit on the game of (two-handed) chess, of which, however, only six have come down to us.

Comment:

Although the verses of the "Caturaṅgāṣṭaka" are - in comparison, e.g., with the chess text of the Mānasollāsa (cf. p. 10) - certainly not very old, it must be emphasized that also such younger texts are worth studying as they can give us valuable information on the later development of chess in different parts of India. In this connection it is interesting to note that the text investigated by Dr. Rajendran does not show any Persian or Arabic influences. In so far as the metres of this text are rather complicated -

Dr. Rajendran mentioned *sragdharā, vasantatilakā* and *Śārdūla vikrīḍitā* - and its language not always easy to understand, it can be compared with other late Sanskrit texts on chess like the Vilāsamaṇimañjarī.

This voluminous text was dealt with by Mr. M. D. Paradkar in the last paper of the 1st session on: "Caturaṅga Vilāsa-Maṇi-Mañjarī A Sanskrit work on chess" (*Abstracts Pondicherry*, p. 3). In his lecture Mr. Paradkar described the circumstances under which the Vilāsamaṇimañjarī, a work of more than 273 pages in the Kolhapur edition of 1937, was written and gave a summary of its contents. While its introductory part deals, among other things, with three different ways of playing chess called *haindusthāna* (North Indian), *kārṇāṭa* (South Indian) and *vailāyata* (European) and mentions the rules of the promotion of the pawn, the bulk of this voluminous work is concerned with 100 chess problems and their solutions.

Comment:

Mr. Paradkar should be encouraged to continue his valuable studies of the Vilāsamaṇimañjarī, for there are some aspects which need further clarification and make its comparison with other rather late texts on the rules of chess desirable. Very interesting is, e.g., verse 8 of the introductory part (called *prastāvanā* in Sanskrit) which I interpret in a different way than Mr. Paradkar.

It says that the minister, as far as its moves are concerned, should be equal to the king and that the chariot moves two squares aslant, jumping over the foot soldiers.'[5] The move of the chariot is comparable to that described in the already mentioned Mānasollāsa,[6] but it is unclear whether the author of the Vilāsamaṇimañjarī - verse wanted to say that the minister moves exactly like or only similar to the king (Sanskrit *tulya* can mean both) in that it takes one step in the four diagonal directions, not also in the four cardinal directions. The Vilāsamaṇimañjarī also displays characteristics which link it to Harikṛṣṇa's Krīḍākauśalya (19th CE.), e.g., in verse 18 of the *prastāvanā* where it is mentioned that the king, if it has not been given check, may once leap like a horse (cf. Krīḍākauśalya, v. 372).

2. Approaching the Roots of Chess

The second session centred on the question of the origin of chess. The problems pertaining to this subject were specified by Mr. Egbert Meissenburg in his paper: "Some Notes on the State of Chess Research Especially in Connection with Proto-chess" (*Abstracts Pondicherry*, pp. 30-33; *Abstracts and Papers*, pp. 21-23). Mr. Meissenburg complained that, compared to the relatively detailed documentation of Arabic chess (which is, above all, the merit of R. Wieber's thesis from 1972), the state of research regarding Indian chess was still in its infancy.

He pointed out that the primary task to overcome this deficiency had to be to collect and systematize all references to chess in the literary and archaeological sources and to collaborate them with the facts already known to us.

He further emphasised that such a tremendous task could only succeed if all scholars involved in the subject - chess historians, Indologists etc. -were willing to cooperate.

Mr. Meissenburg formulated five questions on which according to his opinion the future research work should concentrate:

1. "Who": by this Mr. Meissenburg means the question whether chess was invented by a single person (as, e.g., Sir William Jones believed) or whether it is the product of an evolutionary process (as, e.g., is assumed by M. Eder and J. Averbach, cf. pp. 16;17).
2. "Where", i.e., the problem should be solved whether chess has indeed its origin in India or in China, Iran or elsewhere.

3. "When", i.e., is it possible to specify the time of the origin of chess. As is well known, the opinions uttered so far in this respect range from 3000 B.C. to the middle of the 5th CE.

The following problems were subsumed by Mr. Meissenburg under the questions no. 4 "How" and no. 5

"Why": Is chess a reality-orientated transfer of the forces of the Indian army onto the gaming board? Is it a pure game of numbers or has it developed from magic squares? Is it a combination of a race game and a strategic game? Does it have its roots in astronomical symbolism and the techniques of divination? Has the rule that the king must not be taken anything to do with the conquest of India by Alexander the Great? Did the game originate in Buddhist circles or was it inspired by Brahmanical ideas? Last not least: was it originally a two-handed game of intelligence or a four-handed dice game?

The three remaining papers of this session were concerned with some of these problems and tried to answer them.

To prove that the place of the origin of chess in all probability is not China was the intention of Mr. Koichi Masukawa's paper: "About the Origin of Chess; Criticisms on the Publications in China and on the Common Notion in Europe" (*Abstracts Pondicherry*, pp. 37-38). Mr. Masukawa criticized two recent works dealing with the history of chess in China: Song Fu's *Stories of Xiang Qi History* from 1981 and *A history of Chinese Xiang Qi* written by Zhang Ru in 1991.

The main theses of these publications are: 1. The forerunner of Chinese chess (Xiang Qi) is a game called Liu-bo; 2. Xiang Qi was invented by the emperor Wu-Di of Bei Zou; 3. Bao Inn Xiang Qi is an earlier stage of Xiang Qi; and 4. Xiang Qi was introduced from China to other surrounding countries.

Mr. Masukawa demonstrated that all four of these theses are untenable. Especially worth mentioning is his refutation of the assertion that Xiang Qi is an invention of Wu-Di, for the book composed by this king is a work on astronomy, not on games. A few European scholars, however, had erroneously adopted the idea of Wu-Di's invention of chess because they had not realized the ideographic variation of the letter "xiang" which also means "shape" and "figure" and must not necessarily point to chess.

Comment:

Mr. Masukawa's implicit conclusion that chess did not originate in China - according to his view there is no proof of its existence in China before the 8th century - clearly substantiates arguments already advanced earlier, e.g., by Richard Eales in his book: *Chess. The History of a Game* (London 1985). Eales emphasises "that Chinese chess can only be proved to be in existence by c. 800, almost two centuries after its appearance is documented in India and Persia" (p. 33) and that Needham's so-called divination theory according to which the central characteristics of chess have developed from astrology is not conclusive (p. 34).

If, therefore, the assumption that chess originated in China can quite safely be ruled out, there is much more evidence that India was its birthplace and that it developed on the model of the old Indian army. This was shown by Dr. C. Panduranga Bhatta in his paper "Indian Origins of Chess - An Investigation" (Abstracts Pondicherry, p. 47). Dr. Bhatta stressed that the description of the rules of chess in the relevant Sanskrit literature (to which belongs, e.g., the above-mentioned Mānasollāsa) betrayed the warlike character of the game by the frequent use of the terms *caturaṅga* and *vyūha*: while the former expression indicated that the four chess pieces of chariot, horse, elephant and foot-soldier symbolise or correspond to the military forces of chariots, cavalry, elephants and infantry, *vyūha* signified the various possible arrangements of the pieces on the board and had evidently been adopted from the Sanskrit literature on the conduct of war where it means battle array.'[7]

Further evidence adduced by Dr. Bhatta for the Indian origin of chess and its conception as a war game is:

1. the roles of the chariot and the elephant in the Indian warfare between the 4th century BCE. and the 1st to 2nd CE.
2. the group of seven ivory figurines from Afrasiab; and
3. the rule of the invincibility of the king in chess which has its root in the doctrine of the divinity of the king emerging during the post-Vedic period.

Comment:

The result of Dr. Bhatta's paper is very clear and essentially substantiates that of my own investigations as well as of other scholars:[8] the Indian (two-handed) game of chess, which in the Mānasollāsa is called *caturaṅga*, and its pieces are derived from the old Indian army and its constituents; it is a transfer of the above-mentioned four branches of this army onto the gaming board. Therefore, I still subscribe, contrary to scholars like Prof. Hollander,[9] to the view that the Indian game of chess reflects certain cultural and social circumstances. It can be shown "that the power of the single chess pieces as described in the Mānasollāsa, especially that of the chariot and the elephant, reflects the structure and organisation of the Indian army as it already operated in pre-Christian times up to the 3rd or 4th CE.[10] I do not deny that chess is, considered from a theoretical point of view, an "artificial structure that can also be described in mathematical terms" and that "the names and shapes of the piecesî create a net of their own" which can be "substituted" by other similar nets.[11] What I doubt, however, is that these modern theoretical considerations played any role with the emergence of chess in India.

While the papers by Mr. Masukawa and Dr. Bhatta were thus concerned with the question "Where (did chess originate)", the contribution by Mr. Manfred Eder titled "Approaching the Roots of Chess by Trying A Definition In Historic Context"[12] (*Abstracts Pondicherry*, pp. 27-29; *Abstracts and Papers*, pp. 8-9) referred to the questions "How" and "Why".

As it is often unclear which regulated way of playing, we mean when the term of chess is used in connection with investigations pertaining to the origin of board games, Mr. Eder pointed out the necessity of giving a deinition of the term which means to find a common denominator that can be accepted as the origin, as the first appearance of the game of "chess". He proposed to sketch a "family tree" the visible part of which represents the already known development after the origin of chess and the invisible part of which are its roots which are mostly hidden from our view.

By focussing one's attention on the spot where the object appears one is supposed to find what Mr. Eder called the "chess-point" which can be reached from two diametrically opposed directions: the present time from which we look backwards down to the earliest proof of chess and the past from which we look forwards to the same "chess-point".

Furthermore, Mr. Eder explained that besides the characteristic "two-handed chess" there was a second, equally important criterion, namely "giving check" which means the rule that the king must not be taken. For Mr. Eder it is this immunity of the king which constitutes the game of chess, which is its "idea-bearing concept" and its very essence. He considers the introduction of the rule of the invincibility of the king as key-event which is without equal in the long history of chess: with the combination of two opposing concepts, that of a warlike game which aims at the enemy's defeat and that of the humane aspect of the invincibility of the king "chess" was born. This constellation is called "chess-point" by Mr. Eder.

Comment:

Mr. Eder's impressively shrewd theory has a consequence which he did not expressly mention in his lecture: the game which till now we were used to call four-handed dice chess does not fall under his definition outlined above and consequently can no longer be called chess because its rules allow any of the four kings to be taken.[13]

In this connection it may be quite useful to point out that the Indians themselves evidently did not find it necessary to draw such a sharp distinction, at least as far as the Mānasollāsa's passage on chess is concerned. In this text both games, two-handed chess and the four-handed form, are described in one and the same chapter (12), and for both of them the same terminology is used: the two-handed game being played without dice in which the king must not be taken is given the name *khelana caturaṅgākhya* - "the game called *caturaṅga*"-, and the passage in which it is described ends with: *iti caturaṅgavinoda*: "this is the amusement (achieved by playing) *caturaṅga*". On the other hand, the four-handed game, in which it is allowed to take any of the four kings, is likewise called *caturaṅga* which is evident from the colophon of the passage where it is described: *iti caturaṅgaśikṣā*. "this is the art of (playing) *caturaṅga*"; and the whole 12th chapter which, as mentioned above, comprises both descriptions, that of the two-handed as well as that of the four-handed game, ends with the words: *iti caturaṅgakrīḍā.* "this is the *caturaṅga*-game". So, one has the impression that the author of the Mānasollāsa found it not so important whether the king was allowed to be taken or not. What mattered was that both forms were played with the four branches of the (chess)-army.

In addition to the papers by Mr. Meissenburg, Mr. Masukawa, Dr. Bhatta, and Mr. Eder, also the written contributions by Jurij Averbach, Isaak Linder, Franco Pratesi, Alessandro Sanvito and Kenneth Whyld, which are contained in the *Abstracts and Papers* only, belong to the range of themes of the second session.

The first four of them are related to Mr. Meissenburg's questions nos. 1 ("who") and 4 ("how") while the paper by Mr. Whyld deals with the question "where".

Mr. Averbach's contribution: "To the Question of the Origin of Chess" (*Abstracts and Papers*, pp. 5-6) is principally a summary of his article *Wie das Schachspiel entstand* which appeared in "Schach-Journal" 1 (1991), pp. 51-64. Mr. Averbach assumes six successive stages of the development of the game of chess:

1. At the beginning, there was *aṣṭāpada,* a running game played by four players with dice on a board of 8 x 8 squares.
2. The pieces used in this *aṭāpada*-game were substituted by miniature chariots.
3. These chariots were made to compete, with the result that the running game developed into a war game.
4. After that all four arms of the Indian army — chariots, elephants, cavalry, and infantry — appeared on the board.
5. Because of reasons pertaining to certain political

circumstances in North India during the 6th CE. the war game for four players was transformed into a game for two participants. This change automatically entailed the idea of checkmate.

6. Finally, due to Greek influence, the use of the dice was given up which meant relinquishing the principle of *karma.*

Comment:

The clarity with which Mr. Averbach presents his theses is very impressive, although I have slight reservations about some of his statements.

First, there is no clue what kind of game *aṣṭāpada,* which is mentioned in some religious writings of the Buddhists and Jains, really was. In the Buddhist Vinaya Piṭaka, which can be roughly dated between the 4th and the 3rd BCE., it is said (Vin II 10,17; repeated at Vin III 180,22) that some sinful monks played the *aṣṭāpada* - and daśapada -games.

There are, however, no further details, neither about the character nor the rules of this game; and this also holds true for several texts belonging to the Jaina canon which show that their authors apparently knew *aṣṭāpada* as a kind of board game. In no case it is described as a game with dice for four players as assumed by Mr. Averbach.

Secondly, it seems that the Bhārhut-relief mentioned by Mr. Averbach in his article in the "Schach-Journal" (p. 57) is a rather questionable testimony of the existence of the four-handed dice chess in pre-Christian times. It is unlikely that it depicts four players. If it did, they would sit on the four sides of the board which is not the case.[14] The first reliable testimony of the four-handed dice chess is the 16th chapter of al-Bīrūnī's kitāb fi taḥqīq mā I-hind from which is evident that its author also knew the two-handed game. So, in my view it remains somewhat problematic to see the four-handed dice chess as the precursor of the two-handed game.

Finally, it is not quite clear how the use of dice is related to the concept of *karma*, which is a typically Indian notion existing from about the middle of 1st millennium BCE. to the present day in Hinduism, Buddhism and Jainism. The doctrine of *karma* means that the actions of a human being in his present life inevitably determine his lot in his future existence.

If he lives a righteous and sinless life, this will lead to his rebirth on a higher level of existence, e.g., as a god. Bad actions, however, will result in his being reborn on a lower level, e.g., as an animal. Thus, the *karma* works quite mechanically, and it has nothing to do with chance.

Like Mr. Averbach, Mr. Linder too assumes that the game of chess developed in an evolutionary process which he demonstrates once more in his contribution "My Personal Opinion on the Origin of Chess" (*Abstracts and Papers*, pp. 19-20). According to his opinion, there are three stages of development: *caturaṅga, shatrang* (*chatrang*) and the modern game of chess. As is well known, Mr. Linder was one of the first scholars who interpreted the Sanskrit term *caturaṅga* as four-handed dice chess.

He takes the view that the earliest evidence of the use of the word in this sense is Bāṇa's Harṣacarita from the first half of the 7th century CE. This four-handed game was then transformed into a game for two players which happened, as Mr. Linder conjectures, either during the Kushan period (2nd/1st to 3rd /4th CE) or in the 5th-6th CE. under the reign of the Hephtalites at the latest and which can be explained by "the new socio-cultural conditions of life including the evolution of the military art and the growing role of Buddhism with its self-awareness of the individual and priority of reason." (*Abstracts and Papers*, p. 19).

Mr. Linder also mentions that the names of some chess pieces were changed by the Persian speaking peoples of Central Asia. The observation of such changes is important as they allow scholars "to trace ethnic and cultural links and the specific ways in which the game was adopted by different peoples, determined by differences in their domestic and social life." (p. 20).

Mr. Linder rightly emphasises that only a multi-disciplinary study of the game of chess, which includes historical, ethnographical, literary and above all archaeological evidence, will lead to new results concerning the question of the origin of chess.

Comment:

Although Mr. Linder's line of reasoning sounds convincing, the above-mentioned problem of the still unproven priority of four-handed chess over the two-handed form remains. Mr. Linder's quotation of Bāṇa's Harṣacarita is no proof that the former was already known at that time.

The passage in question — *aṣṭāpadānāṃ caturaṅgakalpanā*: "the fourfold [army] was only arranged on *aṣṭāpada*-boards" — could just as well refer to the two-handed chess.

While Mr. Averbach and Mr. Linder try to elaborate various, relatively clearly defined stages in the development of the game of chess, Mr. Franco Pratesi expounds general considerations on "Proto chess -A Framework for Pondicherry" (*Abstracts and Papers*, pp. 24-26). Defining chess "as the 'standard' game between two players without dice" and protochess as "any earlier, significantly different variant suggested but without applying this name to boardgames played with identical men or pebbles"

(*Abstracts and Papers*, p. 24), Mr. Pratesi suggests several hypotheses which he thinks are possible regarding the origin of chess:

1. Proto chess did not exist. Chess being played with six different pieces was practically a new creation which did not presuppose a step-by-step evolution from board games played with identical pieces.
2. Proto chess was a primitive war game played with two or more different pieces from which chess developed by a gradual increase in the number of different pieces up to six.
3. Proto chess existed among other board games:
   a) as a race game, e.g., the four-handed dice game mentioned by al-Bīrūnī, from which chess developed by the transformation of the second king into the new minister.
   b) as a kind of hunting game.
   c) as a form of dice game.
4. Certain forms of proto chess were derived from other uses of a board as an abacus or in connection with astronomy, divination and other arts and sciences.

Comment:

Although Mr. Pratesi understands his contribution as a tentative framework leaving open which of his hypotheses should be preferred for proto chess, he intimates that in his view nos. 2 and 3 are not very likely to prove true. As far as no. 2 is concerned, Mr. Pratesi points out that there is evidently no "documentary evidence supporting the hypothesis of a gradual increase in the number of different men on the chess board", and with regard to no. 3a) he rightly observes that till now we lack any definite proof that chess developed from the four-handed dice chess as a form of proto chess (cf. above, my remarks on the contributions by Mr. Averbach and Mr. Linder).

Mr. Sanvito's contribution "Some Remarks upon the Origin of Chess" (*Abstracts and Papers*, pp. 27-28) is exclusively concerned with the question of whether chess is an invention or whether it developed in an evolutionary process (cf. the first of the five questions formulated by Mr. Meissenburg). Tackling this problem, Mr. Sanvito assumes that the difference between the invention-theory and the evolution-theory does not necessarily need to be as great as generally assumed and thinks it possible that both opposites do not exclude each other but are complementary.

He imagines "that the eventual inventor created this game, as a simulated game of war, not from nothing at a single blow, but, on the contrary, he might draw his inspiration looking at some board game and looking at this game he had the idea to 'invent' the game of chess" (p. 27).

Comment:

In his contribution, Mr. Sanvito takes up an idea which quite similarly has already been suggested by M. Eder in his attempt to define the game of chess in its historical context. Mr. Eder believes that the development towards the "chess-point" (cf. p. 16) was an evolutionary process, whereas the introduction of the rule that the king must not be taken may be called an invention.[15]

Is India the country of the origin of chess or not: this is the subject of Kenneth Whyld's contribution: "The Birthplace of Chess. Some Reflections" (*Abstracts and Papers*, p. 29) in which he contrasts the arguments for India with several counterarguments. The points speaking in favour of India are:

1. that the earliest chess terms are in Sanskrit from

where they have been adopted into the Persian and Arabic languages.

2. the Firdausi legend which describes the arrival of chess from India.
3. Folklore about India as the birthplace of chess.

The counterarguments — which in Mr. Whyld's opinion tend to outweigh the clues that chess originated in India— are:

1. Sanskrit is only one member of a family of languages. Other closely related languages, e.g., Avestan, were used outside India.
2. Firdausi's description of chess as coming from "Hind": this area has been interpreted by some scholars as Khuzistan, by others as signifying the region around Baluchistan.
3. Firdausi's story of the transposition of the two games of chess and nard was intended to extol the virtues of Khosros I. Judging it from an objective point of view, it seems unlikely as "there would be more merit in 'cracking' chess than nard".
4. The proliferation of the (conflicting) Indian legends about the creation of chess may be attributed to the rich narrative tradition of India.

Moreover, Mr. Whyld mentions that "while chess flourished in Baghdad in the 9th century, the earliest reliable account of chess playing in India date only from the 11th century".

Comment:

Commenting on some of the counterarguments adduced by Mr. Whyld, I would like to point out that

1. as far as I know, the etymology of the name of the game as well as that of the pieces is well-established: while the Middle Persian *catrang* directly developed from

Sanskrit *caturaṅga*, the other terms were semantically imitated: *hastin* (elephant) as *pīl*, *aśva* (horse) as *asp*, *ratha* (chariot) as *rahv*, *padāta* (foot-soldier) as *padātak* and *rājan* (king) as *śāh*.[16] There is no serious attempt to derive these terms from Avestan or another Indo-European language.

2. the term *hind* etymologically derives from "Sind", i.e., the region around the lower course of the Indus River. Already in some younger inscriptions of Dareios I. this area, which had been conquered shortly after 518 CE. and annexed to the Persian empire as a province, was called "Hi(n)dus". It is, however, quite possible that Firdausi, who lived very much later (ca. 934-1021 CE.) and sometimes stayed as a guest at the court of Mahmud of Ghazni, understood by "Hind", corresponding to the area which had been conquered by that ruler, not only Sind proper, but the entire region along the rivers Ganges and Yamunā.
3. the earliest evidence for (two-handed) chess in India is not as late as Mr. Whyld assumes; the description of the moves of the chess pieces in Rudraṭa's Kāvyālaṁkāra (9th century CE) seems to indicate that at that time the game of chess must already have had a certain tradition.

3. Chess and Yoga

Surprising as the connection between these two fields for a Westerner may be, the papers presented in this part of the symposium gave an interesting insight into the relationship between them.

In his paper on "Application of Yoga to Chess: An Observation" (Abstracts Pondicherry, pp.15-16) Mr. Chakradhar Behera demonstrated how yogic exercises, e.g., the practice of various *āsana-s* (sitting in peculiar postures) and *prāṇāyāma* (breath-exercises) - can be made useful for playing a better game of chess. It is through Yoga that a chess-player acquires the power of concentration which is necessary to win the game. Moreover, Mr. Behera pointed out that eating vegetarian food and abstaining from meat, smoking and alcohol are equally important for a yogi as well as for a good chess-player.

The utilisation of yoga for chess was also covered by Mr. D. Sakthignanavel in his contribution: "Scientific Approach of Yoga Towards Chess" (*Abstracts Pondicherry*, p.10). Yoga, he said, "trains in a slow and steady manner to develop the mental, moral and physical fitness of chess-players."

In her paper "Yoga and Chess" (*Abstracts Pondicherry*, pp. 11-12) Ms. Yogacharini Meenakshi Devi Bhavanani was careful to stress that the relationship between these two fields is a mutual one. "Yoga methodology", she said, "may be useful for the chess-player, and a good chess-player may find that his prowess in this game also makes him a good Yogi" (p. 11). Therefore, a good and well-trained chess-player, who can foresee the consequences of each of his moves on the board, will, according to Ms. Bhavanani, also develop an understanding of the law of karma, whereas the yogi's capacity to perceive the workings of the karmic forces makes him also able to foresee the moves in a game of chess more easily.

Mr. V.G. Krishna Murthy gave a lecture on "The Human Mind - Genesis and Growth - Thesis - Brief Report" (*Abstracts Pondicherry*, pp. 13-14) in which he traced the gradual development of mind during the evolution of man. Furthermore, he had one of his pupils perfectly performed various asana-s. He emphasized how very important it was for a good chess player to do these exercises regularly. More information on Mr. Krishna Murthy's theses may be found in his book Yoga and Chess (Vijayawada 1994).

4. Anthropology, Archaeology and Chess

The range of themes dealt with in the 4th session made clear that the intricate problems of the origin and development of chess are not only a matter of textual research but also necessarily involve other disciplines. The first lecture was given by Prof. (Ms.) R. Vasantha on "Chess Play as Depicted in Bhārhut Sculpture" (*Abstracts Pondicherry*, p. 48) which was dealing with two quite different subjects:

a) the probable roots of chess and

b) the interpretation of the board game represented in the Bhārhut relief.

In the first part of her lecture Prof. Vasantha argued that chess was genetically linked to magical and religious rituals which have been known in India from ancient times. In her view it is associated with the belief that the life of human beings is influenced by the nine celestial bodies[17] each of which relates to a particular number.

If these numbers are arranged in a diagram of 9 **x** 9 cells, one obtains what Prof. Vasantha called the "Vedic square", which she believes to be the basis of a complete mathematical system and the numerical model of the universe.

While the upper horizontal and outer left rows of this diagram contain the numbers from 1 to 9 (starting from the top left-hand corner), the numbers of the other squares of each row are obtained by "arithmetic progression". This means, e.g., that the 2nd row starts with the sequence 2-4-6-8 and the 3rd one with the sequence 3-6-9. If, however, the sum "x" exceeds 9, the next member of the sequence is produced by the difference $x-9$ (which, e.g., in the case of the 5th cell of the 2nd row means 10 – 9 =1).

Prof. Vasantha asserted that it is from this "Vedic square" that chess and other board games were derived, the moves of the pieces being closely related to the movements of the celestial bodies and their numerical symbolism.

Furthermore, she pointed out that by joining those cells that show the same number certain geometrical diagrams are obtained which "represent to ourselves our real-life relationships and experiences."[18] These diagrams are linked to board games in so far as every move of a piece result in similar geometrical patterns. At the same time the interrelationship between these patterns is, according to Prof. Vasantha, also helpful in deciding the "compatibility" between different persons.

As far as Prof. Vasantha's explanation of the origin of chess is concerned, the question remains how the *aṣṭāpada* the board of 8 x 8 squares on which chess is usually played, is related to the "Vedic square" of 9 x 9 squares. It would also be very important to know whether there is literary evidence for the "Vedic square" and its numerical symbolism. Irrespective of these questions it is obvious that Prof. Vasantha's view is in a certain way connected with the position of Ricardo Calvo who, taking up the hypothesis of Johannes Kohtz about the "jumping rook", maintains that the moves of the chess pieces historically derive from the numerical arrangement of the so-called Safadi board, which means a magic square of 8 x 8 cells.[19]

With respect to R. Calvo's opinion it may be observed the board used for playing chess was doubtlessly also used for mathematical calculations, especially that of the arithmetic progression 1-64 and that it served as a magic square where the numbers of the arithmetic progression are distributed in such a way that the addition of the numbers of each row and file as well as of the two diagonals results in the same sum. But there is no reason to suppose that the game of chess developed from the use of the board as a magic square. In this connection it seems quite useful to have once more a look on the Mānasollāsa quoted above. After the paragraph on chess this text continues, in the verses 623cd-632, with a description of the knight's move which is performed on what F. Bernhauer considers as the earliest evidence known so far for the magic square of the Safadi-type.[20]

The way in which both these descriptions are juxtaposed seems to exclude the possibility that the game of (two-handed) chess (and its variants) is genetically linked to the knight's move on the magic square.

In the second part of her lecture Prof. Vasantha attempted a new and, in some points, quite surprising interpretation of the well-known and much discussed relief of the Bhārhut stupa on which four men in pairs on the opposite sides of a gaming board are shown. She believes that

1. the 6 square objects depicted beside the upper left corner of the gaming board, which so far were thought to be either coins or dice, are nothing else than a "scoreboard" on which the scores of each pair of players are marked.
2. the single rectangular object depicted beside the lower left side of the board is a die.

The pictures available for Prof. Vasantha's lecture did not allow a definite answer to the question whether the board, which is split in two halves, has 6 x 5 or 6 x 6 cells.

Discussing the rules according to which this board game was possibly played, Prof. Vasantha asserted that there are four players playing with pieces which are depicted as dots on the board: "the players move their individual pawns and try to check-mate the pawns of the opposite player. Probably, the four players might have started the game from the four corners of the board, each player moving his pawns towards his opponent on the opposite side. The two players on each side possibly played as partners in the game."[21]

Comment:

Without doubt Prof. Vasantha's interpretation of the Bhārhut relief is an important and innovative contribution to its future investigation.

It has, however, already been pointed out that the assumption of four players taking part in the game is not very likely (cf. p. 18).

As so many different suggestions have already been made in the past regarding the explanation of this gaming scene, I deemed it necessary to make a fresh, comprehensive investigation which, apart from recording the secondary literature so far written on this subject, compares it with similar artefacts such as the representation of a gaming board at Bodhgaya. The results of this project, which is sponsored by the "Förderkreis Schach-Geschichtsforschung e. V.", will probably be published in 1998.

Investigating the history of chess, backgammon, Pachisi etc., one should always be aware that all these games are not only a set of abstract rules but often also reflect significant elements of human behaviour. They must be seen in the wider context of gambling which may be said to be a universal trait comparable to man's physical functions.[22]

Overlapping with magical, religious, and social aspects, they are a highly important field of research for anthropologists and ethnographers.

In the light of these facts, it is deplorable that many board games as potential sources of anthropological information, which, like Pachisi, one hundred years ago were still widespread in India, are nowadays rapidly vanishing. Therefore, Dr. Irving L. Finkel's project on the anthropological investigation of the board games of India is of great significance. Presenting his paper on: "Outline Plan for an Anthropological Investigation of the Board Games of India "(*Abstracts and Papers*, pp. 11-18; title in the *Abstracts Pondicherry*, p. 43: "Indian Board Games and The Anthropological Survey: The Pursuit of Information") Dr. Finkel pointed out that especially about games of alignment, war games and race games the matter was very urgent.

The investigation is to be based upon two sources of information:

a) in the case of living games on interviews with persons who know how to play them and on immediate observation, which allows to determine the geographical distribution of an individual game:

b) on the representation of gaming boards scratched on pavements, temple walls and public places.

The primary goal of Dr. Finkel's project is "to survey the distribution of board games in India at large" (*Abstracts and Papers*, p. 12) which can be achieved with the help of field agents and anthropologists working for the Anthropological Survey of India. Being equipped with a special questionnaire, which will be especially useful in the case of such complex games as Chaupar or Mancala, they are expected to collect information regarding the geographical location of a particular game, its regional name, and its rules (number of players, type, and number of pieces etc.). Dr. Finkel's project will also include an investigation of the local equipment for board games, i.e., the material and decoration of the boards, dice, and gaming pieces.

Comment:

It is to be hoped that the reference work Dr. Finkel has promised because of his campaign can appear as soon as possible. For me, who as an Indologist is especially concerned with the history of Indian religions, it would be very interesting to get some more information on those games which reveal a particular religious background. A game of this kind is, e. g., the "Chaupar of knowledge" (*jñāna caupar*) which is mostly Vaiṣṇava in character, but also has Jain, Buddhist, and even Muslim variants. One of the still unanswered questions is, whether it originated in Buddhist or in Hindu circles.[23]

The 4th session was rounded off by a lecture on the "Historical Development of chess in India."[24] held by Dr. A. Ramachandran.

5. Chess and Regional Literature

While the classical Sanskrit literature has been thoroughly scrutinized for references to chess and other board games, comparatively little research has been done so far on the description of these games in other Indian languages. Therefore, the lectures of the 5th session were so highly important. All four of them focussed on the languages and literatures of South India.

Mr. P. V. N. Nambudiripad, who is the author of a book on various games of chess as well as of several chess-orientated articles published in newspapers and magazines, reported on "Some References and Chess Literature in Malayalam" (*Abstracts Pondicherry*, p. 20). He pointed out that chess is mentioned for the first time in Malayalam literature in the so-called Payyannoor Pattu of the 13th century. Further references can be found in poetical works, ballads and popular folk songs which have been composed between the 14th and 18th century CE.

From Prof. (Mrs.) V. Balambal's lecture on "Chaturanga in Folk Games of Tamil Nadu" (*Abstracts Pondicherry,* p. 23) we learnt that Tamil literature yields only very little information on chess. Therefore, her main interest was on several folk games-she mentioned Tayakattam, Tanjavurkattam, Sokkatan and others-which are, like the four-handed chess, played in combination with dice.

Comment:

Prof. Balambal's explanations invite the conclusion that these folk games have never or only rarely been dealt with in literary descriptions because they have been handed down mostly orally. Therefore, any investigation of their rules and possible varieties as well as of the question when and where they are played will very much depend on the knowledge of local informants, a fact which underlines once more the importance of Dr. Finkel's project.

Considering the significance of oral information with respect to individual board games, Mr. D. Sakthignanavel's paper was particularly welcome as he gave an account on "Existing Chess Related Chaturanga Games in South India" (*Abstracts Pondicherry*, pp. 25- 26) which was not based on any literary sources, but on his own personal knowledge of these games. Mr. Sakthignanavel described four board games which are played to the present day all over South India: two different types of Nehr Kodu, Nera and Adu Puli (Goat and Tiger).

Especially worth mentioning seems the third game, Nera, as it evidently falls under the group of war games with moves along the marked lines of a board and leap capture. The players, each of whom has sixteen pieces, move alternately, and a capture is made by jumping over an enemy piece on to a vacant point beyond.

Murray H.J.R., has recorded several variants of this type of game in his book A History of Board Games Other Than Chess.

According to his investigations, they are not only played

in different regions of India but are also known in many other parts of the world.

The variants which come closest to the Nera-game have been described by Murray under the nos. 4.2.21, 25, and 26 (p. 67).[25]

A game like Nera called *smaśānadyūtakaṅkaṅkrīḍā* ("game played with small stones on a cemetery") is also mentioned in v. 256ff. of the Krīḍākauśalya, an encyclopedia of games from the 19th century written in Sanskrit.

The fourth game, Adu Puli, evidently belongs to the group of hunt games, the general aim of which is to obstruct the moves of the "tigers". According to Murray (p. 107ff.), variants of this game are played in different parts of India under the names of Bagh bandi or Bagh guti (with 2 tigers and 20 goats), Sher-bakar (with 2 tigers and 19 goats), Bagh-bukri (with 3 tigers and 13 sheep), Mudrunggum (with 4 tigers and 16 sheep), Bhagchal, Bhagchakar, or Chahrachel (with 4 tigers and 20 goats) and Kaooa (with 1 tiger and 7 *kaooas*)[26]

Also, the Krīḍākauśalya mentions four variants of Adu Puli played with 1 tiger and 3 goats, 2 tigers and 8 goats, 4 tigers and 28 goats, and 3 tigers and 16 goats (vs. 306-316).

At first sight, the title of Mr. T. V. Gopalaiyer's paper: "Chess play in Tamil literature" *Abstracts Pondicherry*, pp. 41-42) seems to be at variance with Prof. Balambal's observation that Tamil literature contains only very few references to chess.

From the details of Mr. Gopalaiyer's lecture it became, however, clear that he referred to a form of "chess" or board game played in combination with dice.

The textual sources upon which he based his investigations — e.g., the Tolkappiyam and the Sangam literature composed between the 1st and 3rd centuries CE. — yield information about:

1. the social status of the players (common people, but also princes)
2. the material and making of the board (drawn on the ground; made of gold)
3. the number of dice (rectangular or round; methods of throwing them and counting the pips)
4. the place where and the opportunities at which the game was played.
5. the role of betting in the game.

Comment.

Mr. Gopalaiyer's and Mr. Sakthignanavel's papers lead me to a concluding remark on the terminology used by them. They apply the terms "chess" and *caturaṅga* in a rather broad sense. Contrary to what had been demanded by Mr. Eder, Mr. Gopalaiyer refers to the game of chance he describes as "chess", while in Mr. Sakthignanavel's usage all the games mentioned by him are "*caturaṅga* games".

It seems that both expressions have developed into a kind of generic term for all kinds of board games.[27]

6. Chess in Contemporary Literature and General Aspects

Altogether four lectures dealing with very different aspects of chess were given in this session. Dr. P. Marudanayagam was concerned with "The Game of Chess as a Literary Symbol" (*Abstracts Pondicherry*, p. 17), examining its role in a wide range of mostly English plays, poems, and novels (e.g., Shakespeare's "The Tempest", Lewis Carroll's "Through the Looking Glass").

The contribution: "On Computational Aspects Of The Game Of Chess", jointly authored by Dr. Chandragupta,

S. Warnekar, Ms. Anjali and V. Betawadkar (*Abstracts Pondicherry*, pp. 35-36), was another attempt to prove that chess is fundamentally based on mathematics, which seems also apparent in the well-known legend of the inventor of chess who is given one grain of wheat for the first square of the board, two for the second, four for the third etc. The main idea worked out in this lecture is that chess as it is played in its present form falls into 5 distinct phases which partly correspond to mathematical processes (e.g., the 2nd stage called "phase of increasing combinations" is said to be based upon a geometrical progression).

Like Dr. Wakankar, J. Averbach, Prof. Petzold and other chess historians also Ms. G. Vasanthi takes it for granted that chess originated from the four-handed dice game called *caturaṅga.* This became evident from her paper: "Genesis of The Game of Chess and Chess Pieces" (*Abstracts Pondicherry*, pp. 44-45) in which she also traced the spread of the game from India via Persia and the Arab empire to Europe and outlined the history of the names and the moves of the individual chess pieces.

Finally, the report given by the British archaeologist Dr. M. Soar on finds of gaming planograms ("boards") in the Kailāsanātha temple of Ellora[28] demonstrated how closely entwined the literary and archaeological sides of chess research may be. During her fieldwork Dr. Soar discovered that the said building contains depictions of gaming boards with pieces on them which exactly tally with a passage in the Mānasollāsa describing a backgammon-like game.[29]

7. Workshop on Gaming Pieces

The workshop, which concluded the symposium, was governed by Mr. Eder's paper titled: "Which Indian Gaming-Pieces or Chessmen are the Predecessors of the (so-called) Arabian-Islamic Style?" (*Abstracts Pondicherry*, pp. 39-40; *Abstracts and Papers*, p. 10).

Proceeding from the assumptions

a) that originally natural objects like pebbles, seeds, nuts, and cowrie-shells were used for playing.

b) that such primitive, elementary "gaming pieces" were then differentiated in size, shapes and colours to arrange them in a kind of hierarchy and

c) that later they were "designed" artificially and artistically into miniature-like images of living beings such as animals, Mr. Eder holds that also the very first chessmen were figurative representations of the four arms of the Indian army. He further believes that parallel to this chess already even from the beginning may have been traditionally played with simple, non-figurative chess pieces. In this connection Mr. Eder challenges the view shared by many chess historians that the chessmen of the so-called Arabic-Islamic style are "abstractions" from figurative representations the origin of which is attributed to the Koran's alleged prohibition against the depiction of living beings. Instead, he assumes that they have developed in an evolutionary process from those elementary archetypal formes.[30]

Mr. Eder's lecture mainly consisted in the presentation of several items from collections of ancient gaming pieces and chessmen which were compared and vivaciously discussed together with a very attentive audience.

It was the intention of the workshop to present at least a part of the wide variety of "playthings" for chess (and its precursors) and to determine which of these objects may be of Indian origin, possibly even to specify from which regions of India and how old they probably are.

Although many questions in this respect were left unsolved, one can be sure, that the interest and commitment shown by our Indian colleagues will lead to further results.

Symposium on Approaching the Roots of Chess, Pondicherry University, 26th-29th November 1996

Irving Finkel second, Koichi Masukawa third from left and extreme Right: Siddharth Y Wakankar

Left to Right: Andreas Bock Raming, Ms. R. Vasantha, Egbert Meissenburg, Irving Finkel, and other participants

From Left to Right: second Egbert Meissenburg, third C Panduranga Bhatta and other participants.

From left to right:
Rajendran C, Manfred A.J. Eder, Siddharth Y Wakankar, C Panduranga Bhatta, Ms. V. Balambal, Ms. R. Vasantha, Irving Finkel, Andreas Bock Raming, C. S. Radhakrishnan
Back row:
Third from the left: J. Krishnan, fifth Chakradhar Behera, sixth Sampath Kumar

Left to Right: Manfred A.J. Eder, Egbert Meissenburg, Andreas Bock Raming, C PandurangaBhatta

Left to Right: Rajendran C, Siddharth Y Wakankar, Manfred A.J. Eder

Left to Right: S.V. Narayanan, C Panduranga Bhatta, Yogacharini Meenakshi Devi Bhavanani, Narasimhachary M, Egbert Meissenburg.

Left to Right: Koichi Masukawa, Egbert Meissenburg, Andreas Bock Raming

Left to Right: Narasimhachary, M, Egbert Meissenburg, Manfred A.J. Eder.

Left to Right: Egbert Meissenburg, Andreas Bock Raming, Ms. R. Vasantha.

B. Report on the Gaming Pieces and Chessmen Exhibited in the Museums of Madras and Hyderabad

The second main part of the present article gives a short description of some highly interesting gaming pieces and chessmen which Mr. Meissenburg, Mr. Eder and I discovered at the following places:

1. Government Museum, Madras
2. Salar Jung Museum, Hyderabad
3. State Museum of Archaeology, Hyderabad
4. Government Museum, Hyderabad
5. The fortress of Golconda and the tombs of the kings of the Qutb Shāhī dynasty.

1. The Government Museum at Madras

This museum is the second oldest (founded in 1851) and one of the most important museums of the Indian sub-continent. From our point of view, it was above all the "Mohenjo-Daro"-section[31] which presented us with several surprises.

Among numerous small objects (from beads, weights, cones, and seals to figurines and rattled) we Found

Illustration No. 1: Four Pottery Gamesmen

The four "pottery gamesmen"- (not yet published?)-are comparable with other "gaming pieces" found at Mohenjo-Daro, which however, are made from shells' material[32]. In shape they are very similar to each other, some even identical.

Illustration No. 2: A Black Stone Amulet

Which were in the centre of our attention

Illustration no 3 features a part of them from a private collection.

The designation "amulet" of the black-stone-object is questionable in so far as a group of these items.

Illustration No. 4

Differing in size and one of them coloured white, would also justify the question whether they are gaming pieces.

The same question might apply to 2 x 4 objects defined as "pottery cones" (**Illustration no 5**) which could as well

Illustration No. 5

have been used for playing (on a board?), and this could have also been the case with the so-called "pottery rattles".

Illustration no 6 which being made of shells' material, more likely appear to be "gaming pieces".

Illustration No. 6

Illustration No 7: Examples of gaming pieces from Mohenjo-Daro from a private collection.

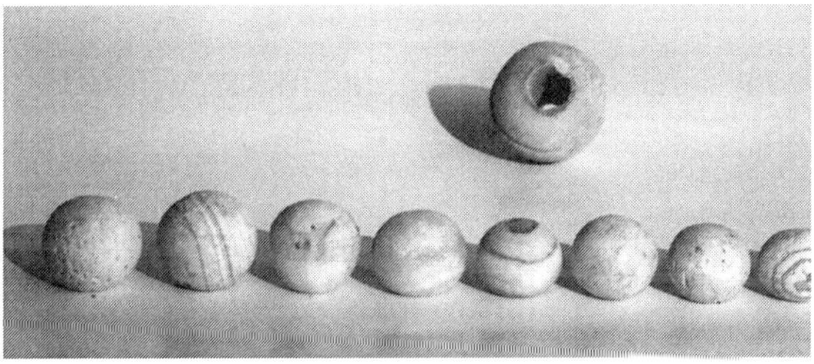

Illustration No. 7(a): A "bone bead"

Illustration No. 8 could as well be considered as a "gaming piece" due to its similarity with many objects very close to it, found in Pakistan/India and being part of private collection.

Illustration No. 8

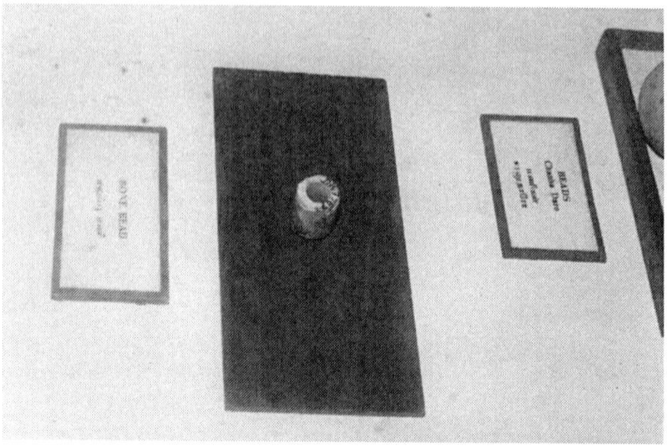

(also compare illustration no. 18, featuring a similar object found within the fortress of Golconda).

The many small objects presented in a showcase featuring finds from "Peddamudiyam" could also include the one or the other gaming piece (within the so-called "spindle-whirls"-group?

Illustration No. 9

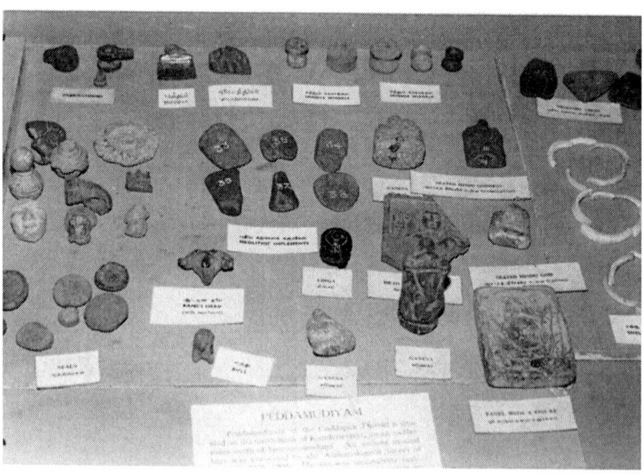

Prof. (Mrs.) V. Balambal, Department of History of the University of Madras, has promised to investigate these items.

Further observations and information.

Numerous stone-sculptures in the Government Museum from large to small ones, represent the motif of an "elephant" which should be made the subject of further investigations in connection with the concept of an elephant representing a piece with different functions within the ensemble of a chess-set. Every visitor of the Coins Department of the Museum who reads the following description of some Kuṣāṇā coins will be reminded of the notable influence of the Indo-Greek rulers of Bactria[33] on India:

"The coins of the Kanishka group employ only Greek characters, Kanishka introduced the Iranian title 'Shaonana Shao', 'King of Kings' instead of the Greek 'Basileus Basileon'. On the reverse of their coins are found a series of gods and goddesses, Iranian and Indian. On the reverse of Vasudeva's gold coins is found Śiva accompanied by his bull. The appearance of the skill and craftsmanship of the Indians may be noticed on the Kuṣāṇā coins. The coinage becomes more Indian than Greek"[34]

It may be added that cast and die-struck coins were introduced in India about the middle of the 3rd century CE. by the Indo-Greeks. The legends on the reverse were written in Prakrit with Kharoṣṭhī script, the obverse being reserved for legends written in Greek. The image on the obverse always represents a royal portrait, while a Greek deity is shown on the reverse. Subsequent dynasties continued this tradition (i.e., a royal portrait on the obverse and a divine figure on the reverse) until about 600 CE. Other foreign dynasties in India - the Scythians, Parthians and Kuṣāṇās - continued to use Greek letters, but rulers of Indian origin - the Guptas and Sātavāhanas - replaced them with the Brāhmī script.

In the view of this far-reaching significance of the Indo-Greek rule on the Indian coinage the question arises whether possibly there has also been an (Indo-) Greek influence on the history of Indian board games. In this respect one may recall J. Averbach's assertion that the Greek board game "petteia" may have played a role in the development of chess.[35]

Apart from the Government Museum we also visited the Government Oriental Manuscripts Library of the University of Madras, where in a showcase we discovered, much to our surprise, a manuscript on chess and the knight's moves which had been reported by S. Y. Wakankar in his article from 1986 as not available there[36] the Caturaṅgavihāra by Krishnaraja Wodeyar III. With the kind permission of Dr. S. Soundarapandian, the curator of the Manuscript Library, we carefully examined the manuscript, which is written in Sanskrit and Marathi.

It is hoped that this important work, which, as a matter of fact, among the 30.000 or so manuscripts kept at the Manuscripts Library seems to be the only one dealing with chess, can be published as soon as possible.

2. The Salar Jung Museum at Hyderabad

The Salar Jung Museum has got almost all its gaming pieces and chessmen on exhibition which have been described in the museum's brochure titled: The Game of Chess (Rare Art Collections in the Salar Jung Museum), published by the museum, sponsored by Sanghis. There are altogether about 15 chess sets variously made of porcelain, ivory and other materials coming not only from India, but also China and Europe. Moreover, the Salar Jung Museum is also in possession of several rare Chaupar sets.

An important source of information is also the museum's collection of rare manuscripts illustrating the game of chess.

Especially worth mentioning are

— the *Qaweid Wa Zawabit-e-Shatranj in Urdū* by Syed Mustafa Shatir Hyderabadi, dated 1894 A.D.

— the *Sardar Nama* written in Persian by Sher Mohd. Khan Iyman-a-Hyderabadi in 1796 A.D., which is a treatise on chess dedicated to Sardar-Ul-Mulk Ghansi Miyan during the period of Asaf Jah II.; and

— the *Risala Dar Shatranj Bazi* in Persian dating from the 19th century.[37]

Visiting the museum, we also had the honour to be received by Dr. I. K. Sharma, the Director of the Museum, who was so kind as to comment on the provenance and possible age of Indian chessmen shown to him on photographs from private German collections. It was suggested that a possible reprint of the above-mentioned brochure should also contain a description and discussion of some of these objects.

We are very much obliged to Prof. (Mrs.) Dr. R. Vasantha of the Krishnadevaraya University of Anantapur for having arranged this meeting for us.

3. The State Museum of Archaeology at Hyderabad

In the State Museum of Archeology at Hyderabad we were introduced by our guide, Dr. Bharat Bhushan to the curator Mr. P. Jogi Naidu and his team who warmly welcomed us.

As far as chessmen are concerned, the museum is in possession of a Chinese "Puzzle-Ball"-set

Illustration-10: of around the mid19th century: (with some defects which, however, can be touched up)

In a showcase presenting small toys and gaming objects such as animals made of ivory, playing cards, stick-dice, and the like.

Illustration 11: A group of about 25 chessmen was discovered

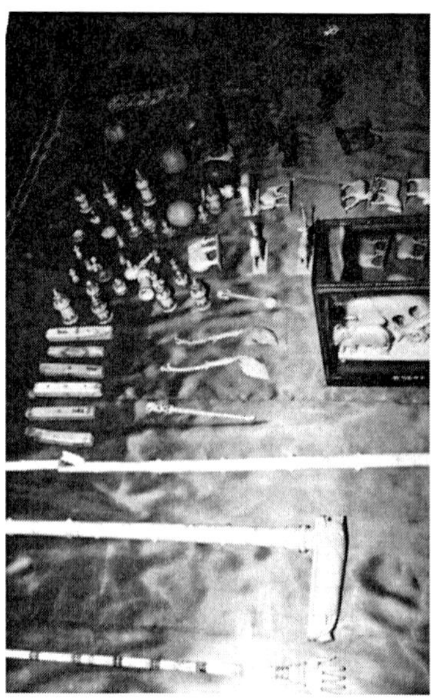

Illustration 12: Which-at first sight-would not appear to belong to "our game".

Mr. Naidu and his team could, however, be convinced by showing him all the pieces of a complete set fabricated in the same pattern and decoration, here from a private German collection:

Illustration No. 13

While Europeans are used to call such sets "Muslim" and to date them to the 19th century, Mr. Naidu insisted that this was "Hindu" and as early as the 17th century.

Illustration No. 14: "A nice Chaupar-set together with two sets of 3 stick-dice each (probably 19th/20th century)

Further information:

Mr. Mohd. Safiullah, one of Mr. Naidu's assistants and a member of the Numismatic Society of Hyderabad, in his capacity as an archaeologist informed us about excavations taking place at Kondapur.[38]

It is to be expected that among the antiquities unearthed at this place also chess pieces will come to light. Already more than 15 years ago, J. E. van Lohuizen de Leeuw had pointed out a little terracotta horse from the 2nd or 3rd century CE. (In the possession of the Government Museum, Hyderabad - see our illustration no 17) excavated at this site which has a close parallel with the oldest chessman known so far, a chariot made of ivory from Mantai (Ceylon).[39]

4. The Government Museum at Hyderabad

This museum had numerous surprises for us which - with

the kind permission of its Director, Dr. Sidharth -, we were allowed to photograph:

— A miniature painting on which a round of people is depicted playing "Chandal Mandal", a sort of Chaupar-game.

Illustration No. 15

— Two Zebu-bulls-Illustration no 16-and a horse-illustration no 17-(2nd /6th century CE.) which could have been gaming pieces or toys; this horse is the object described by von Lobuizem de Leeuw.

Illustration No. 16

— A horse rearing up depicted in a wooden door-frame tall as a man, similar in design to the "knights" of the 17th century (see catalogue).

Illustration No. 17

— Old (round) playing cards

5. The Fortress of Golconda and the Tombs of the Kings of the Qutub Shāhī Dynasty

The highlight of the open entrance hall of Golconda is a tiny but wonderful exhibition of small objects excavated at this site.

One of the showcases contains "ivory objects" as they are described of which at least one-illustration no 18, on the right, possibly even two (also the item on the left) could be gaming pieces.

Illustration No. 18

Our friends in India are kindly requested to assist us in further research. The answer should not be too difficult if the objects could be inspected more closely instead of looking at them through their glass cover.

Some general observations of possible importance for further research:

When visiting the tombs of the Qutub-Shāhī kings, a dynasty ruling from 1507 to 1687, Mr. Eder concluded that the architecture of these structures provided the basic concept for the design of various Indian styles of chessmen. To him, there is no doubt that the figures of the so-called Indian-Muslim chess sets as well as famous 'Visakhapatna"- sets (made in the East of Andhra Pradesh) inherited their typical features from the same pattern after which the dome-shaped roofs and the minarets of these tombs were built.

Illustration No. 19

Illustration No. 20

Illustration No. 21

It remains to be seen, however, whether this assumption can be substantiated by further research (Prof. Holländer, Aachen, and Prof. (Mrs.) Vasantha, Anantapur, India promised studies).

Asking people what they know about the provenance as age of "Pachisi" gaming pieces, we had problems in making ourselves understood.

The reason is that the game which Europeans know as Pachisi (the precursor of our game of ludo/"Mensch-ārgere-Dich-nicht") has obviously many different names India, Chaupar being apparently the most common one. Is it possible that the British brought the name "Pachisi" along from India to the occident and made this term popular here?

Every region, however, seems to have a regional or even local term for this game and plays it according to principally the same rules which, however, are from case to case slightly modified.

A Final Note

We were told by Dr. Bhatta, the organizer of the symposium "Approaching the Roots of Chess" that, while preparing the project, he got in touch with nearly 80 museums all over the Indian subcontinent but was eventually left without substantial information from them.

Much to our surprise we learnt during our visits that a museums' people we talked to knew about the event at Pondicherry. Thus, we may look forward to obtaining many more contributions from their side for another congress in India which we hope Dr. Bhatta will organise in the next few years.

As the most recent attempt we established contact to the Raja Kelkar Museum at Pune (near Bombay) which is said to be famous for holding one of the largest collections of antique Indian chessmen in India, the country, where chess most probably was born.

Appendix

Note to footnote 31

On a chart the visitor of this section is informed in the following way:

"Antiquities from Mohenjo-Daro. About 5000 years ago when Egyptians and Sumerians were building magnificent temples, but living in mud huts, a highly developed urban civilization flourished in India, relics of which have been discovered at various sites in Sind, the Punjab and Baluchistan, especially at Mohenjo-daro — "the place of the dead" in Sindhi in the Indus Valley.

At that time, Sind and Baluchistan had a heavier rainfall and supported a larger population than they do now, and the original city at Mohenjo-daro must have been considerably larger than its ruins, though these are about a square mile in extent. A definite scheme of town-planning is obvious, for the streets, some of them about 30 ft. wide, run-in straight lines aligned as a rule from east to west and north to south.

The houses were two or three stories high, the walls being of brick with mud plaster, and there were underground drains made of excellent bricks. But no temple or shrine has been discovered.

The arts and crafts known to the people of Mohenjo-daro included sculpture, bead-making, spinning, and weaving and working in gold, silver, copper, shell, bone, and ivory. The script they used, yet undeciphered has been found engraved on stone seals.

As no traces of iron have been found, that metal was presumably unknown at the time when this civilization flourished. Copper was the most important metal and bronze and copper tools existed side by side with those of stone. Mohenjo-daro was thus of copper or bronze age.

For reasons unknown to us, this prosperous ancient town seems to have been slowly deserted. Mohenjo-daro was essentially a city of traders, whose business activities had wide ramifications.

There was close economic and cultural relation between Mohenjo-daro and ancient cities in Mesopotamia as is shown by the occurrence in the latter region of types of seals, carnelian beads, knobbed pottery, representations of mother goddesses, horned deities, composite animals, sacred tree-spirits etc., that are found at Mohenjo-daro; and the probable trade route between the two areas can still be traced. But Mohenjo-daro had peculiarities of its own, such as highly developed brick architecture, and the worship of the *linga* and possibly of a deity resembling Śiva."

Remembering Andreas

Dr. Andreas Bock-Raming left us for a better place a few months ago and we will never be able to fill the gap created by his sad demise. His contributions such as "A pioneering study of the game of caturaṅga as recorded in the Mānasollāsa of Someśvara" and his articles such as "The Varieties of Indian Chess Through the Ages", "The literary Sources of Indian Chess and Related Board Games", "An Analytical Assessment of the Contribution for the Symposium on Approaching the Roots of Chess, Pondicherry University, 26th-29th November 1996 together with a report on the game pieces and chessmen exhibited in the Museums of Madras and Hyderabad" and "The Gambling Scenes of Bharhut and Bodh-Gaya-A Critical Assessment of Their Previous Interpretations and Some New Suggestions" are of invaluable help in reconstructing the game of chess. A very humble and scholarly personality and a renowned Indologist will forever be missed.

INDIAN ORIGIN OF CHESS—A SUMMARY

The purpose of this chapter is to reassess the issues connected with the Indian origin of chess. A study of references to implements associated with board games namely, board, pieces, dice, and gamesmen found in Sanskrit literature and unearthed by archaeological excavations throw fresh light on some of the unsolved problems of the early history of chess. It is further argued here that the concept of the divinity of the king which is found in Sanskrit literature led to the concept of immortality and inviolability of the king both in war and in the game of chess. The concept of righteous war (*dharma-vijaya*) is another unique ancient Indian concept which has exercised considerable influence on the game of chess, in which two opposing parties agree to respect each other's king.

Caturaṅga and *Buddhibala*

Siddharth Y Wakankar says that the Sanskrit words *caturaṅga* and *buddhibala* are translated by one common word chess in English which is not correct. Ordinary persons my doubt that these two words denote one game. However, it may be noted here that *caturaṅga* and *buddhibala* are not two different games but are the two stages in the development of the same game as will be clear from the following facts, as gleaned from their earlier Sanskrit descriptions.

Caturaṅga and *Buddhibala* are distinguished as shown below:

- *Caturaṅga* is played with the dice and the moves of the pieces were regulated by the throw of the dice. Whereas, in *buddhibala* there is no dice, and the moves are the result of the reasoning, talents of the players.
- There are stakes or bets in the *caturaṅga* based on the dice, while in *buddhibala*, there are no stakes in the absence of the dice.
- In *caturaṅga* the pieces are moved as per the throw of the dice, while, in *buddhibala*, they are independently moved.
- In *caturaṅga*, the king is helped by his four-fold army of elephants, chariots, horses, and foot-soldiers, while in *buddhibala*, the *pradhāna* or *vazir* or *mantri* (minister), is an ally that is out of the four-fold army.
- In *caturaṅga* there are four kings, and the two opposites kings are friends. In *buddhibala*, there are only, two kings and they are enemies of each other.
- The *ratha* (chariot) or *nauka* (boat) in the *caturaṅga* is replaced by *uṣṭra* or camel (bishop) in the *buddhibala*.
- In *caturaṅga*, a king could be captured and killed, while in *buddhibala*, the king can never be killed, but only check mated.[1]

Chess as the Product of an Indian Genius

P. Thime Observes:

"Surely, a civilization that gave birth to the grammar of Pāṇini can easily be trusted to have also produced a game that was above the grasp of children and could be played for the sheer joy in puzzling out intricate problems of an abstract nature."[2]

This observation deserves to be investigated further. Nothing is known of Pāṇini's life except the fact that he was born in the extreme Northwest of India during c. 500 BCE. His Aṣṭādhyāyī, which fixed the form of Sanskrit grammar once and for all, consists of some 4000 aphorisms of the greatest brevity.

This brevity is achieved by the invention of an algebraical system of notation of a kind not found outside the grammatical schools. Pāṇini's grammar is composed in what is called *sūtra* style (aphoristic style). The aphoristic style (aphorisms) dated from perhaps the 8th century BCE to the early Christian era. It is a terse statement well suited for meditative thought, such as the game of chess itself revolves around. The brevity, which the *sūtra* style of Pāṇini's grammar aimed at and achieved, was due to the fact, that all instruction was still oral and dependent on memory.

Chess is a game between two individuals who use their skills and intelligence to wrest a win. It is an imaginary one between two minds. It demands extraordinary steadiness of mind and concentration. The ancient Indians developed various strategies to gain concentration.

We may mention one such method, which is unique to them. *Astāvadhāna* is a Sanskrit word meaning 'eight-fold concentration'. It is very difficult and rare literary feat in Sanskrit.

The poet scholar creates extempore metrical composition according to specification given by eight questioners at a time. It demands exceptional qualities of multiple concentration, memory, imagination, and quick thinking. *Avadhāna* is an act of a poet instantly composing poetical lines on the assigned metre as desired by the confronting poets or questioners and answering all their tricky problems in high powers of instant poetical compositions and the power of recalling the answers in order. This act is clearly a mind-blowing exercise exhibiting multiple powers of mind, the powers derived through highest concentration of mind meditation. It will be highly beneficial to conduct more research on such strategies of ancient India as they may throw more light on origin of chess.

One more fact which strengthens our contention that the game of chess originated in a period of high intellectual activity is the tradition enshrined in the Shahanāma of Firdausi and in Chatrang Namak that chess was introduced from India to Persia in the reign of Khusrau Nushirman (531-579 CE). This fact is accepted by the chess historians as a plausible hypothesis.[3]

The Origin of Chess in Relation to War and Peace

The story found in Chatrang Namak (pre 800 CE) confirms the theory that originally chess was played as a war game. Even the later texts dealing with chess often refer to its connection with battle. Harikṛṣṇa's Bṛahajjyotiśārṇava in its sixth chapter dealing with chess, refers to its connection with battle. He refers to the movements of the king and says that the king adopts straightforward and crooked methods according to the situation. He is brave, intelligent, and daring: always caring for the safety of his subjects. The idea is, that just like an actual king, he behaves in this game as well.[4]

Hellmut Rosenfeld observes: "*Chaturanga* had been invented as a game for kings for the purpose of learning strategic war skill from the world of political teaching books in the beginning of the first millennium BCE. This became a game of intellect for two persons without dice round about 550 A D."[5]

Egbert Meissenburg observes that "chess as a kind of strategic exercise for war, with a transport of the members of the Indian army on *aṣṭāpada* in accordance with the reality, seems the most plausible idea of the game's origin"[6]

In his article "Chess 1,300 years ago" Issak Linder observes: "An answer to the question of where the game might have originated can be obtained from the figure of the elephant, an animal not only characteristic of India but one also employed in warfare there in ancient times."[7]

Pavle Bidev in his article entitled "How old is chess?"[8] observes that before Harṣa, the Indian army was not *caturaṅga,* but *triaṅga* under the dynasty of Gupta for 250 years (from 280, Chandragupta I, to Bhanugupta +530).

It is further stated by him that Harṣa (606-647CE) ordered the reorganization of his army to include the recently forgotten war chariots (*rathas*), and so his army became *caturaṅga* and fulfilled the condition sine qua non for the creation of chess, a vivid example before his eyes which enabled him to follow his war game, *caturaṅga.*

An army was known in ancient India as *caturaṅga* constituting elephants, cavalry, chariots, and infantry. Vedic literature does not seem to have noticed a four-fold division of the army, but rather a three-fold one because the use of elephants in wars had not come into vogue. But in the earliest records of the Buddhist age, we find mention of armies composed of elephants, cavalry, chariots, and bowmen. Megasthenes also gives a description of the military caste-which is well organized and equipped for war, containing men-at-arms, war-horses, war-elephants, and chariots.[9]

The four kinds of armies were generally arranged in the form of *vyūhas* for offering an organized attack to the enemy. The deployment and the drawing up of the army in array form is the chief part of the plan of battle which should be arranged in accordance with the nature of the ground.

Kautilya, the famous political thinker of ancient India speaks of specific arrays called *sama, viśama, hasti, rathi, aśva* and *patti vyūhas.* In all these arrays the four-fold forces are used.

Harikṛṣṇa's text refers to two arrangements in chess that are successful in warding off the opponent's attacks just like the wheel-like arrangement (*cakra-vyūha*) in actual battle. *Cakra-vyūha* is an arrangement of the army in the form of a wheel with the king or general at the centre, so that it is difficult for the enemy to get to the centre. This passage also strengthens the argument that the ancient Indian army consisted of *caturaṅga* and not *triṅnga.*

The more accurate facts available regarding the military organization of various kings in ancient India also indicate that generally armies consisted of four divisions only. The well-known *akṣohiṇī* forces of the *Mahābhārata* war also consisted of the same four-fold division. The *caturaṅga* (four-fold) conception of army continued for a very long time.

Gradually the use of chariots in war declined, and we have no mention of it the army of Pulakeśin II (641 CE) if we may rely on the authority of Yuan Chwang[10] (Hiuen Tsang). Again, in the Kuram Pallava grant[11] of 650 CE which describes the battle of Peruvala Nallur, only elephants, horses, and footmen are mentioned and not chariots. Further, in the history of the Chola kings of South India, during the succeeding centuries mention is only made of the other three divisions of the army. The chariots, as instruments of war, are not mentioned and this is a clear indication that they must have become obsolete by that time.

The Gunalghar copper plate[12] of Vainyagupta omits chariots from the convention units '*hasty-aśva-rath-padātam senāṅgam syācctuṣṭhayam'* and thus suggests the rare use of them.

However, Kālidāsa, the famous Sanskrit poet who is supposed to have flourished under the Gupta kings, mentions the four columned army, namely *padāti (infantry), aśva-rūḍha (cavalry), gaja-rūḍha (elephants) and ratha-rūḍha (chariots).*[13]

The Origin of Checkmate

Manfred A.J. Eder[14] in his paper has concluded that the two war armies agreeing themselves to respect the king, the enthroning of the fidated king, that is 'differentia specifica', a classification difference, which defines chess.

He also observes that "In a war-game, the stated concept of which is to destroy the enemy, the 'king' becomes inviolable, fidated," the consequences and the range of this refinement of a game-concept are immense. The war-like game of two parties with the kernel element of the immortality of the king is proposed by him as the origin of 'chess point". The point stressed by Eder is the element of the immortality of the fidated king as a game's rule.

Petzold, in his article of 1991 on the origin of symbolic meaning of chess, argued that the invincibility of the king in chess is a Persian invention. But Bock-Raming has rejected this theory of Persian invention based on the evidence provided in the Mānasollāsa of Someśvara. There are many more points which strengthen the argument of Bock-Raming. Some significant points are as follows:

In the *Rigveda,* one king alone, namely Purukutsa, has been once described as semi-divine (*ardhadeva*). This does not prove the acceptance of the divinity of the king by the age.

When a popular assembly (*samiti*) could despose a king, the theory of the latter's divinity was not likely to take root in society.[15] The growing sway of religious ideas and notions produced an atmosphere in the Brāhmaṇa period which was more favourable to the notion of the divinity of the king.[16] Victories of the king began to be attributed to the favour of Indra, and very often the latter's epithet began to be transferred to the former.

The Gods Agni, Savitar and Bṛhaspati were believed to enter the person of the king, when he was being anointed at the coronation. Some of the sacrifices he performed were declared to enable him to obtain parity with Gods.[17] The mystery of the multitude obeying one king was explained by some on the grounds that he was the veritable symbol of the chief of Gods (*prajāpati*)[18] The Mahābhārata states that the *God* Viṣṇu himself entered the body of the first king.[19] Thus, an atmosphere was created during the post-Vedic period, which was very favourable to the doctrine of royal divinity.

The advent of the Kushana dynasty in the 1st century CE further strengthened this tendency. The Kushana kings claimed to be the sons of Gods (*devaputra*) and represented themselves on their coins as descending from clouds and surrounded by divine flames.[20]

Divinity has been claimed for the king by some Smṛtis and Purāṇas. Manu says that the king is verily a great divinity in the human form, his very body is formed by the creator by taking particles from the bodies of the divine guardians of the eight quarters.[21]

The Viṣṇnupurāṇa and the Bhāgavatapurāṇa say that several divinities reside in the person of the king.[22] The efforts of the medieval dynasties to trace their origin to the Gods Brahmā, Rāma or Lakṣmaṇa also presuppose a desire to emphasize their divine origin. When the theory of incarnation (*avatāra*) became popular, kings began to be regarded as the incarnation of Gods. Thus, the kings Chandra and Govindachandra of the Gahadwala dynasty were regarded as the incarnations of Brahmā and Hari respectively.[23]

The Nāradasmṛti[24] goes to the extent of maintaining that the person of even a wicked king was inviolable because of his divinity. Rājataraṅgiṇī also enjoins regard for even a vicious king.[25]

Thus, we have the clear evidences in ancient Sanskrit works and inscriptions regarding the divinity of the king which makes him immortal and inviolable, a feature which probably entered the game of chess.

When society in ancient India became organized and a warrior caste (*kṣatriya*) came into being, it was felt that the members of this caste should be governed by certain human laws. It was further believed that the observance of these laws would lead them to heaven, while non-observance would lead them into hell.

We have no evidence to indicate the existence of an accepted code of fighting during Vedic period. The literary evidences at our disposal prove that in the post-Vedic period, particularly during the epic period, a code has begun to govern the waging of wars.

The ancient lawgivers, the reputed authors of Dharmaśāstras, codified the then existing customs and usages. Thus, the law books and the epics contain special sections on royal duties and the duties of common warriors.

It would be beneficial for scholars interested, in the early history of the game of chess, to study the rules which restrained the warrior's whims and ennobled his character and conduct.

The principles regulating the warfare are elaborately described in the Dharmasūtras and Dharmaśāstras, the Epics, and the Arthaśāstra treatises of Kauṭilya, Kāmandaka and Śukra.

Hospitality, the sacredness of the refugee, the law not to forget a kindness and not to refuse to fight when challenged are some characteristic features of fair fighting according to the Epic code.[26]

Ancient Indian military science recognizes two kinds of warfare-the *dharma-yuddha* and the *kūṭa-yuddha.* Dharma-*yuddha* is war carried out on the principles of dharma, meaning here the laws of kings and warriors (*kṣatra*-dharma). In other words, it was a just and righteous war which had approval of society.

There is no evidence to suppose that the literature of the Vedic-period contemplated any clear distinction between dharma-*yuddha* and *kūṭa-yudda.* It was only in the post-Vedic period that a code came into being. In the post-Vedic period, it was believed that a monarch desirous of dharma-*yuddha* should conform to the code of ethics enjoined upon warriors and that waging a war without regard to moral standards degraded the institution into mere animal ferocity.[27]

The art organizing of war in ancient India had become a game, which was to be played according to certain specified rules and principles. Fairness as well as equity was insisted on even in battles. Unethical fighting was strictly prohibited. It has many implications. The need for equality of war-equipment on both the sides was emphasized. Thus, no one having arms could fight with a person having no arms, nor could one have superior arms with a person having inferior arms. The division of the dharma-*yuddha* and the *kūṭa-yuddha* was in the epic tradition.[28]

But dharma-*vijaya, asura-vijaya and lobha-vijaya* occasionally mentioned in the Epics and Purāṇās seems to have been an innovation of Kauṭilya, author of the Arthaśāstra. *Dharma-vijaya* is an equivalent of dharma-*yuddha*, while *lobha-vijaya* and *asura-vijaya* come under the category of *kūta-yuddha.*

The term *dharma-vijaya* occurring in the inscriptions of king Aśoka was a puzzle to Aśokan scholars since they took it for granted that Aśoka was a Buddhist and connected the term with the Buddhist dharma, interpreting it to mean 'conquest by morality.'

According to Kauṭilya, dharma-*vijaya* meant that a conquering king was satisfied with the acknowledgement of his over-lordship by the inferior and defeated powers as also by others. The motive was to avoid war as far as possible, and to promote peaceful and diplomatic relations with neighbours and foreigners. This was the mission on which Aśoka sent not missionaries, but political envoys.

In the *lobha-vijaya* the aim of the conqueror was to covet the territory and the treasure of the enemy. In the *asura-vijaya* the enemy is captured and deprived of his kingdom, treasure, sons, and wives. After the deadly Kalinga war Aśoka inaugurated a policy of dharma-*vijaya* in his foreign politics.[29]

Thus, Aśoka gave a new orientation to the traditional policy of the Mauryas which was imperialism and expansion and that resulted in the end of the era of political *digvijaya* (conquest by sword) and ushered in the glorious period of dharma-*vijaya* or conquest by spiritual force of non-violence. Aśoka called on his sons and grandsons "not to think of new conquest by sword, but to think of conquest by mildness and gentleness.[30] Aśoka's pious aim was to be a *dharmika dharmarāja* in and beyond his kingdom.

About the ideal of a *dhārmika-dharmarāja,* the following

dictum has been laid down by the Buddhist text *Dīgha-nikāya.*[31]

"Two careers are open to a superman, i.e., that of an *arhat* (a Buddhist dignity) or of a *chakravarti dhārmika dharmarāja,* who conquers the four corners of the earth, not with the sword of steel, but with the sword of love".

An important tradition of dharma-*vijaya* was that a king, having conquered the capitals of his foe, should invest there a prince of the royal race of that country with the royal dignity.[32] Following this tradition Lord Rāma gives territories of Ceylon back to Vibhīṣaṇa, the brother of the conquered monarch.[33]

According to Kauṭilya one must reinstate on the throne the sons of the dead king, thereby, the conqueror could be obeyed from generation to generation.[34] Normally the defeated king was reinstated on the throne. But if the enemy king had met with his death in battle, his son or nearest relative was installed on the throne on terms of subordinate alliance.

Many political authorities gave their unqualified support to the cause of peace. They recognized that the tittle of rivals existed not mainly as enemies, but as collaborators in the building of a civilization based on the principles of mutual toleration and co-operation.

The dharma-*vijaya* was a kind of warfare where diplomacy and conciliation were pressed into service to avoid actual fighting as far as possible. The dominating personality of the conqueror evoked regard from alien states amounting to an acknowledgement of his superiority or equality. According to the precept of fair fighting (dharma-*vijaya*) the kingdom of the enemy should not be annexed, and no bodily punishment should be inflicted on the person of the king or his commander.[35]

The Chinese traveller Hiuen Tsang records a tradition according to which "Whenever a general is despatched on a warlike expedition, although he is defeated and his army destroyed, he is not himself subjected to bodily punishment, only he must exchange his soldier's dress for that of a woman."[36]

The practical implementation of this policy by the ancient kings of India is recorded in some inscriptions also. Different cases of dealing with the conquered kings are mentioned in the Allahabad pillar inscription of Samudragupta. The conqueror, in most cases, was satisfied with the acknowledgement of his over-lordship and many rulers who were captured in his wars were set free.[37]

According to the Sanskrit drama composed by Kālidāsa, the two defeated kings, namely Mādhavasena and Yajñasena, were allowed by King, Agnimitra to establish their rule and to govern their people peacefully.[38]

The Gupta rulers followed this usage of restoring a fallen king to his throne and cultivating relations of good-will with them. This policy was continued even in succeeding ages and Buddha's teachings inspired Harṣavardhana, the last great Hindu emperor in the seventh century AD to fulfill the ideal of *chakravarti*. About him Bāṇabhaṭṭa, his poet laureate says: "Universal monarchs do not undertake military expeditions, they do not get tribute from any kingdom, yet they become masters of the whole earth, only by their irresistible spiritual influence.[39]

Sanskrit literature in general is replete with such technical terms as *cakravartin, sārvabhauma, sāṁrāt, parameśvara, paramabhaṭṭāraka* and others. The Amarakośa, a Sanskrit lexicon, makes the following distinction in various technical terms of rulers: *chakravartin* or *sārvabhauma* is one whose empire extends to the seas, and lastly *sāmrat* is one who performed the *rājasūya* sacrifice and who was the head of a circle of kings, acknowledging his sovereignty. The term *cakravartin* means "a holy king turning the wheel". The wheel is emblematic of temporal and spiritual powers.

Another highly significant story related to the invention of Shatranj, and the origin of check mate contained in a famous old book entitled "Nafāyis-ul-Fūnūn" or Precious Things in Science", is worth repeating here. Major Raverty gives a detailed story related to this matter in his article "The Invention of Chess And Backgammon".[40] An abridged version of the same is given below which serves our purpose.

Sahsih (Sahasī), also known as Laj-Lāj, son of Dāhir, which latter was one of the ancient rulers of Sind (and the last of the Rais or kings of Sind, who fell in battle fighting against the 'Arabs, when they subdued that territory in 94 H.-712-13 CE-, was also called Dāhir.).

Rai Bhalīt, by some called Rai Baghil, who was never contended on wars against his neighbours, at last became afflicted with some painful disorder which precluded him from sitting on a horse, or on an elephant: and he was passionately fond of military operations, and "setting squadrons on the field," he assembled the sages, and all the most sagacious and ingenious persons of his court and of Sind, and said,

"As you are all aware that I am afflicted with this complaint, I desire that you would devise some contrivance, whereby, without being obliged to sit on horse-back or on an elephant, I may still be able to occupy myself in the (semblance of) warfare, so that I may divert my thoughts from brooding over this disorder afflicting me, and thereby obtain some relief"

Sahsih (Sahasī), otherwise Laj-Lāj, then came forward, and said, "I have in my possession an expedient whereby this difficulty may be solved and remedied, and the Rai obtain the alleviation he seeks." Thus, saying he arose, and having gone to his own dwelling, he soon returned, bringing along with him the game of chess complete, a cloth to play it upon, and the chessmen, all of which he had invented. Rai Bhalit was so excited with delight and told Sahsih, "Demand of me, O sage whatever thou mayest desire, and I will grant it unto thee." Sahsih, thanking the king replied:

I merely ask that a single grain of wheat may be placed on the first square of the chess-cloth and doubled every time on each succeeding one. For example, on the first square one grain of wheat on the second two, on the third, four, and on the fourth, eight, and so on: and when the number of squares on the cloth shall have been computed after this manner: be pleased, O Rai! To command that that quantity of wheat be made over to me".

When Rai Bhalit heard this, as he supposed, modest request, he exclaimed to those present in his assembly, in the most contemptuous manner: "I was desirous of bestowing upon him something of great value, and he has instead, merely asked for the most insignificant and paltry thing possible!" to this Sahsih replied: "This is the request that I desire to make, if the Rai shall be pleased to grant it, I do not desire anything more, and shall be quite satisfied with that."

The Rai, who commanded that what he had asked for should be given to him. But when the revenue officials began to make their computation, to carry out the Rai's commands, they, in a great fright, dispatched one of their members in his presence, who represented saying,

"In the whole of our country such a quantity of wheat cannot be obtained as would be required to carry out the Rai's commands respecting Sahsih."

When Rai Bhalit heard this statement, he was filled with amazement, and could not believe it: and he commanded that all the revenue officials should be summoned before him, and show how they arrived at, as he conceived, such an absurd conclusion.

When the revenue officials, appeared before him, he required them to show how they made out that there was such difficulty, nay impossibility, in complying with what Sahsih had asked for; and what they thought it would be advisable to do under the circumstances. They replied, that if the wheat produce of the whole world could be collected, it will not come up to the quantity required to carry out the Rai's command.

On hearing this, Bhalit was still more amazed than before, and he felt certain that they could not be speaking the truth; and he felt commanded that they should proceed to prove their statement clearly and fully.

Several arithmeticians accordingly assembled for the purpose; and after making their calculations, declared that it was beyond the power of anyone to comply with Sahsih's request. The way in which they proceeded to prove this was, that, having placed one grain of wheat on the first square, and doubling the number each time, when they reached the sixteenth, it was proved that the quantity then amounted to 32,760 grains of wheat, and when the nineteenth square was reached, what revenue officials computed, was equivalent of the produce of one city with its dependent lands and villages.

For the fiftieth square it was found that the produce of 1,024 such cities would be required; for the sixtieth square, the produce of 1,048,576 cities; and for the sixty-fourth or last square, 16, 777, 216 cities!

But taking the surface of the whole earth into account, if there should be one city on every square mile even, there would not be sufficient to furnish the quantity of wheat required to carry out the promise given to Sahshih, much less the cities and their lands and villages contained in the Rai's dominions. Hearing this astonishing statement, Rai Bhalit turned his face towards Sahsih and exclaimed; Oh sage! thy genius and sagacity in inventing this game of chess are as nothing compared with the astonishing kind of reward which thou hast chosen for it."

As it was found thus to be impossible to comply with Sahsih's request, whether he received or accepted any other reward, the chroniclers do not say.

Rai Bhalit used to be constantly occupied in playing the game up to the tune of his death. His wife named the male child born to her of Rai Bhalit as Shāh. In one of his more distant expeditions, Shāh was dangerously wounded in an encounter, and died of his wounds. No one in the court could venture to break this sad news to his mother.

According to a story one of her sons requested sages of Sindh to adopt some means of demonstrating to his mother how her husband was situated at the time of death; and one of them succeeded in doing by means of the game of chess, in which he had managed to interest her. He took the chessmen and chequered cloth and showed her how the game was played.

During the game the Shāh Bādshāh, or Shāh, the king, on the board or cloth, became *shāshdār*, or unable to move, and the foot-men, the elephant (the Bishop or Europeans), the Horse-man (the Knight or, Chevalier), and the Wazīr or Queen, surrounded the Shāh Bādshāh or

King, on all sides, when the players exclaimed: "Shāh māt" or Shah, the king, is undone or destroyed," and having no move left, and no means of flight or retreat, he perished accordingly, and the game was won.

The wise men who were present during the playing of the game, now succeeded in showing the Rāi (Queen) that this game represented the situation and positions of the King.

Being unable to move, finding himself in this position, out of his great pride, and the chagrin at the helpless state he found himself in, died, and thus became "Shāh Māt" or undone-Check-mated. Rāni thus became convinced as to the cause and manner of her son's death. She now learnt the game and began herself to play it: and whenever the "Shāh Māt" came about, she would melt into tears at the remembrance of her son's fate.

It is from these words "Shāh Māt", that words "Check Mate" are derived, showing how words during ages, handed down, from one race of people to another, become vitiated. The word "Māt" is derived from the Arabic māta, "he is dead": and used in Persian to signify 'conquered', 'subjected', 'reduced to the last extremity' etc. This story is significant as it throws some new light on the origin of check mate.

Major Raverty also mentions how and in what manner the game of chess was first introduced into Iran-Zamin or the ancient Persian empire.

He narrates the story of Nūh-shīrwān receiving an envoy from the Rai of Sind who brought the chessmen and the cloth. Nūh-shīrwān, and the learned men of his court, never having seen anything of the kind before, were, of course, quite unable to understand the game, and were at a loss to explain it. At this time his famous minister Būzur Jamhir, who had lost one of his eyes in the punishment given by the king Nuh-shīrwān, was brought to the court and he attempted to play the game of chess with the Sindī envoy. Būzur Jamhir lost the first game, but improved on the second, which was a drawn game, and beat the Rai's envoy in the third, and checkmated him!

Būzur Jamhir did not invent, as some have supposed; for it had been known long before, as Major Raverty had already shown.

The pieces in the game of chess were, at first, wooden figures having the human form: and what is known now as the King, was then called Shāh Bādshāh, from Shāh son of Rai Bhalīt.

The Castle or Tower of the present was they styled the Rukh after fabulous bird, the Bishop of the present day, was them the Fīl or Pīl ('f' and 'p' are permutable) or Elephant, and was sometimes called the Camel; the Knight or Chevalier was known as the Faras, or Asp, signifying a Horse; the Queen was styled Farz, or Farzin, or Farzī, or Farzān, and also Wazirī or Minister; and the Pawn or Foot soldier or Common Man, was called Piyadah as those words signify. "Shashdār" means "Confounded," "Distressed," "Astonished," "Useless for a square," "Tied up;" and Shāh Māt," as before mentioned Shāh Bādshah, or Shāh, the King, is reduced to the last extremity, conquered," etc.

The names used in India differ somewhat, most of them being derived from the Sanskrit language.

The wise and accomplished Khalīfah, Al-Māmūn, son of Harūn-ar-Rashīd, composed some lines on chess, which literally are as follow:

> "Upon a square of red-dressed leather,
> Two friends, for generosity well-known,
> Re-call war to mind, and thereon stratagems invent,

Without the guiltiness of shedding blood therein,
This assaults that, and that assails this.
And the eye of vigilance sleepeth not.
Behold the ingenious foes! How skillfully they move
Between two hosts, without banner or drum."

William Jones remark related to the invention of chess is worth recalling here:

"If evidence be required to prove that chess was invented by the Hindus, we may be satisfied with the testimony of the Persians, who though as much inclined as other nations to appropriate the ingenious inventions of a foreign people, unanimously agree that the game was imported from the west of India together with the charming fables of Vishnusharman, in the sixth century of our era: it seems to have been immemorially known as *Chaturanga*, that is, the four *anga's*, or members of an army, which are said in the Amaracosha to be *haśtyaswarathapadātam* or elephants, horses, chariots and foot soldiers: and in this sense, the word is frequently used by Epic poets in their descriptions of real armies. By a natural corruption of the pure Sanscrit word, it was changed by the old Persians into *Chatrang*, but the Arabs, who soon after took possession of their country, had neither the initial nor final letter of that word in their alphabet, and consequently altered it further into *Shatranj*, which found its way presently into the modern Persian, and at length into the dialects of India, where the true derivation of the name is known only to the learned: thus has a very significant word in the sacred language of the Brahmanas been transformed by successive changes into *axendrez, scacchi, echecs*, chess, and by a whimsical concurrence of circumstances, given birth to the English work check, and even a name to the Exchequer of Great Britain".[41]

Saliant Points from the Research conducted in the last decade

Before concluding it is worth highlighting some salient points that emerged from the research conducted in the last decade regarding the origin of chess.

The Editors of Sedentary Game of India made the following observation:

In the last five decades, however, not a single article on sedentary game has come out in the Journal of Asiatic Society, and except a few commendable works by C. Panduranga Bhatta, S Wakankar and Krishnamurthy, Indian scholars have hardly taken any initiative to contribute to this field.[42]

One realizes how much new research remains to be undertaken, and therefore how many discoveries might remain to be made.

Only a few scholars, even in recent times, have fully grasped that the study and comparison of board games has relevance on many levels, contributing to history, anthropology, sociology, psychology, and indeed other disciplines.[43]

The essential points in favour of India being the country of origin are quoted in the detailed article of Mark, Michael.[44]

- Earliest reference in India literature, earlier than allusion in other languages
- The gaming pieces in the early chess correspond to the four branches of the Indian army
- In Persian literature, it is stated, that chess came from India to Persia
- In other countries, the name of the game is etymologically derived from the Indian denomination of *caturaṅga*

- The denomination and conception of the game are purely Indian and show no imported elements.

Prof. Dr. Renate Syed firmly believes that Mahārājādhirāja Śarvavarman sent chess along with other presents to his Western neighbour in Sasanian Persia, around 550 CE, following an advice given by the political theory in texts like the Arthaśāstra and Nītisāra: To consolidate peaceful conditions, a king should send presents to a mighty and still peaceful neighbour as expression of good will and appeasement.

The Northwest was from Indian perspective, a dangerous direction: All foreign invasions, as recently the Huns, came from the Northwest into India. So why not appease and pacify potential aggressors with valuable gifts in those remote areas?[45]

She stresses the point that Chess, *caturaṅga* was invented in India in the 4th or 5th century CE and is mentioned for the first time by the poet Bāṇa in the early 7th century at Harṣavardhana's court in Kannauj, which was probably the birthplace of the game. King Śarvavarman Maukhari sent the *caturaṅga* around 570 A.D. to Persia a present to Khusrau Anushirvan, the Sasanian king. Bāṇa's Haṣacarita not only contains the oldest Indian reference to the game of chess, *caturaṅga*, played on the 64-square board called *aṣṭāpada*, but also gives a hint to terracotta chessmen in the phrase *pārthiva-vigrahāḥ*, which is not only to be rendered as "fights among kings", but as "earthen figures" as well. Chess, it seems, was played at Harṣa's court in Kanyakubja/ Kanauj in the first half of the 7th century A.D. with earthen figurative chessmen.

Before the game *caturaṅga* was invented-so her thesis-the theoreticians of warfare used similar terracotta as means to teach strategy and tactics of battles in sand-tables. Further,

Bāṇa's *adhikaraṇa-vicāraḥ* can be read as *adhika-raṇa-vicāraḥ* and translated as 'Thoughts on further battle(s), pointing at continuous discussions on warfare'.[46]

In her opinion to understand why a particular battle was lost or was successful, it is plausible that simulation of that battle, using a model representing the actual army with terracotta figures (elephants, horses...), was highly effective. It is quite probable that from such a didactic model the game of *caturaṅga* developed in times of peace i.e., after the second half of the sixth century CE. By training strategic abilities and providing entertainment, this formalized game kept the name and nature of the Indian army, called *caturanga.*

It is worth quoting the observation of Rajendran C who says, "...during Bāṇa's lifetime, *caturaṅga* or the Indian chess was relatively new game.

It seems to have originated out of the fusion of two different traditions:

One is the old board game tradition which used *aṣṭāpada* square board and the other is the symbolic representation of the fourfold Indian army. Bāṇa seems to have marvelled at this invention; he also credits the emperor, his patron, as the agent under whom the game came to be popular."[47]

The final and an irrefutable conclusion comes from Manfred AJ Eder when he says,

"My Claim is: Chess originated in India, neither in Persia, nor in China. The game of chess came down to us-based upon Renate Syed's conclusive and convincing theory-from what she calls a 'Didactic Model', a sort of sandpit-exercise of *caturaṅga,* the term for Indian army, respectively its four wings (Syed 2001a).

I trust and believe in the following Research Results:

- The German Iranist and Philologist Werner Sundermann explained with great clarity, brevity, and precision, that Sanskrit term *catur-aṅga* is the Original from which *Chatrang* and Shatranj respectively, the Persian and the Arabian names for the game, have been created.
- There are several references to "*Aṣṭāpada*" and "*Caturaṅga*" by Bāṇa in his "Harṣa-Carita"- according to the Indologist S.R. Goyal (Goyal 1978/79) written between 617-625 AD-illustrating King Harṣa's court in Kanauj, where *Caturaṅga* as a Game already existed at that time, probably played with terracotta-figures.
- This has been independently confirmed by recent re-readings of this Sanskrit-text by the Indologists and Sanskritists Renate Syed and the Indian Sanskrit -Scholar Chettiarthod Rajendran (Rajendran 2007).
- The German Iranist Manijeh Abka'i-Khavari (Abk'i-Khavari 1998, 1999, 2001) newly investigated all early well-known middle-Persian texts, ending up with three conclusions which are proved by them:
    1) Chess Originated in India
    2) The Indian King from Kanauj (Ray from Qonnuj-identified by Syed as Mahārājādhirāja Śarvavarman Maukhari) sent a game of chess to Iran at the time of Chosrow I Anushirwan (531-579AD)
    3) Which was presented in Ctesiphon, the ancient capital of Persia, consisting of a planogramme ("board") with 64 fields and two rows of 16 gamesmen each in ruby and emerald - non-figurative!
- And last but by no means least, Antonio Panaino, Iranist in Bologna, who translated "Wizarisn I Catrang"

into Italian, summarized in English (Panaino 1999)- I quote

"Sasanian chess was clearly based on an Indian model, where the ancient traditional four-fold division (*caturaṅgabala*) of the army [...] influenced the arrangement of this war-game"

My personal conclusion from investigating gaming-pieces "in lots", especially those from "Indian"- (and ex-Indian-!) territories, over almost 20 years, has taught me, that the origin of what so far is called "Arabian-Islamic" Chessmen has its home-base in India-just like the game itself-and therefore for the future should be called "Indian-Islamic"! Or even better:

of traditional Hindu Origin."[48]

Leander A. Feiler says, "All these arguments and findings in favour of India being the origin of chess do not apply in comparable number to any other candidate country... To find further confirmation, a systematic archaeological excavation campaign in Kannauj, the former capital of king Harsha and the Maukharis, is essential, whereby the archaeological context and dating of the finds will become possible. Since 2007, the FSG has been proposing such systematic archaeological excavations."[49]

We must record two very significant archaeological discoveries as they support our hypothesis that chess originated in India.

The first discovery of the earliest known chess pieces in 1977 in Afrasiab, an ancient site near the city of Samarkand, located in modern-day Uzbekistan. This discovery was made by Jurjij F. Burjakov, an archaeologist and historian who had been part of a major excavation project carried out by the Uzbekistan Academy of Archaeology.

Afrasiab Chessmen

Five Chessmen

Dice and Chess

Samarkand, where Burjakov made his discovery, is considered one of the oldest inhabited sites in the world. Situated on the historical trade route linking China and the eastern Mediterranean region (the famous 'Silk Road'), the city has achieved prominence several times throughout its long history as one of Central Asia's greatest metropolises.

Delicately made from ivory, the seven Afrasiab chessmen are currently housed at the State Museum of Samarkand. It is generally believed that all seven pieces were made sometime between the late 6th and early 8th centuries of Common Era.

The seven chessmen, all of which are heavily worn (indicating considerable use), are small, ivory carvings depicting soldiers and contemporary battle equipment. They are all representational in shape (rather than abstract).

The chessmen consist of two foot-soldiers (pawns) bearing shields and short swords; a war elephant (bishop) with a rider in battledress; a vizier (queen) with two horses; two mounted riders with sword and shield (knights); and a Shah (king) on a three-horse chariot.[50]

The second discovery is related to five chessmen made of Stone which Professor Burjakov commented full of enthusiasm in a report over three pages in Russian, translated by Jelena into German, to make a historic document dated May 3rd, 2009 (20:29). He draws special attention to the shape of the figures, their jewelry and decoration, their ritual cultic symbolic, deeply expressing Indian roots.

Example: the floral rosettes on the shields, the lotus-blossoms symbolysing sun and light; in India lotus flowers also mean the miracle of Buddha's birth, meaning immortality.

Manfred A.J. Eder says that "except for the fact that the Stone of the five chessmen is Slate which points to Gandhara (nowadays Pakistan, formerly India), we have no idea about a possibly more likely location of their production...we may determine the age of the Stone-pieces next to the age of the Afrasiab group, i.e., around 700 A.D. in spite of the fact, that stone alone does not allow to measure age."[51]

NOTES AND REFERENCES

Part-I
Dice Play in Sanskrit Literature

Chapter-1: Introduction

1. JRAS, 1904, pp. 355-7.
2. Gurupūjākaumudī, Leipzig, 1896, pp. 1-4.
3. Orientalia Neerlandica, Leiden, 1948, pp. 349ff.
4. JRAS, 1908, pp. 823-8.
5. VIJ, vol. 1, No. 1, March 1963, op. 141-153.
6. JRAS, 1898, Part 1, pp. 117-141.
7. The Mahābhārata, an Ethnological Study, pp. 243-93.
8. Die Suparṇasage, pp. 83ff.
9. Das Wurfelspiel im alten Indien.
10. ṚV, X.34.
11. VS, X.28.
12. VS, XXX.18.
13. TS, 1.8, 9.
14. AV, IV. 38, 1-4.
15. Ibid., VI.118.
16. Āśva. Gṛh., II.7, 12.
17. Āpa. Dha., II.10.25.

18. Manu Smṛti, IX.221-22, 224-26.
19. Arthaśāstra, III.20.
20. Aṣṭādhyāyī, II.1.10.
21. Jātakas Nos. 62, 91, 360, 481 and 545.
22. Kāmasūtra, I.3-14.
23. Ibid., III.1.22.
24. Ibid., IV.12.
25. Kṛtyatattva, p. 452.
26. Dharmasindhu, p. 106.
27. Nirṇayasindhu, p. 191.
28. Tithitattva, pp. 135-137.
29. Festivals, Sports, and Pastimes of India, B.J. Institute of Learning and Research, 1972, p. 18.
30. AV, IV.38.
31. Āpa. Gṛh., VII.18-1; Hir. Gṛh., II.7.1.
32. Nirṇayasindhu, p. 202.
33. ASINIS, No. 22.
34. ASIAR, 1908-09, p. 85.
35. The Stūpa of Bhaṛhut, p. 94.
36. Bhaṛhut, pp. 95-96.
37. Ellora, Plate No. 38.
38. Taxila, vol. 2, pp. 662-663.
39. Report on Kumrahar Excavations by Dr. A.S. Altekar and V.K. Misra.
40. OHRJ, Vol. X, 1961, Nos. 1 and 2, pp. 1-4.

Chapter-2: References to gambling in the Vedas, Brāhmaṇas, Āraṇyakas and Upaniṣads.

1. AB, II.16 and KB, XII.1.3.
2. Nirukta, IX.8.
3. Ṛgvidhāna, III.51-54.
4. AV, IV.38.1.
5. AV, IV.38.3.
6. AV, VII.52.9.
7. AV, VII.114.3.
8. Bṛhaddevatā, VII.36&37.
9. Sarvānukramaṇī, II.10.34.
10. HIL, Vol. 1. pt. 1, p. 98.
11. History of Sanskrit Literature, p. 107ff.
12. Mysterium und Mimus im Ṛgveda, p. 377ff.
13. Die Suparnasage, p. 83ff.
14. History off Indian Literature, Vol. I, pt. 1, p. 99n.
15. Bhāratīya Vidyā, vols. XX & XXI, p. 8.
16. Hymns of the Ṛgveda Not Employed in the Solemn Rituals, p. 67.
17. ṚV, I.41.9.
18. Ibid., II.12.4.
19. Ibid., II.29.5.
20. Ibid., I.92.10.
21. Ibid., V.85.8.
22. Ibid., VII.86.6.
23. Ibid., X.42.7.

24. Ibid., X.43,5
25. Ibid., X.27.17.
26. Ibid., X.116.9.
27. Ibid., I. 124.7.
28. Ṛgvedic Culture. p. 325.
29. VS, X.28.
30. MS, IV.4-6.
31. TS, I.8.16.
32. VS, XXX.18.
33. VS, XXX. 8.
34. VS, XXX.22.
35. ṚV, I.112-24.
36. VS. XXXIV.29.
37. KS, XV.4 and MS, II.6.5 and IV.3-8.
38. AV, IV.38.1-4.
39. See his commentary on AV, IV.38.1.
40. AV, VII.52.3, 7&8.
41. AV, VII.109.2.
42. Kauśika Sūtra, 41.10-13.
43. Ibid., 7.19.
44. AV, IV.17.7.
45. Ibid., IV.16.5.
46. Ibid., VI.70.1.
47. Ibid., II.2.5.
48. Ibid., V.31.6.

49. Ibid., VI.118.1-2.
50. Ibid., VI.118.3.
51. Ibid., XII.3.46.
52. Ibid., XlV.1.35 & 36.
53. Ibid., XlV.3.52.
54. Kauśikasūtra, 30.8-10.
55. See his gloss on the above text.
56. AV, VI.38.3.
57. Adyar Library Bulletin, XXV, pts. 1-4, 1961, p. 211.
58. Paippalādasṁhitā, I.49.1.
59. Ibid., 1.49-4.
60. AB, VII.15-4.
61. Ṛgveda Brāhmaṇas, p. 302.
62. TB, I.7.3.
63. Ibid., 1.7.10.
64. Ibid., III.4.16.
65. SB, V.4.4.
66. SB, V.3.1.
67. SA, XII.3.
68. Ch. Up., IV.1.4.
69. Ibid., VI.I.3.1.

Chapter-3: Dice-play in Sūtra literature and Smṛtis

1. KSS, XV.6-2; XV.7.5 to 21; ASS, XVIII.18-16, XVIII.19,1-5, V.19, 1-4; V.20; BSS, II.7-10; XXII-19; LSS, IV.10, 22-23; BhāSS, V.12, 1-7; MSS, 1.5, 5-16.
2. TS, I.8.16-1.

3. BhāSS, V.12, 1-7.
4. MSS, I.5.5.7.
5. Āpa.Gṛh., II.1-81.
6. Hir. Gṛh., II.7.1.
7. See Haradatta's gloss on Āpa. Gṛh., VII .18.3.
8. Āśva. Gṛh., I.56.
9. Āpa. Dha., I.1.3.12.
10. Ibid., II.7.16.12.
11. Ibid., II.10.25.
12. Ibid.
13. The Social and Military Position of the Ruling Caste in Ancient India, p. 67n.
14. Bau Dha. II.1.28.
15. Gautama Dharmasūtra, I.2.23.7.
16. See above.
17. Viṣṇusmṛti, V.138.
18. Ibid., III.50.
19. Manusmṛti, IX.221-22, 24.
20. Ibid., IX.225.
21. Ibid., 226.
22. Ibid., 258.
23. Ibid., XII.45.
24. Ibid., IV.74.
25. Ibid., II.171 (179).
26. Ibid., III.151.

27. Ibid., III.159&160; see also the gloss of Medhātithi on these verses.
28. Ibid., VIII.159.
29. Ibid., VII.46.
30. Ibid., 47.
31. Ibid., 50.
32. Ibid., 52.
33. Manusmṛti, IX.227.
34. See his Introduction to SBE, Vol. XXV, p. 1xxx.
35. History of Dharmaśāstra, Vol. I, p. 337.
36. ṚV, X.34.
37. M.Bh. Udyoga, 37.19.
38. Manusmṛti, IX.228.
39. YS, II.199-203.
40. Ibid., I. 138.
41. Ibid., II.267.
42. BS, XXVIII, 1.
43. NS, XVI.1
44. NS, I.8
45. See above.
46. SBE, Vol.33, P.223. This reference is found in the Nepalese Manuscript only.
47. Ibid., I.43.
48. Ibid., I.159.
49. KSSā., verse.934.
50. Nirukta, IX.7.

51. Ibid., IX.8.
52. See his gloss on Nirukta, IX.8.
53. Nirukta, IX.8.
54. See his gloss.
55. Nirukta, V.22.
56. Ibid.
57. Ibid.
58. ṚV.I.41.9.
59. Nirukta, III.16.
60. Aṣṭādhyāyī, II.1.10.
61. Ibid., I.4.43.
62. Ibid., II.3.58.
63. Ibid., II.3.59.
64. Ibid., II.3.60.
65. MS, I.6.2.
66. Aṣṭādhyāyī III.3.70.
67. Ibid., VIII.2.77.
68. *Ādyūnaḥ and paridyūnaḥ* mean greedy and sorrowful respectively.
69. Aṣṭādhyāyī II.3.57.
70. Ibid., II.1.40.
71. Ibid., IV.4.2.
72. Ibid., IV.4.19.
73. Ibid., V.2.9.
74. Kāmasūtra, I.3.14.
75. Ibid., III.1.22.

76. Ibid., I.3.14.

77. Ibid., III.1.22.

78. Arthaśāstra, VIII.3.

79. Ibid. According to Piśuna, in hunting there is the danger of robbers, enemies, wild animals and forest fires.

80. Arthaśāstra, VIII.3.

81. Ibid., VIII.3.

82. Ibid.

82a Ibid., VIII.3.

83. Ibid., III.20.

84. Śukranītisāra, I.108.

85. Ibid., 109.

86. Ibid., 302.

87. Ibid., 141.

88. Kāmandakīyanītisāra, XIV.66.

89. Ibid., XV.44-49 & 54-55.

90. Bṛhatsaṁhitā, IX.34.

91. Ibid., X.6.

92. Milindapañha, III.44.

93. Dhammapada, verse, 252.

94. Mahāvastu Avadhāna, Vol. III, p. 169.

95. SBE, Vol. X, p.18.

96. Jātaka No. 62.

97. Jātaka Tales, p. 250f.

98. Jātaka No. 481, Jātaka Tales, P.351f.

99. Jātaka No. 91, Buddhist Parables, Vol.1, p.379f.
100. Buddhist Parables, Vol. I, p. 379f.
101. Jātaka No. 545, The Jātaka, p.133f.
102. Jātaka No.360, Jātaka Tales, p.68f.
103. Sūtrakṛtāṅga, I.2.3., 23&24.

Chapter 4: Dice-play in the Epics and Ancient Classical literature

1. The Rāmāyaṇa, II.75-41.
2. Ibid., V.9-31.
3. Ibid., V.14-15.
4. M.Bh., Sabhā, Ch. 48 to 74.
5. Ibid., Vana, Ch. 52 to 79.
6. Nalopākhyānam, ed. by Monier-Williams, Preface, I-XV.
7. Ibid.
8. M.Bh., Virāṭa, 68.30-36.
9. Ibid., 31.
10. Ibid., Sabhā, CXXXV, 21-2.
11. Ibid., 58, 11; 63.1.
12. Ibid., Droṇa, 85, 27 & 28.
13. Ibid., Udyoga, 128.6&7.
14. See above.
15. M.Bh., Vana, 13.7&9.
16. Harivaṁśa, II.61, 21-54.
17. Ibid., II-61.39.
18. Bhāgavatapurāṇa, X.61, 28-38.

19. Brahmapurāṇa, CCI, 1-23.
20. Viṣṇupurāṇa, V.28, 1-23.
21. Brahmapurāṇa, CLXXI, 1-24.
22. Ibid., CLXXI, 28-38.
23. Caturvargacintāmaṇi, Kālanirṇaya, p. 616. See also Ādiyapurāṇa quoted in Caturvargacintāmaṇi.
24. Dr. K. Krishnamoorthy's article entitled "*Jūju*" in Kannada Viśvakośa, vol. Vlll, pp. 287-289.
25. Skāndapurāṇa, I. 1-34, 56-88.
26. Ibid., Kāśīkhaṇḍa, Ch. 88.
27. Agnipurāṇa, CCXLI, 40.
28. Raghuvasṁśa, VI.18.
29. Ibid., IX.7.
30. Kirātārjunīya, I.7.
31. Ibid., Xl.47.
32. Śiśupālavadha, VIII.32.
33. Kādaṁbarī, p.87.
34. Ibid., p.126. See also DKC, Ucchvāsa, II, p.22.
35. Ibid., p.143.
36. Ibid., p.296.
37. Ibid., p.177.
38. Ibid., p.214.
39. Harṣacarita, p. 19.
40. Daśakumāracarita, Ucchvāsa, II, pp. 76-77.
41. Ibid., VIII, pp. 196-97.
42. Ibid., II, p. 66.

43. Avantisundarīkathāsāra, VIII, 41-44.
44. KSS, LXXIV,138-150.
45. Ibid., LXXIV,177-182.
46. Ibid., CXXI,72-186.
47. Ibid., CXXI,188-199.
48. Ibid., XCII,14-27.
49. Ibid., LII, 292-96.
50. Ibid., LXXIII, 175-81.
51. Ibid., CXXI,33-68.
52. Ibid., XXV.
53. Ibid., XXIV. 57-60.
54. Ibid., LVI. 237-424.
55. M.Bh., Vana, 58-14.
56. KSS, LVI, 293.
57. M.Bh., Vana, 59.7.
58. See Nīlakaṇṭha's gloss on the above text.
59. KSS, LVI, 311.
60. Ibid., LVL, 307.
61. Bṛhatkathāmañjarī, XV, 344-70.
62. Ibid., 347.
63. Ibid., V, 24, 233; IX, 817-36; 977-79; X, 67-83; 85-124; XV,152-53.
64. Śukasaptati, Story 1.
65. Ibid., V.33.
66. Pañcatantra, I.391.
67. Ibid., I.58.

68. Mahāsubhāśita-saṁgraha, Vol. I, p.149.

69. Ibid., Vol. I, Verse, 1310.

70. Ibid., Vol. II, Verse, 3680.

71. Ibid., Verse, 3685.

72. Subhāṣita-sudhā-nidhi, Dyūta-paddhati, 1-9.

73. Mahāsubhāṣita-saṁgraha, Vol. I, p.132.

74. Subhāṣita-ratna-bhāṇḍgāram, p.330.

75. Kuṭṭanīmata, Verse, 11.

76. Ibid., Verse, 996.

77. Ibid., Verse, 894.

78. Dūtavākya, Verse, 8.

79. Ibid., Verse,11.

80. Ibid., Verse,12.

81. Dūta-ghaṭotkaca, Verse, 24.

82. Cārudatta, Act II.

83. Mṛcch. Act II, Verse,1.

84. Ibid., Act II, Verse, 5

85. Ibid., Verse, 6.

86. Ibid., Verse, 9.

87. Ibid., Act II, p. 78.

88. Ibid., Act II, Verse, 7.

89. Ibid., Verse, 8

90. Ibid., Act IV, p. 172.

91. Ibid.

Chapter 5: Analysis of the Game of Dice

1. KāSS, XV-6-2; Āśva. GṛhG II-7-10.
2. Gautama Dharmasūtra, I-2-23.
3. See his gloss on the above text.
4. Manusmṛti, IX.223.
5. Ibid., IX.223.
6. NS, XVI.1.
7. Mallinātha's Commentary on Kirātārjunīya, I.7.
8. ṚV, II-29-5; V.85-8; X.34-3,7&10.
9. VS, XXX.18.
10. See his gloss on VS, XXX 18.
11. TB, III.4.16.
12. See his gloss on TB, III.4.16.
13. ṚV I.92.10; II.12.4; IV.20.3; AV, IV.16.5.
14. Aṣṭādhyāyī, IV.4.2.
15. ṚV, X.34.5. The *vibhītaka* tree is botanically known as Terminalia Bellerica. In the Ṛgveda the word used is *vibhidaka* whereas in later literature it is found as *vibhitaka.*
16. See his gloss on TS, I.8.16.
17. JRAS, 1908, July, p.827.
18. Ibid.
19. BSS, XXII.19.
20. M.Bh., Virāṭa, I.25.
21. Harivaṁśa, II-61-37.
22. Aṇḍabhūta Jātaka (Jātaka No.62).

23. Mṛcchakaṭika, Act IV, p.160.
24. The Indus Civilization, p.179.
25. Taxila, vol. 2, p.663.
26. VPJ (Jātaka No. 545).
27. M.Bh., Virāṭaparvan.
28. NS, XVI.1.
29. The commentary on NS, XVI.1.
30. Ibid.
31. Keśavavaijayantī on Viṣṇusmṛti, V.135.
32. Aṣṭādhyāyī, II.1.10.
33. Arthaśastra III.20.
34. Mohenjo-Daro and the Indus Civilization, Vol. II, p.551.
35. The Indus Civilization, p.179.
36. ASIAR, 1908-9, p.85.
37. The Stupa of Bharhut, p.94.
38. Taxila, Vol. 2, pp. 662-663.
39. OHRJ, Vol. X, 1961, Nos.1&2, pp.1-4.
40. ṚV, X.34.1 & 9.
41. AV, IV.15-12; TS, III.4-8.
42. ṚV VIII. 4-3.
43. Vedic Index, Vol. 1, P. 80.
44. Ibid.
45. See his gloss on Nirukta, IX.8.
46. See his gloss on ṚV, X.34 1.
47. See his gloss on M.Bh., Sabhā, 56.3.

48. Nirukta, IX.8.
49. ṚV, X.43.5.
50. AV.V.31-6; VI.70-1.
51. See his gloss on Nirukta, V.22.
52. ASS, V.19.2.
53. BSS, II.7.
54. BhāSS, V.12-4.
55. Āp. Dha., II.10-13.
56. See his gloss on the above text.
57. Dīghanikāya, XXXIII-27.
58. Pāṇini was aware of the word *aṣṭāpada* being used in a technical sense. Aṣṭādhyāyī VI-3-125: *aṣṭanaḥ saṁjñāyām.* Alaka while commenting on Haravijaya of Ratnākara (canto XII, Verse 9) explains the word *aṣṭāpada* as *tasya hi paṅktau paṅktau padāṣṭakopetatvādaṣṭāpadamiti saṁjñā.*
59. See his gloss on Dīghanikāya, XXXIII-27.
60. Rāmāyaṇa, I.5.16.
61. See his gloss on the above passage.
62. Harivaṁśa, II.61.46 & 54.
63. Viṣṇupurāṇa. V.28.23; Brahmapuāṇa, Ch. 201, Verse. 23.
64. VJP, Jātaka No. 545.
65. Kāmasūtra, IV.4.
66. India and Indology, p. 302.
67. The Stūpa of Bharhut, p. 94.
68. OHRJ, Vol. X, 1961, Nos.1&2.

69. See Introduction to Caturaṅgadīpikā by Manomohan Ghosh, p. xxvii.

70. The Indus Civilization, p.179.

71. India and Indology, p. 302.

71a. Andreas Bock-Raming, "The Game Board in Indian Chess and Other Board Games", Abstracts, International Symposium on Approaching the Roots of Chess, Pondicherrry University, 1996, pp.6-7.

72. See his gloss on ṚV. I.41.9.

73. See his gloss on TS. I-8-16.

74. See his gloss on VS. X.28.

75. Mṛcch., Act II, Verse 5.

76. See Prthvīdhara's gloss on Mṛcch., Act II, Verse 5.

77. SB. V.3.1.

78. Cārudatta, p.97.

79. M.Bh., Sabhā, 59.9.

80. See his gloss on the above text.

81. DKC, Ucchvāsa, II, p. 76.

82. AKS, Ch. VIII, Verse, 42.

83. Mahābhāṣya on Pāṇini's Rule, 5.2.9.

84. The Indus Civilization, p.179.

85. ṚV, X.34-6.

86. Ibid., I.100.9.

87. Ibid., IX.97.58.

88. Ibid., X.42.9.

89. ASS, V.20-1; KāSS, XV-7-18.

90. Aṣṭādhyāyī, III-1-21.

91. M.Bh., Sabhā, 58.13.
92. See his gloss on M.Bh., Virāṭa, 50.24.
93. JRAS, 1892, p.127.
94. ṚV, I-132.1.
95. Ibid., V. 60.1.
96. Ibid., X.102.2.
97. Vedic Index, Vol. I, p. 4.
98. AV, VII.109.1.
99. ALB, Vol. XXV, p. 202ff.
100. See his gloss on AV, VII.109.1.
101. ALB, Vol. XXV, p. 202ff.
102. AV, IV.38.1.
103. AV, VII.109.3; Paippalāda, IV.9.5.
104. Paippalāda, I.72.4.
105. AV, VII.50.9.
106. See his gloss on AV, VII.109.1.
107. SB, V.4.4.
108. VS, XXX.18.
109. Aṣṭādhyāyī, III.1.21.
110. See his gloss on M.Bh., Virāṭa, 50.24.
111. M.Bh., Vana, 78.22.
112. Paippalāda, I.49.4.
113. See his gloss on M.Bh., Virāṭa, 50.24.
114. Ibid.
115. M.Bh., Ādi, 67-78, Svargārohaṇa, 5.21.

116. See his gloss on VS, X.28.
117. See his Bhāṣya on Ch.Up., IV.1.4.
118. See his Bhāṣya on the above text. See also Nīlakaṅṭha's gloss on M.Bh., Virāṭa, 50.24.
119. See his gloss on ASS, V.20.1.
120. See his gloss on VS, X.28.
121. Orientalia, Neerlandica, p. 354.
122. Profs. A.B. Keith and Haug are emphatic that the concept of *yugas* is only later.
123. ERE. Vol. I, p. 200.
124. See his gloss on AB, VII.15.4.
125. See AB edited by him, part 2, 464.
126. See his notes on AB, VII.15.4 in Ṛgveda Brāhmaṇas, p. 302.
127. See his gloss on SB, XIII.3.2.
128. Mṛcchakaṭika, Act II, Verse 9.
129. See his gloss on the above text.
130. Mṛcchakaṭika, Act II, Verse 1.
131. VPJ (Jātaka No. 545).
132. Amarakośa, III.171.
133. Medīnikośa, 17.261.
134. Anekārthasaṁgraha, Verse 265.
135. Orientalia Neerlandica, p. 351.
136. M.Bh., Sabhā, 58.9.
137. See his gloss on the above text.
138. M.Bh., Vana, 13.13.

139. Ibid., Droṇa, 130.20.

140. Ibid., Karṇa, 74.15.

141. AV, XIV.1.38.

142. ṚV, VIII-81.1, XI. 106.3.

143. YS, II.199.

144. Mitākṣarā on YS, II.199.

145. Aṣṭādhyāyī, III.3.70.

146. Amarakoaś, II.751.

147. M Bh., Sabhā, 59.8.

148. Ibid., 56.3.

149. See his gloss on the above text.

150. M.Bh., Droṇa, 130.20.

151. See his gloss on M.Bh., Sabhā, 76.24.

152. Orientalia Neerlandica, p. 357.

153. Das Würfelspiel in alten Indien, 49, 50.

154. M.Bh., An Ethno. study, p. 243f.

155. See his gloss on TS, I-8-16.

156. M.Bh., An Ethno. study, p. 243.

157. ASS, V-19, BhāSS, V-12.

158. ṚV, X-34-8 & 12.

159. Ibid., 8.

160. Vedic Index. Vol. I, p.4f.

161. See his gloss on X.34.8.

162. Das Würfelspiel in alten Indien, 25.

163. ASS, XVIII-19-1; V-19-4; MSS, I-5-7.

164. M.Bh., Vana, 34.4.

165. See his gloss on the above text.

166. See Zimmer, Altindisches Leben, 284.

167. Das Würfelspiel in alten Indien, 25ff.

168. M.Bh., Vana, 72-76.

169. Orientalia Neerlandica, p. 350f.

170. M.Bh., An Ethno. study, p. 243f.

171. AV, VII-114-5.

172. Orientalia Neerlandica, p. 360.

173. ṚV, X-34-2.

174. Dīghanikāya, XXXIII.27.

175. Orientalia Neerlandica, p. 361.

176. M.Bh., Sabhā, 59-7.

177. See his gloss on the above text.

178. Orientalia Neerlandica, p. 362.

179. The following texts refer to *treta* and *dvāpara*:
    a. Paippalāda, I.49.4.
    b. M.Bh., Virāṭa, 50.24.
    c. Sutrakritāṅga, I.2.3.23.
    d. Mṛcchakaṭika, Act II, Verse 9.

180. Mahābhaṣya on Pāṇini, II.I.10.

181. JRAS, July 1980, p. 823ff.

182. Orientalia Neerlandica, p. 362.

183. Kāśikā on Pāṇini, II.1.10.

184. Aṣṭādhyāyī, II.1.10.

185. Mahābhaṣya on Pāṇini, II.1.10.

186. DKC, Ucchvāsa, II, p.76.

187. Jayamaṅgalā on Kāmasūtra, I.3.14.
188. Kāmasūtra, I.3.14.
189. PIHC, 1939 (Third Session, Calcutta), p. 241f.
190. NS, XVI.3.
191. M.Bh., Sabhā, 59.4.
192. Ibid., Sabhā, 21.
193. KSS, CXXI. 90.
194. Ibid., CXX1.82.
195. Brahmapurāṇa, Ch. 201, Verses 1-23.
196. Ibid., 201.20 & 22.
197. M.Bh., Sabhā, 68, 24.
198. Ibid., 33.
199. KSS, LXXLV, 48.
200. M.Bh., Sabhā, 67.50.
201. Ibid., Udyoga, III.6.8.
201a M.bh., Sabhāparva, 59.16 &18.
202. Ibid., Sabhā, 68, 9.
203. History of Dharmaśāstra, Vol. III, p.542.
204. M.Bh., Udyoga, II. 9.11.
205. Mṛcch., Act II, p. 76.
206. Jātaka No. 91.
207. NS, XVI. 5.
208. M.Bh., Sabhā, 67.47.
209. The Gambler's Hymn, stanza 4.
210. M.Bh., Sabhā, 66,4.

211. Ibid., 71, 19.

212. Ibid., 67, 5a.

213. Ibid., Sabhā, 67, 5b.

214. Ibid., 67.7.

215. Ibid., 48-49.

216. Ibid.,68.1.

217. Ibid., Sabhā, 68, 3b, 4b.

218. Ibid., 20 & 21.

219. Ibid., 23 & 24.

220. Ibid., 68. 32.

221. Ibid., 35.

222. Ibid., Vana, 61. 3-5.

223. KSS, LXXIV, 80-81.

224. M.Bh., Sabhā, 68.38.

225. Ibid., 39.

226. Ibid., 47.

227. Introduction to Sabhāparvan (A Critical Edition), Bhandarkar Oriental Research Institute, 1944, p. xxix.

228. JOR, Vol. XVIII, part III, 1951, pp. 170-178.

229. AIOC, 1961 (21st Conference at Srinagar), p.14.

230. M.Bh., Vana, 61-14.

231. Ibid.,16.

232. KSS

Chapter 6: Gambling Houses-Rules and Regulations and their Implementation

1. ṚV, X.34.6. *sābhameti kitavaḥ*
2. VS, XXX.18; TB, III.4.16.
3. AV, V.31.6.
4. Āśva. Gṛ. Sūtra, VII.ii.10.12.
5. See his gloss on Āpa. Dha., II.10.25.
6. YS, II-201.
7. NS, XVI.8.
8. M.Bh., Sabhā, 56.18, 20c, 22a, and 22b.

8a Harivamsa, II.61.23.

9. Kathā-sarit-sāgara, Taraṅga, LXXIII, Verses. 189-90.
10. Avimāraka, Act III.
11. Arthaśāstra, III.20.
12. DKC, Ucchvāsa, II, pp.76-77.
13. Ibid.
14. Ṛgvedic Culture, p. 325.
15. Ibid.
16. See his gloss on ṚV, I.124.7.
17. M.Bh., Sabhā, 69.4-5.
18. Ibid., 8.
19. Ibid., 69.9.
20. The Social and Military Position of the Ruling Caste in Ancient India.
21. See his gloss on TB, III-4-16.

22. TS, I.8.9; see Sāyaṇa's gloss on SB, V.3.1.
23. SB, V.3.1; MS, II.6.5; KS, XV.4.
24. See his gloss on Āpa. Dha., II.10.25.
25. YS, II.199.
26. See his gloss on YS, II.199.
27. YS, II.200.
28. See his gloss on the above text.
29. See his gloss.
30. BS, XXVIII.2.
31. NS, XVI.2.
32. Ibid., 5.
33. Ibid., 2.
34. Arthaśāstra, III.20.
35. KSSā. 937.
36. YS, II.201.
36a. KSSā, 940.
37. AP, Ch. 257, Verses. 35 & 49.
38. Mṛcch., Act II, Verse 2.
39. Ibid., Act II, p. 172.
40. Ibid., Act II, p. 94.
41. Ibid., Act II, Verse 3. See also Darduraka's remark after insulting *sabhika,* Act II, p. 84.
42. Ibid., Act VI, P. 222.
43. DKC, Ucchvāsa, II, p. 76.
44. Ibid., p. 77.
45. KSS, Ch. XCII, Verses. 19-22.

46. YS, II.202; NS, XVI.4.
47. Mitākṣarā on YS, II.202.
48. KSSā., 943.
49. BS, XXVIII.9 & 10.
50. KSSā., 942.
51. BS. XXVIII.6.
52. KSSā, Verse 941.
53. Arthaśāstra, III.20.
54. ṚV.V.85.8.
55. Ibid., II.29.5; X.34.3, 3, 7 & 10; AV, VII.50.1; VS, XXX.8.22.
56. AV, XII.3.52.
57. M.Bh., Sabhā, 59.5.
58. See his gloss on Viṣṇusmṛti, V.135.
59. YS, II.201; NS, XVI.7.
60. BS, XXVIII.8.
61. Viṣṇusmṛti, V.135.
62. YS, II.2.2.
63. NS, XVI.6.
64. BS, XXVIII.7.
65. Arthaśāstra, III.20.
66. Ibid.
67. Mṛcch., Act II, pp. 72-87.
68. Ibid., p. 84.
69. See the order of Māthura in Mṛcch., Act II. p. 84.
70. Mṛcch., Act II, Verse 12.

71. KSS, CXXI, Verses 85-86.

72. Ibid., Verses 35-36.

Part-II
Origin of Chess in Sanskrit Literature

Chapter-1: Introduction

Texts

[T 1] Ghosh, Manomohan [Ed.]: Śūlapāṇi's Caturaṅga Dīpikā. A Manual of Four-Handed Dice-Chess. Critically Edited. Calcutta 1936.

[T2] Kulkarni Haldikar, C.R. [Ed.]: Vilāsamaṇimañjarī- Kolhapur: School and College Book Stall 1937.

[T3] Shrigondekar, G.K. [Ed.]: Mānasollāsa of Somadeva. Vol. 111. Baroda 1961, Gaekwad's Oriental Series 138 (Vol. I. 1925. Vol. Il. 1939).

Literature

1. Bock-Raming, Andreas, Ein bisher unbeachtet gebliebener Sanskrit-Text zum indischen Schachspiel, sein Inhalt und seine Bedeutung fur die Schachgeschichte in: Schach Journal, Berlin, 3. Jg., 1993, No 1/ 1993, 71-77.

2. Bock-Raming, Andreas, The Varieties of Indian Chess Through the Ages in The Chess Collector, London, vol. IV, 1993/94, April 1994, 17-2 1. First part of the lecture given Amsterdam November 27, 1993, on the second conference of the chess historians in the Initiativ-gruppe Königstein. Abridged version in Programe for the Second Conference of the Chess Historians, Seevetal, Meissenburg 1993, pp. 3-4.

3. Bhatta C. Panduranga, Dice-Play in Sanskrit Literature

A Study, 1985. See "Is Chess derived from dice-play", pp. 119-125.

4. Wakankar Siddharth Y, A Survey of Sanskrit Works on the Game of Chess, 1986, pp. 293-303.
5. See above reference no. 2.
6. Calvo Ricardo, Thesen in Programme for the Second Conference of the Chess Historians Seevetal, Meissenburg, 1993, pp.3-4.
7. Holländer Hans, Thesen zur fruh und Vorgeschichte des Schachspiels in print for Homo Ludens IV, München/Salzburg 1994. Enlarged print version of the lecture given Amsterdam November 27, 1993, on the second conference of the chess historians in the Initiativ-gruppe Königstein shortened version in: Programe (see [09]), pp. 8-9.
8. Chakravarti Chintaharan, Sanskrit Works on the Game of Chess in The Indian Historical Quarterly, Calcutta, 14, 1938, pp. 75-79.
9. See above reference no. 4.
10. Murray Harold James Ruthven, A History of Chess, Reprinted 1962, 1969, [1988].
11. Macdonell Arthur Anthony, On the Origin and Early History of Chess in Journal of the Royal Asiatic Society of Great Britain and Ireland for 1898, pp.117-141.
12. Murray H.J.R, How Old is Chess? In British Chess Magazine, Leeds, 56, 1936, pp. 585-587.
13. Bidev Pavle, "New investigations about chess origin", in: Mail Chess, Beograd, vol. 5, 1951/52, No 7, November 1951, pp.9-15; No 9 (January 1952), pp. 3-13.
14. Hellmut Rosenfeld, On the Morphogenesis of Games,

especially of Chess and Playing Cards in The Playing Card Journal of the International vol. IX, N O 3, 1981, pp. 69-82 [pp.70-73].

15. Hellmut Rosenfeld, Die Beziehung der europäischen Spielkarten zum Orient und zum Ur-Schach in Archiv für Kulturgeschichte, Köln/ Graz, 42, 1960, pp.1-36. Reprint of complete volume Nedeln 1971. [Urschach] pp. 24-35.

16. Warner Lauterbach, die ältesten Schachdokumente und ihre Bedeutung fur die Schachgeschichte in: [Engelhardts] Schach Taschen Jahrbuch 1960, 7. Jg., Berlin Frohnau [1959?], pp.30-39.

17. Hellmut Rosenfeld, Zur Vor und Frühgeschichte und Morphogenese von Kartenspiel und Tarock in Archiv für Kulturgeschichte, Köln/Wien, 52, 1970, pp.65-94 [pp. 80-86].

18. Bidev Pavle, How Old is Chess in British Chess Magazine, St. Leonards on Sea, 107, 1987, 214-217.

19. Bidev Pavle, Zum angeblichen altindischen Würfelvierschach-in: Europa-Rochade, Maintal, 1988, No 4, April 1988, pp. 27-28.

20. Petzold Joachim, Das Königliche Spiel. Die Kulturgeschichte des Schach[s]. Mit einem eleitwort von Lothar Schmid. Stuttgart: Kohlhammer 1987. P.239, (l) S. m. Diagr. u. Abb. 4.

21. Paul Thieme, Chess and Backgammon (Tric-Trac) in Sanskrit Literature, 1962, pp.204-216.

22. Görschen Fritz Clemens, Schach. Das Kriegsspiel aus dem Wunder lande Indien. Eine schachgeschichtliche Abhandlung, Winsen/Luhe, Meissenburg 1980 [1982]. 80 S. m. Diagr. 8.

23. Pratesi Franco, Gli scacchi in India in Scacchi e

Science Applicate, Venezia, vol. 8, 1990 [1991], pp. 5-10.

24. Schlingloff Dieter, Zu den Spielszenen von Bharhut und Bodhgaya in Schachhistorische Forschung. Namen Daten Meinungen Literatur. Eine Übersicht nit den Stand per 30. November 1991 zusamengestellt von Egbert Meissenburg, Seevetal 1991, pp.7-9.

25. Syed Renate Das caturaṅga im Mānasollāsa und einige Bemerkungen zum Schach in Indien in Beiträge des Südasien Instituts der Humboldt Universität zu Berlin, Berlin, Heft 6/ 1993, Berlin [1994], pp. 93-132.

 Revised version of the chess part of author's inaugural dissertation [Habilitations schrift] "Spiele der Menschen, Spiele der Götter- Dyūtakrīḍāvilāsalīlā - Gestalt und Bedeutung des Spiels im Alten Indien" (University Munich, October 1993, unpublished).

26. See above reference no 2.

27. See above reference no 3.

28. Needham Joseph, Science and Civilisation in China. With the collaboration of Wang Ling and the special co-operation of Kenneth Girwood Robinson. Volume 4. Physics and Physical Technology. Part I. Physics, Cambridge 1962, 1972, Gr.8, pp.314-334, The Magnet, Divination, and Chess.

29. Schmidt Rainer, Urschach und die Vorgeschichte des Xiangqi. In Schach Journal, Berlin, 3. Jg., 1993, No 1/ 1993, pp.78-85.

30. Pratesi Franco, Un'altra possibile origine per gli scacchi in Scacco, Mondovi, anno 25, 1994, Aprile 1994, pp.162-164.

31. Averbach Jurij, Wie das Schachspiel entstand. Erstveröffentli chung. Aus dem Russischen übersetzt

von Otto Dietze in Schach-Journal, Berlin, 1, 1991, No l, pp. 51-64.

32. Josten Gerhard, Schachist Himmel und Erde, Köln [Selbstverlag] Gerhard Josten 1993. 54, (l) S. m. Diagr. 29 cm Br.

33. Josten Gerhard, Urschach aus Uruk. Köln [Selbstverlag] Gerhard Josten 1993. 54, (2) Bl. n. Zeichn. 29 cm Br.

34. Eder Manfred, Wo entstand der Königstein und wie? Neue schachgeschichtliche Forschungsimpulse durch die Initiativ-gruppe König stein. Ein Meinungsbericht - nicht ganz ohne Schlusfolgerungen in Schach-Journal, Berlin, 2, 1992, No 3/ 1992, pp.13-31.

35. See above reference no. 12.

Chapter 2: Origin of Chess in Sanskrit Literature

1. Sir William Jones, On the Indian Game of Chess, in Asiatick Researches, London, vol. II, 1790, pp.159-165.

2. Caturaṅgadipīkā of Śūlapāṇi, ed. Manomohan Ghosh, Calcutta 1936, pp.1-8.

3. Sir William Jones, see reference no 1 above.

4. Murray H.J.R., A History of Chess, Oxford 1913. Reprinted in 1962, 1969, [1988].

5. Richard Eales, Chess. The History of a Game, London 1985, pp. 19-35.

6. Pandit V.D., 'The Origins of Chess' in Chess Notes, Geneva, 8, 1989, issue 2, No 44, p.29.

7. Bob Meadley, 'The Origins of Chess' in Chess Notes, Geneva, 8, 1989, issue 3, No 45, May-June 1989, p.55.

8. Hugh Myers, The Origins of Chess in Chess Notes, Geneva, 8, 1989, issue 3, No 45, pp. 55-56 with answer of V.D. Pandit page 100 and replies by Hugh Myers and Bob Meadley, pp.100-102.

9. Paul Thieme, 'Chess and Backgammon (tric-trac) in Sanskrit Literature in Indological Studies in Honour of W. Norman Brown, ed. Ernest Bender, New Haven 1962, pp.204-216.

10. Macdonnell A.A., 'Origin and Early History of Chess' in Journal of the Royal Asiatic Society of Great Britain and Ireland, N.S.

11. Paul Thieme, Op. Cit. p.216.

12. See introductory verses in Caturaṅgadīpikā of Śūlapāṇi, pp.1-5.

13. Ibid.

14. Caturaṅga-taraṅgiṇī, Manuscript preserved in the library of the Nepal Government.

15. Bṛhajjyotiṣārṇava printed by Venkateshwar Steam Press, Bombay in Saka 1822 (1900), VI. 20.

16. Ibid., VI. 20.

17. Ibid., VI.20,1.18.

18. Ibid., VI.

19. Ibid., VI.

20. S.C. Banjeri does not give these verses as attributed to Kālidāsa in his book Kālidāsa Apocrypha, Varanasi, 1989.

21. Bṛhajjyotiśārṇava, VI,20,1959; uṣṭrasya gaṇanā nāstrimarudhanvādikalpitā

22. Ibid. VI .20.4.

23. Ṛgveda, VI. 47.26; Atharvaveda, VI. 125, 75, 1-7.

24. See also Arthaśāstra X .4; Kāmandaki, 20.4.

25. McCrindle, John Watson, Ancient India as described by Megasthenes and Arriani Being a translation of the fragments of the Indica of Megasthenes, 1877, 1926, Frag. 34.

26. The Harṣacarita of Bānabhaṭṭa, Translated by E. B. Cowell and F.W. Thomas. (Second Edition), Delhi, 1968, pp. 224-225.

27. Watters II, p. 239. See also Department of Letters, 1927, pp.38-39.

28. South Indian Inscriptions, Vol. I, p. 153.

29. Richard Eales, op. cit., p. 27.

30. The Epic of the Kings, Shah-Nama the national epic of Persia by Ferdowsi. Translated by Reuben Levy. Revised by Amin Banai, London, Henley, and Boston 1967, 327-329; Murray, op. cit., pp. 156-7.

31. Pandit V.D., op. cit.

32. See under *caturaṅga* in Kannada Viśvakośa, University of Mysore.

33. Kāmasūtra, I.3.14.

33a. Bṛhajjyotiśārṇava, VI .20.3.

34. Richard Eales, op. cit., p. 24

35. Ibid., p. 26.

36. Bṛhajjyotiśārṇava, VI .20, 2 and 3.

37. In the Parsee book, Gulistan written by king Sekhasadisi in Hijra year 656 (1235CE) it is mentioned that an ancient king of Hindustan taught this game to an Iranian king (mentioned in Kannada Viśvakośa).

38. Mentioned in Mysore Gazetteer II i -pp. 416-17 and G. R. Josyar in his History of Mysore and Yadava Dynasty, p. 197, without reference to manuscripts or printed editions.

39. See under caturaṅga in the Card Index maintained in the Adyar Library, Madras (now Chennai).

40. Śrītattvanidhi, O.R.I., Mysore, No A. 852.

41. Ramachandra Dikshitar V.R., War in Ancient India, Reprinted Delhi 1987, p.156.

42. Arthaśāstra, p.140; Kāmandaki, 19, 23 and 25; Śukra IV.7; Agnipurāṇa 228.6; Jātaka vol. VI, p. 298, vol. II, p. 66, 70, 71, vol. III, pp. 157 and 161.

43. Tylor, Edward B, Anthropology. An introduction to the study of man and civilization, London 1892, p. 307.

44. Ramachandra Dikshitar V.R., War in Ancient India, p. 155.

45. Ibid.

46. Ibid.

47. Ibid., page 156.

48. Ṛgveda, X. 34, 8 and 12.

49. Tridib Nath Rai, The indoor and outdoor games in Ancient India in Proceedings of Indian Historical Congress, 1939, 241-261.

50. Panduranga C Bhatta, Dice-Play in Sanskrit Literature, 1985, pp. 7-63.

51. Rāmāyaṇa, I.5. 12.

52. See Tilaka's commentary on Rāmāyaṇa, I.5.12.

53. See Amṛtakaṭaka commentary on Rāmāyaṇa, 1.5. 12, published by Oriental Research Institute, Mysore, 1965.
54. Harivamśa, II.61, 21-54.
55. Olden Berg (Edited), vol. II, p. 10; vol. III, p. 180.
56. Sacred Books of the Buddhists, vol. II, p. 9.
56a. M.Bh. Sabhāparva, 59.9.
57. Panduranga C Bhatta, Op. cit., p 60.
58. Paul Thieme, op. cit., P. 215.
59. H.J. R. Murray, op. cit., p. 156-157.
60. Amarakośa, II. 498a.
61. Ṛgveda, II.92-2; Śatapatha Brāhmaṇa XIII.
62. Rāmāyaṇa, I. 69.3.
63. Ibid., VI.3.25.
64. Ibid., II. 94.3 ff. For the word caturaṅga and its constituents vide Ramāyaṇa I. 18-10, 1.49. 11-12.
65. Mahābhārata, Vanaparva 52 to 79.
66. See his commentary called Bhāratabhāva Pradīpa on Mahābhārata, Virāṭaparva, I.25.
67. Mahābhārata, Sabhāparva, 56.3.
68. Ibid., Droṇaparva, 130.20.
69. Ibid., Karṇaparva, 74. 15.
70. Even Manu refers to *vyūhas* in his Manusmṛti, VII. 187-188
71. Arthaśāstra, X. 3.
72. Kauṭilya mentions *maṇḍalas* in Arthaśāstra, 6.2, 24-29.

73. Kauṭilya is placed in 324-300 BCE by the Sanskrit historians.

74. Mahābhārata, Bhīṣmaparva, 20. 18.

75. Ibid., 100,2 f., Śalyaparva, 7.20.

76. Ramachandra Dikshitar, V.R., War in Ancient India, Op.cit., p. 270.

77. Arthaśāstra, X. 6, 9-23, 25-29, 31-33, 35-38 and 42.

77a. Murray, Op.cit, pp. 39-41; Meissenburg, Egbert: Das Schachapiel in der mittelpersischen Literatur, Forschungsbericht, Bibliographie, Text-und Schrifttumsnachweise; Winsen/Luhe 1976. 4. Sanvito, Alessandro: Testimonianze trascurate; In: L'Italia Scacchisstics, Milano, anno 78, 1988, N. 997, Novembre 1988, pp. 350-353, 376.

77b. Murray, Op.cit., pp. 156-157.

78. Caṁpūrāmāyaṇa, V. 38.

79. Bṛhajjyotiśārṇava, V.151.

80. Bṛhajjyotiśārṇava, VI. 20.46.

81. Linder, I [saak], Chess I,300 Years Ago in Sport in USSR, Moscow, 1978, No I (179), pp. [26]-28. Burjakov, Jurij F, Zur Bestimmung und Datierung einiger der ältesten Schachfiguren. Der Fund von Afrasiab <Samarkand> in Antike Welt, Mainz, 25. Jg., 1994, Heft l, pp. 62-71 (translated from the Russian original published in Sovetskaja Archeologija, Moscow, vol. 24, 1980, No 3, pp. 162-172). Eder, Manfred, Die Schachfiguren von Afrasiab. Fragen die Wissenschaft zur Deutung, Zeitstellung und Ikonographie in Antike Welt, Mainz, 25. Jg., 1994, Heft 1, pp. 71-78.

82. The Cambridge History of India. Vol. I. Ancient India. Edited by E -J. Rapson. Second Indian Reprint, Delhi [etc.] 1962, p.262.
83. Mahābhārata, Sabhāparva, 59. 16 and 18.
84. Caturaṅgadīpikā, Op. cit., p. 2.
85. Mahābhārata, Sabhāparva, 59, 16 and 18.
86. Ibid., Sabhāparva 68-69.
87. Arthaśāstra, X.6.
88. Kāvyādarśa, III.80.
89. Kāvyālaṅkāra, V.2.
90. Jacobi, Hermann, Ueber zwei ältere Erwähnungen des Schachspiels in der Sanskrit Litteratur in Zeitschrift der Deutschen Morgenländischen Gesellschaft, vol. 50, 1896, pp.227-233.
91. Sarasvatīkaṇṭhābharaṇa, vol. II, pp.277, 278.
92. Tridibnath Ray, The indoor and outdoor games in Ancient India. Proceedings of Indian Historical Congress, 1939, pp.241-261 [p.252].
93. Aṣṭādhyāyī, VI.3.125.
94. Agrawala, V.S., India as known to Panini, 1962, p.166.
95. Murray, H.J.R., A History of Board Games other than Chess, Oxford 1952, p.133-4. Brown, W. Norman: The Indian Games of Pachisi, Chaupar, and Chausar in India and Indology, Selected Articles by W. Norman Brown, Delhi [etc.] 1978, pp.287-302 (reprinted from Studies in Indian Linguistics. M.B. Emeneau Sastipurti Volume, Poona,1968, PP. 46-53).
96. Aṣṭādhyāyī, III-1-75.

97. Paul Thieme, Op. Cit., p.208.

98. Mahābhāṣya, vol. I, 439.1.8 ff.

99. Paul Thieme, Op. Cit, p.208.

100. Ibid.

101. Subhandhu's Vāsavadattā. Ed. by L. Gray, New York 1913, p.191.

102. Paul Thieme, Op. Cit, does not mention Subhandu in connection with chess.

103. Amarakośa, III. 171.

104. Vreese, K. de: The Game of Dice in Ancient India in Orientalia Neerlandica, Leiden 1948, pp. 349-362 (p.351).

105. Thomas, F.W., The Indian Game of Chess in Zeitschrift der Deutschen Morgenländischen Gesellschaft, vol. 52, 1898, pp.271-2, and vol. 53, 1899, 364-5.

106. Medinīkośa under the word *naya.*

107. Dśakumāracarita, Ucchvāsa, Il.76.

108. Jayamaṅgalā on Kāmasūtra, I.3-14.

109. Murray, H.J.R., A History of Chess, 1913, p.51.

110. Harṣacarita of Bāṇabhaṭṭa, text of the Uchhvāsas I-VIII. Edited with an Introduction and Notes by P.V. Kane, Bombay 1918, Delhi [etc.] 1986 [Third reprint], p.24.

111. Haravijaya, XII.9.

112. Hermann Jacobi (see above note 90), pp. 225f., Macdonell (see note 10), pp.124.

112a. Mṛtasanjīvinī on Piṅgala's Chandaḥsūtra, I.3. See also Journal of Royal Asiatic Society, 1896, p.122.

113. Vikrama's Adventures; or, Thirty-Two Tales of the Throne, edited in four Different Recensions and Translated with an Introduction by Franklin Edgerton, 2 vols. Cambridge/Mass. 1926, story no. 27, verses 31-35.

114. McKay, Ernest John Henry, The Indus Civilisation (On the Results of the Excavations in the Province Sind 1921-1931) London 1935, p. 179. See also Marshall, John Hubert, Mohenjo Daro and the Indus Civilisation. 3 vols., London 1931, p. 552.

115. See Petzold, Joachim: Auf der Suche nach dem Ursprung des Schachs in Deutsche Schachblätter/ Schachreport/Deutsche Schachzeitung, Hollfeld, 1990, No 5, pp. 65-66. Sanvito Alessandro: Un ritrovamento che fara discutere in Mondoscacchi, Roma, vol. 9, 1990, No l, pp.13-15.

116. K. Krishna Murthy, Dice Play and its Archeological Corroboration at Nāgārjunakoṇḍa, Andhra Pradesh in Orissa Historical Research Journal, vol. X, 1961, Nos 1&2, pp.1-4.

117. Indian Antiquary, vol. XXI, 1892, p. 229, note 25.

118. Ibid., vol. X, p.119; also see Rosenfeld, Hellmut, Die Beziehung der europäischen Spielkarten zum Orient und zum Urschach in Archiv für Kulturgeschichte, 42, 1960, pp. 1-36. Petzold, Joachim: Das rätselhafte Relief in Deutsche Schachblätter/Schachreport, Hollfeld, 1988, No 12, 65-66. Bidev, Pavle, Zum angeblichen altindischen Würfelvierschach in Europa-Rochade, Maintal, 1988, No 4, April 1988, 27-28. Schlingloff, Dieter:zu den Spielszenen von Bharhut und Bodhgaya in Schachhistorische Forschung, Seevetal 1991, pp.7-9.

119. Cunningham, A, The Stupa of Bharhut, London 1879, Reprint Varanasi 1962, p.94f. with plate XLV. For the contradictions on the Jataka story represented in this scene refer to Benimadhah Barua, Bharhut, pp. 95-96; Inscriptions on Jatakas and Aradanas unidentified.

120. See Schlingloff, Dieter, Op.Cit.

121. Basham, A[rthur] L, The Wonder That Was India, 1954 (and many reprints), p. 208.

122. Andreas Bock Raming, The Gambling Scenes of Bhārhut And Bodhgayā, A Critical Assessment of Their Previous Interpretations and Some New Suggestions, Asiatische Studien Etudes Asiatiques, LIV.1.2000. Peter Lang, Berlin, pp. 160, 161, 173.

123. McKay, E.J.H, Indus Civilisation, London 1935, pp. 180-181.

124. Linde, Antonius van der, Geschichte und Litteratur def Schachspiels, I. Berlin 1874, pp. 64ff. Linde, Antonius van der, Quellenstudien, Berlin 1881, p. 259.

125. For a discussion on this issue see Murray (note 4), pp. 45-77.

126. Richard Eales, Op. Cit, p. 29.

127. Mahābhārata, Ādiparva, 197-14.

128. Vairāgyaśataka, 43.

129. Skāndapurāṇa, 88.8.

Chapter 3: Analytical assessment of the contributions for the symposium on "Approaching the Roots of Chess", Pondicherry University, 26th-29th November 1996 together with a report on the gaming pieces and chessmen exhibited in the museums of Madras and Hyderabad prepared by Andreas Bock Raming, Freiburg, Germany.

1. Cf., his article Wie das Schachspiel entstand, in: Schach-Journal 1/91, pp 51-64, esp. p. 56; 62; 63.
2. Cf., his book Das Koōnigliche Spiel. Die Kulturgeschichte des Schach, Leipzig 1987, esp. pp.20-40.
3. Cf., also Murray, A History of Chess, pp. 61-62.
4. Cf., verse 5,605.
5. *nṛpatulyo bhaven mantrī gamane śkaṭo bhaṭān/ullaṅghya yāti sadanaṃ koṇena...*
6. See my article: The varieties of Indian Chess through the ages in: Asiatic Studien XLIX,2 (1995), p. 311 and diagram 1 on p. 324.
7. Passages dealing with the conduct of war and the formation of *vyūha*-s may be found, e.g., in the Mahābhārata (compiled between the 2nd century BCE. And the 2nd century CE.), the Arthaśāstra (which in the form we have it today was probably composed on the turn from the 3rd century CE.) and Kāmandakīya-Nītiśāstra (composed between the 4th and 8th century CE.)
8. Cf., e.g., my article mentioned in footnote 6, cf. also R Syed on: Caturaṅga, Anmerkungen zu Alter, Ursprung und Urform des Schachs, in: Beiträge des Sūdasien-Instituts der Humboldt-Universität zu Berlin, H. 8/1995, pp. 63-108.

9. Cf., his article Thesen zur Fruh-und Vorgeschichte des Schachspiels, in Homo Ludens. Der spielende Mensch IV. Internationale Beiträge des Institutes fur Spielforschung und Spielpādagogik an der Hochshule "Mozarteurn" Salzburg. Hrsg.v.Gūnther G. Bauer, 4. Jahrgang 1994, p.19.

10. Cf., p. 321 on my article mentioned above in footnote 6.

11. Cf., Hollānder, ibid., p. 19.

12. On this subject cf., also M. Eder's lecture on: Was ist Schach-im historischen Kontext? [What is Chess-in the historical context]? given at the 2nd Symposium of the "Initiativ-Gruppe Kōnigstein", 26th-28th Nov. 1993, published in: Schach-Journal 1/1994, pp. 20-30.

13. Cf., however, Mr. Eder's lecture mentioned in footnote 12, where he, with reference to the Russian chess historian M. Linder, observes on p. 27: "And if, after all, it could be proved that this two-handed chess developed from the four-handed "chess", a game '*caturaṅga*' played by four parties: chess-in the sense of our 'chess-point' that was not, at any rate not as long as it was possible to beat the king from the game".

14. Cf., D. Schlingloff, Zu den Spielszenen von Bharhut und Bodhgaya, in: Schachhistorische Forschung. Narmen-Daten-Meinungen-Literatur. Eine Ūbersichit mit dem Stand per 30. November 1991 zusammengestellt von Egbert Meissenburg, Seevetal 1991, pp. 7-9.

15. Cf., p. 27 of M. Eder's lecture mentioned in footnote 12 of the article.

16. Cf., G. Bossong, Sermantik der Terminologie: Zur Vorgeschichte der alfonsinischen Schachtermini, in: Zeitschrift fūr Romanische Philologie 94 (1978), pp. 56-57; cf., also S. Powels, Zur Geschichte des

Schachspiels bei Indern und Arabern, in: Studia Semitica Necnon Iranica. R. Macuch Septuagenario ab Amicis et Discipulis Dedicata, Wiesbaden 1989, p. 202.

17. Called *navagraha* in Sanskrit; they are Mars, Mercury, Jupiter, Venus, Saturn, Sun, and Moon, Rāhu (ascending node of the moon) and Ketu (descending node).

18. Page 3 of the typoscript of Prof. Vasantha's lecture which she kindly made available to me.

19. Cf., his article Die Hypothese von Johannes Kohtz, in: Homo Ludens. Der spielende Mensch IV. Internationale Beiträge des Institutes für Spielforschung und Spielpädagogik an der Hochschule "Mozarteum" Salzburg. Ed. by Günther G. Bauer. München/Salzburg 1994, pp. 29-45; cf. also Pavle Bidev's articles: Geschichte der Entdeckung des Schachs im magischen Quadrat und des magischen Quadrats im Schach, in: Schachwissenschaftliche Forschungen Nr. 5 (Jan. 1975), pp. 120-131, and Zur Verteidigung Des Indischen Ursprungs von Schachbrett und Caturaṅga. Part 4: Der Ursprung des Aṣṭāpada [sic!], in: Stammt Schach aus Altindien oder China? Yu Igalo 1986, pp. 152-159, esp. p. 159.

20. F. Bernhauer, Der Rösselsprung im Mānasollāsa, in: Beiträge des Südasien-Instituts, Humboldt-Universität zu Berlin, no.8/1995, pp. 109-122.

21. Page 6 of the typoscript of Prof. Vasantha's lecture.

22. Cf. the introductory chapter of F. Rosenthal's book on: Gambling in Islam, Leiden 1975.

23. Cf., Topsfield's article The Indian Game of Snakes and Ladders, in Artibus Asiae 46 (1985), pp. 203-214, esp. pp. 212f., and I. Finkel, Notes on Two Tibeten

Dice Games, in: New Approaches to Board Games Research: Asian Origins and Future Perspectives. Ed. by A.J. de Voogt. Leiden: International Institute for Asian Studies 1995, pp. 24-47, esp.pp.34ff.

24. Not in the Abstracts Pondicherry.

25. Cf., also the game of the sixteen soldiers described by R. C. Bell, Board and Table Games From Many Civilizations, Dover 1979, vol. I, p. 51.

26. Cf., also Bell, Board and Table Games, vol. II, p. 47, the "tiger game" and J. Averbach, Board Games And Real Events, chapter II: "Baghacal", in: New Approaches to Board Games Research. Asian Origins and Future Perspectives. Ed. by A. J. de Voogt, Leiden 1995, pp. 17-23.

27. Cf., in this connection also Murray's remark on the use of *caturaṅga* in South India and Ceylon (A History of Chess, p. 62.)

28. Neither contained in the Abstracts Pondicherry nor in the Abstracts and Papers.

29. See my article: Untersuchungen zum indischen Wūrfelspiel nachvedischer Zeit I: Das Backgammon nach der Darstellung des Mānasollāsa - [Studies on the Indian dice-play in post-Ved times I: Backgammon according to the description of the Mānsollāsa], in: Schach-Forschungen 9. Ed. by E. Meissenburg,Seevetal 1995, 18 pages.

30. Cf., also Mr. Eder's two contributions: Mensch - Spiel - Scha: Zehn Thesen zur Entstehung, Entwicklung und Verbreitung Schachspiels, in: Vom Wesir zur Dame. Kulturelle Regeln, Zwang und ihre Brūchigkeit. Ūber kulturelle Transformations am Beispiel des Schachspiels. Ed. by E. Strouhal, Wien 1995, pp. 181-185, esp. p. 182 and the same: From Gaming-

Pieces Chessmen- Which was the Way, presented at the International Colloquium "Board-Games of Academia", Leiden, 9-13 April 1995.

31. Note see Appendix

32. Cf., J.M. Kenoyer, Muschelarbeiten der Indus-Zivilisation, in Vergessene Stādte am Indus-Frūhe Kulturen in Pakisan vom 8-2 Jahrtausend v. Chr., Aachen 1987, p. 227, fig. 205; cf. also by the same author: Shell Industries at Mohenjodaro, Pakistan, in: Interim Reports vol.1 (Editors: Michael Jansen and Gūnter Urban), Aachen and Rome 1984, pp. 99-115. More information on gamesmen coming from the Indus-civilization may, e.g., be found in: Ernest J.H. Mackay, Chanhu-Daro Excavations 1935-36, Varanasi, Delhi 1976, pp. 169f. and J Marshall (ed.), Mohenjo-Daro and the Indus Civilization, Vol. II, Delhi/ Varanasi 1973, pp. 478; 557; 559.

33. Occupying present-day Afghanistan, Bactria is the ancient name of the region between the Hindu Kush Mountain range the Oxus.

34. Coins of India Through the Ages, Government Museum Madras 1995, p. 2.

35. Cf., his article Wie das Schachspiel entstand, in: Schach-Journal 1/1991, p. 62.

36. S. Y. Wakankar, A Survey of Sanskrit Works on The Game Of Chess, in: Journal of the Oriental Institute, University of Baroda 35 (1986), p. 298.

37. Information on the altogether 8.500 manuscripts in the Arabic, Persian and Urdū languages on other subjects like history, biography etc. may be found in the Salar Jung Museum Guidebook, Hyderabad 1990.

38. Kondapur is a small village situated in Medak district at 70 kms to the Northwest of Hyderabad.

39. J. E. van Lohuizen de Leeuw, A unique piece of ivory carving - the oldest chessman, in: South Asian Archaeology 1981. Proceedings of the Sixth International Conference of the Association of South Asian Archaeologists in Western Europe. Held in Cambridge University 5-10 July 1981 (Ed.: B. Allchin, with assistance from R. Allchin and M. Sidell). Cambridge etc. 1981, p. 247f. In a subsequent article, however, van Lohuizen de Leeuw opined that the Kondapur horse was not a chessman but formed a group together with a lion and a bull which she interpreted as cosmological animals, i.e., symbolic representations of the quarters of the sky; C. Sivaramamurti Commemoration Volume. Vol. II. Delhi 1987, pp. 369-371.

Chapter 4: Indian Origin of Chess: A Summary

1. Siddharth Y. Wakankar, "Chaturanga, Buddhibala and Their Literary Description", Abstracts, International Symposium on Approaching the Roots of Chess, Pondicherry University, 1996, pp.4-5.

2. Thime, P Indological Studies, American Oriental Society, 1962, p. 216.

3. Eales, Richard, Chess: The History of a Game, Ishi Press, 1985, pp. 19-35.

4. Bṛhajjyotiśārṇava, VI. 20.46.

5. Rosenfeld Hellmut, Die Beziehung der europäischen Spielkarten zum Orient und zum Ur-Schach in Archiv für Kulturgeschichte, Köln/ Graz, 42, 1960, 1-36. Reprint of complete volume Nedeln 1971. [Urschach] pp. 24-35.

6. Panduranga C Bhatta, Origin and Genesis of Chess, published by Egbert Meissenburg, Seevetal, Germany, 1994, See Introduction.

7. Issak Linder, My Personal Opinion on the Origin of Chess, Approaching the Roots of Chess, Abstracts and Papers presented to the Organisers and Participants of the Symposium at Pondicherry University, 1996.
8. "The Origin of Chess", The Chess Collector Supplement, Vol. I Number 2, July 1996.
9. Indra, Ideologies of War and Peace in Ancient India, Vedic Research Institute, Hoshiarpur, 1957.
10. Watters II, p. 239; See also Dept. of Letters, 1927, pp. 38-39.
11. South Indian Inscriptions, Vol. I. p. 153.
12. Ibid., p. 341.
13. Raghuvaṁśa, IV. 29, 30, 32, 40, 62, 71, 82, 85; VII. 36, 59.
14. See his paper "Approaching the Roots of Chess by trying a definition in Historic Context" presented at the International Symposium on "Approaching the Roots of Chess" held at Pondicherry University, India, 26th-29th November 1996.
15. Ṛgveda, IV. 42. 8-9.
16. Aitareya-Brāhmaṇa, VIII. 2.
17. Śatapatha Brāhmaṇa, XII.4.4.3.
18. Ibid., V.1.5.14.
19. Mahābhārata, XII. 39.128.
20. The Catalogue of Coins in the Punjab Museum, Vol. I, Pl. XVII.31-33.
21. Manusmṛti, VII. 5.4.
22. Viṣṇu-purāṇa, I.13.14; Bhāgavata, IV.13.23.

23. Indian Antiquary, XVIII. 15; Epigraphia Indica, IX. 31.19.
24. Nāradasmṛti, XVIII.31.
25. Rājataraṅgiṇī, I.72.
26. Indian Historical Quarterly, Vol. I. p, 270.
27. Raghuvaṁśa of Kālidāsa, XVIII, 47 and 68, (See Mallinātha's commentary on it).
28. Rangaswami Aiyangar, K.V, Rājadharma, Adyar, 1941, pp. 140-143.
29. See Ramachandra Dikshitar's paper in Woolner Commemoration Volume, Lahore.
30. See his *Rock Edict XIII.*
31. Dīgha-nikāya XIII, Lokkhana Suttanta.
32. Viṣṇupurāṇa, III, 49.
33. Rāmāyaṇa, IX. 28.
34. Arthaśāstra, XIII, 162.
35. Ibid., VIII, Chapter 16; Manusmṛti, VII, 202ff.
36. Beal, Life of Hiuen Tsang, IV, p. 147.
37. Jayaswal, A History of India, AD 150-350 AD; cf. nature of Samudra-Gupta's conquests.
38. Mālavikāgnimitra, Act. VII.
39. Harṣacarita, IV, Ucchvāsa.
40. Raverty H.G., The Invention of Chess and Backgammon, Sedentary Games of India, Edited by Nirbed Ray and Amitabha Ghosh, The Asiatic Society, Calcutta, 1999, pp.52-55,58,62-63.
41. William Jones, "On the Indian Game of Chess", The Asiatick Researches, Vol. II. pp. 159-165, 1790

under the title On the Indian Game of Chess By the President.

This was the seventh annual deliberation of Sir William Jones as the President of the Asiatic Society of Bengal. Reprinted in Sendentary Games of India, Nirbed Ray and Amitabha Ghosh (Ed.) The Asiatic Society Calcutta, 1999, pp.22-27.

42. Nirbed Ray and Amitabha Ghosh, (Edited), Sedentary Games of India, The Asiatic Society, Calcutta, 1999, p. ix.

43. Irving L. Finkel, The Sedentary Games of India: An Introduction, in Sedentary Games of India, Edited by Nirbed Roy and Amitabha Ghosh, The Asiatic Society Calcutta, 1999, p. 1 and 2.

44. Leander A. Feiler Leander A. Feiler Searching For Traces of the Origin of Chess In India- Chapter III: Visits to Archaeological Museums in the Former Eastern Core Territories of the Guptas, Working Papers, Mission Kannauj, Edited by Manfred A.J. Eder, FSG, Kelkheim/Taunus, 2020, p.127.

45. Renate Syed, Śarvavarman Maukhari of Kanauj and the Way of Chess, *Caturanga,* from India to Persia: Facts and Theories, in Working Papers: Mission Kannauj 2020, FSG, Edited by Manfred A.J. Eder, Kelkhem/Taunus, Germany, 2020.p.68-70.

46. Renate Syed, "War, Peace and Chess, Bana's References to "Terracotta Chessmen" and "Discourses on War" in the Harsacarita." in Working Papers: Mission Kannauj 2020, FSG, Edited by Manfred A.J. Eder, Kelkhem/ Taunus, Germany, 2020, p. 53-63.

47. Rajendran C, "A New Look into the Caturanga Passages in Harsacarita", in Working Papers Mission Kannauj 2020, p.51. Working Papers: Mission Kannauj 2020,

FSG, Edited by Manfred A.J. Eder, Kelkhem/Taunus, Germany, 2020, pp. 48-51.

48. Manfred AJ. Eder, "Proto-Chess: No! Proto Chessmen: Yes!" "New Considerations and Conclusions on the Origin of Chess, Working Papers: Mission Kannauj 2020, FSG, Edited by Manfred A.J. Eder, Kelkhem/ Taunus, Germany, 2020. pp. 73,75,76.

49. Leander A. Feiler, Searching For Traces of the Origin of Chess In India Chapter III: Visits to Archaeological Museums in the Former Eastern Core Territories of the Guptas in Working Papers: Mission Kannauj 2020, FSG, Edited by Manfred A.J. Eder, Kelkhem/Taunus, Germany, 2020, p.128.

50. https://hastingschessclub.co.uk/the-afrasiab-chessmen/ visited on 13/10/2021.

51. Manfred AJ Eder, Working Papers Mission Kannauj 2020, p.117-118.

SELECT BIBLIOGRAPHY

Original Sanskrit Books

Agnipurāṇa, Ed. Hari Narayana Apte, Anandashrama Press Poona, 1977; English Translation by Manmatha Nath W Dutt Shastti, Chowkhamba Publications, 1967.

Aitareya Brāhmaṇa, Ed. Anandashrama Press, Poona, 1977.Translated into English by A.B. Keith, Motilal Banarsidass, Delhi, 1971.

Āpastambha Dharmasūtra, Ed. Chinnaswami Shastri, Jai Krishna Das Haridas Gupta, Benares, 1932; Ed. R. Halasyanatha Sastry, Kumbakonam, 1895.

Āpastambīya Gṛhyasūtra, Ed. Chinnaswami Shastri, Benares, 1928.

Arthaśāstra of Kauṭilya, Ed. and Translated by R. Shama Shastry, Mysore, 1924 & 1967; Translated by P. Kangle University of Bombay, 1963.

Āśvalāyana Gṛhyasūtra, Ed. T. Ganapati Sastri, Trivandrum, 1923; Edited Swami Ravitirtha, The Adyar Library & Research Centre, Madras-20, 1944.

Atharva Saṁhitā, Ed. Sri Venirama Sharma, Chowkhamba Press, 1977; Ed. K.P. Ramachandra Sharma, Sanatana dharma Press, 1929; Translated by W.D. Whitney, Harvard Oriental Series, Motilal Banarsidass, 1971.

Avantisundarī, Ed. S.K. Pillai, Anantashayana, 1954, Trivandrum University.

Avantisundarī Kathāsāra, Ed. G. Harihara Sastri, Kuppuswami Sastri Research Institute, Madras, 1957.

Baudhāyana Śrautasūtra, Ed. Dr. W. Caland, Calcutta, 1904.

Bhāgavatapurāṇa, 5th Edn., Gita Press, Gorakhpur, 1964.

Bhāsanāṭakacakra, Ed. C.R. Devadhar, Oriental Book Agency Poona. 1951.

Brahma Purāṇa, Ed. Hari Narayana Apte, Anandashrama Series, No. 28, Poona, 1895; Translated into Kannada by Venkata Rao, Jayachamarajendra Granthamala No. 30, Mysore, 1942.

Bṛhaddevatā of Śaunaka, Ed. and Translated into English by A.A. Macdonell, Harvard Oriental Series, Motilal Banarsidass, 1965.

Bṛhaspati Smṛti, Reconstructed and Ed. by K. V. Rangaswami Aiyangar, Oriental Institute, Baroda, 1941.

Bṛhat-Kathāmañjarī of Kṣemendra, Ed. Sivadatta and K.P. Parab (2nd edition), Bombay, 1931.

Bṛhatsaṁhitā of Varāhamihira, Ed. Sudhakara Dvivedi, Kashi,1895.

Campūrāmāyaṇa of Bhoja, Ed. Vasudeva Lakshman Shastri, N.S. Press, Bombay, 1914.

Caturaṅgadīpikā of Śūlapāṇi, Ed. Manomohan Ghosh, Metropolitan Printing and Publishing House, Calcutta, 1936.

Chāndogya Upaniṣad (2nd Edition), Gita Press, Gorakhpur, 1954. Ed. Swami Swahananda, R.K. Mutt, 1975; Anandashrama Series 14, Poona, 1890.

Daśakumāracarita of Daṇḍin, Ed. and Translated by M.R. Kale, 4th edition, Motilal Banarsidass, Delhi, 1966.

Gautama Dharmasūtra, Ed. L. Srinivasacharya, Govt. Oriental Library, Mysore, 1917.

Gṛhyasūtra of Hiraṇyakeśin, Ed. J. Kirste, Vienna, 1889.

Harivaṁśa, Ed. Ramanarayana Datta Sastri, Gita Press Gorakhpur.

Harṣacarita of Bāṇabhaṭa, Ed. P.V. Kane, Motilal Banarsidass, Delhi, 1973.

Jātaka, Ed. V. Fausboll (6 vols.), London, 1877-97.

Kādaṁbarī of Bāṇabhaṭṭa, Ed. and Translated by M.R. Kale, Motilal Banarsidass, New Delhi, 1968.

Kāmasūtra, Kashi Sanskrit Series 29, Benares, 1929.

Kāṭhaka Saṁhitā, Ed. Leopold Von Schroeder, 1900.

Kathāsaritsāgara of Somadeva, Ed. Jagadish Lal Shastri, Motilal Banarsidass, 1980; Translated into English by C.H. Tawney, Munshiram Manoharlal Oriental Publishers, Delhi; Indian Reprint, Motilal Banarsidass, 1968.

Kātyāyana Śrautasūtra, Ed. Vidyadhara Sharma, Acyuta Granthamala, Kashi.

Kauśikasūtra of Atharvaveda, Ed. and Translated into English by Maurice Bloomfield, Motilal Banarsidass, 1972.

Kṛtyasāgara of Ratnapāṇi, Ed. Mahaprabhu Lal Goswami, Mithila Research Institute, Darbhanga, 1977.

Kuṭṭanīmata-Kāvya of Damodaragupta, Ed. Jagannatha Pathak, Mitra Prakasan, Allahabad, 1961.

Liṅgapurāṇa, Venkateshwara Press, Bombay, 1924.

Mahābhārata, Ed. with Nīlakaṇṭha's Commentary, ChitraShala Press, Poona, 1929-33; Critical Edition, Bhandarkar Oriental Research Institute, Poona, 1972-76;

Gita Press, Gorakhpur, 1956-58; Translated into English by P.C. Roy. Calcutta, 1884. Translated into Kannada by various scholars up to Droṇa Parvan, Bharat Darshan Printing Press, Bangalore, 1973.

Mahāsubhāṣitasaṁgraha, Ludwik Sternbach, Vols. I & 2, Vishveshwarananda Vedic Research Institute, Hoshiarpur, 1976.

Maitrāyaṇī Saṁhitā, Leopold Von Schroeder, 1881.

Mānasollāsa of Somadeva, Ed. G.K. Shrigondekar, Vol. Ill, Oriental Institute, Baroda, 1961.

Mānavaśrautasūtra, Ed. Jeannette, M. Van Gelder, New Delhi, 1961.

Manu Smṛti, Ed. J.R. Gharpure, Bombay, 1920; Translated into English in Sacred Books of the East, Vol. XXV, 1886.

Matsya Purāṇa, Ed. Sudhindra Natha Vasu, Allahabad, 1916.

Mṛcchakaṭika of Śūdraka, Ed. and Translated by M.R. Kale, Motilal Banarsidass, 1972.

Nāradīyamanusaṁhitā, Ed. Ved Kumari, Jammu & Kashmir Academy of Art, Culture and Languages, 1968.

Nirṇaya Sindhu of Kamalākara Bhaṭṭa, Ed. Panduranga Jawaji, N.S. Press, Bombay, 1905.

Nirukta of Yāska, Bombay Sanskrit Prakrit Series No. 85, 1942.

Nītisāra of Kāmandaka, Ed. T. Ganapati Sastri, Trivandrum Sanskrit Series 14, Trivandrum, 1912.

Paippalāda Saṁhitā, Ed. Durgamohan Bhattacharya, Vol. I, Sanskrit College, Calcutta, 1964.

Pañcatantra of Viṣṇuśarman, Ed. M.R. Kale, Motilal Banarsidass, 1969.

Raghuvaṁśa of Kālidāsa, Ed. M.R. Kale, Motilal Banarsidass,1969.

Rājataraṅgiṇī of Kalhaṇa, Ed. Durga Prasad, Government Central Book Depot, 1892.

Śatapatha Brāhmaṇa, Ed. several learned persons, Laxmi Venkateshwar Steam Press, Bombay, 1940.

Śiśupālavadha of Māgha, Ed. Anantarama Sastri Vetal, Kashi Sanskrit Series 69, 1929.

Śivatattva Ratnākara of Basavarāja, Ed. Oriental Research Institute, Mysore, 1964.

Skānda Mahāpurāṇa, Ed. Kshemaraja Sresthin, Venkateshwara Press, Bombay, 1908.

Śrautasūtra of Āpastamba, Ed. with the commentary of Rudradatta by Richard Garbe, Calcutta, 1882.

Subhāṣita Ratna Bhāṇḍāgāra, Ed. K.P. Parab (5th Edn.), N.S. Press, 1911.

Subhāṣita Sudhānidhi of Sāyaṇa, Ed. K. Krishnamoorthy, Karnatak University, Dharwar, 1968.

Subhāṣitāvali of Vallabhadeva, Ed. Peter Peterson (2nd Edn.). Ed. R.D. Karmarkar, Poona, 1961.

Śuka Saptati, Ed. Sundarlal Jain, Motilal Banarsidass, 1959.

Śukranīti, Ed. Brahmashankaramisra, Chowkhamba Sanskrit Series, 1968.

Taittirīya Brāhmaṇa, Ed. A. Mahadeva Sastri, Mysore, 1911; Ed. Harinarayana Apte, Anandashrama Series, Poona, 1898.

Taittirīya Saṁhitā, Ed. N.S. Sontakke and T.N. Dharmadhikari, Vaidika Samsodhana Mandala, 1972; Translated into English by A. B. Keith, Motilal Banarsidass, 1967.

Vājasaneyī Saṁhitā, Ed. Jaikrishna Dass, Hari Das Gupta, Vidya Vilas Press, 1913; Translated by Devi Chand, Hoshiarpur, 1959.

Vāsavadattā of Subandhu, Ed. L. Gray, Columbia University Press, New York, 1913.

Vīramitrodaya of Mitramiśra, Ed. Jivanand Vidyasagar Bhattacharya, Calcutta, 1875.

Viṣṇu Purāṇa, Ed. Gita Press, Gorakhpur, 1952; English Translation by H.H. Wilson (5 vols.), London, 1864-70.

Viṣṇu Smṛti, Ed. V. Krishnamacharya, The Adyar Library & Research Centre, Madras, 1964.

Vyākarṇa Mahābhāṣya, Ed. Gurukul Bhajjar, Haryana Sahitya Samsthan, 1963.

Vyavahāramayūka of Nīlakaṇṭha, Ed. Vishvanath Narayan Mandlik, Education Society's Press, Bombay, 1880.

Yājñavalkya Smṛti, Ed. Narayana Sastri Khiste and Jaganatha Sastri Hosinga, Benares, 1930.

Books in English

Agrawala, V.S., India as Known to Pāṇini, University of Lucknow, 1953, Second edition, 1963.

Apte, S.S. & Balashastri, Hardas, Glimpses of the Vedic Nation, Sri Kamakoti Publishing House, Madras, 1967.

Apte, V.M., Social and Religious Life in the Gṛhya Sūtras, The Popular Book Depot, Bombay.

Banjeri S.C., Kālidāsa Apocrypha, Varanasi, Chowkhamba Sanskrit Series, 1989.

Basham, A.L., The Wonder that was India, The Fontana Books in Association with Rupa & Co.

Benimadhab Barua, Barhut, Book Il, Indian Research Institute Publications, Fine Arts Series No. 2, 1934.

Bhat, G.K., Mṛcchakaṭika, The New Order Book Co., Ahmedabad, 1953.

Bhatta C. Panduranga, Dice-Play in Sanskrit Literature A Study, Delhi, Amar Prakashan 1985.

Bhatta, Panduranga C., Origin and Genesis of Chess, Published by Egbert Meissenburg Seevetal, Germany, 1994.

Burlingame, E.W., Buddhist Parables, Oxford University Press, 1922.

Chakradar, H.O., Social Life in Ancient India, Susil Gupta (India) Ltd., Calcutta, 1954.

Cowell, E.B., The Jātaka (Stories of the Buddha's Former Births), Cambridge University Press, 1907.

Cunningham, Alexander, The Stupa of Bharhut, Indological Book House, Varanasi, 1962.

Dandekar, R.N., Vedic Bibliography, Karnataka Publishing House, Bombay, 1946.

Devasthali, G.V., Introduction to the Study of Mṛcchakaṭika, Oriental Book House, Poona, 1951.

Dikshitar, V.R. Ramachandra, War in Ancient India, Macmillan and Co., 1948, Madras (2nd edition).

Egbert Meissenburg (Edited), Approaching the Roots of Chess, Abstracts and Papers dedicated and presented to the Organizers and Participants of the Symposium at Pondicherry University, Pondicherry, India, November 26th through 29th 1996.

Francis, H. T. & Thomas, Eales, Richard, Chess: The History of a Game, Ishi Press, 1985.

Franklin Edgerton, Vikrama's Adventures; or, Thirty-Two Tales of the Throne, Edited in four Different Recensions and Translated with an Introduction, 2 vols. Cambridge/ Mass.1926.

Frey, Richard L., Rules of Games according to Hoyle, Fawcett Publications, Greenwich CONN, 1956.

Gharpure, J. R., The Collection of Hindu Law Texts, Vol. Il, part IV, Girgaon, Bombay, 1939.

Gonda, J., A History of Indian Literature, Vol. I, Otto Harpassowitz, Wiesbaden, 1975.

...........Hymns of the Ṛgveda not employed in the Solmn Ritual, North Holland Publishing Co., Amsterdam, Oxford, N.Y., 1978.

Gupta, D. K., Society and Culture in the Time of Daṇḍin Meharchand Lacchmandas, Delhi, 1972.

Held, G.J., The Mahābhārata, An Ethnological Study, London, 1935.

Hopkins, E.W., Epic Mythology, Motilal Banarsidass, 1974.

...........The Social and Military Position of the Ruling Caste in Ancient India, Bharat-Bharati, Varanasi, 1972.

lyengar, P.T. Srinivas, Life in Ancient India in the Age of the Mantras, Srinivasa Varadachari & Co., Madras, 1912,

Jauhari, Manorama, Politics and Ethics in Ancient India, Bharatiya Vidya Prakashan, Varanasi, 1968.

Jayaswal, K.P, Manu and Yājñavalkya, Butterworth & Co. (India) Ltd., Calcutta, 1930.

Jayaswal, A History of India, AD 150-350 AD; cf. nature of Samudra Gupta's conquests.

Jha, Ganga Nath, The Laws of Manu (Vol. I, pt.1), University of Calcutta, 1920.

Jolly, Julius, The Code of Manu, Trubner & Co., Ludgate Hill, 1887.

Kaegi, Adolf, The Ṛgveda (2nd edn.), Amarko Book Agency, New Delhi, 1975.

Kane, P.V., History of Dharmaśāstra, Vols. I & Ill, Bhandarkar Oriental Research Institute, Poona, 1930 & 1946.

Kashikar, C.G., Sutras of Bhāradvāja, Part I, Vaidika Samsodhana Mandal, Poona, 1964.

Katre, S.M., Dictionary of Pāṇini, Part Il, Deccan College, Poona, 1968.

Keith, A.B., The Religion and Philosophy of the Veda and Upaniṣads, Harvard Oriental Series, 1925.

Lakshman Sarup, Nighanṭu and Nirukta, Motilal Banarsidass 1962.

Macdonell, A.A., History of Sanskrit Literature, Munshiram Manoharlal, Delhi, 1958.

Macdonell, A.A. & Keith, A.B., Vedic Index of Names and Subjects, Motilal Banarsidass, Vols. I & Il, Varanasi, 1958.

McCrindle, John Watson, "Ancient India as described by Megasthenes and Arrian"... Being a translation of the fragments of the Indica of Megasthenes, 1877, 1926.

McKay, Ernest John Henry, The Indus Civilisation (On

the Results of the Excavations in the Province Sind 1921-1931) London 1935.

Manfred A.J. Eder and Franz Josef Lang (Edited), Antique Indian Chessmen, Forderkreis Schach-Geschichtsforschung e.V. Kelkheim/Ts, Germany, 1997.

Manfred A.J. Eder, (Edited), Working Papers, Chess Originated in India, Four Contributions, Forderkreis Schach-Geschichtsforschung e.V, Kelkheim/Ts, Germany, 2000.

Manfred A.J. Eder & Irving L. Finkel (Edited), Working Papers "Indian Views", A Collection of Papers on Chess and other Board Games, Forderkreis Schach-Geschichtsforschung e. V, Kelkheim/Ts, Germany, 2001.

Manfred A.J. Eder, (Edited) Working Papers Mission Kannauj 2020, Forderkreis Schach-Geschichtsforschung e.V., Kelkheim/Ts, Germany, 2020.

Marshall, Mohejo-daro and the Indus Civilisation, Asian Educational Services, New Delhi, Vol. II. 2004.

Mainkar, T.G., Mysticism in the Ṛgveda, Popular Book Depot, Bombay, 1961.

Majumdar, R.C., The Vedic Age, Allen & Unwin Ltd., London, 1951.

Marshall, Sir John, Mohenjo-Daro, and the Indus Civilization, London, 1931.

Max Muller, F., Sacred Books of the Buddhists (Translated by various Oriental scholars), Oxford University Press, London, 1843-1922.

Michael Mark, Antique Indian Chess Sets, Forderkreis Schach-Geschichtsforsechung e.V, Kelkheim/Ts, Germany, 1997.

Mitra, Veda, India of Dharmasūtras, Arya Book Depot, New Delhi, 1965.

Muir, J., Original Sanskrit Texts, Vol. V, London, 1884.

Murray, H.J.R., A History of Chess, Oxford 1913. Reprinted in 1962, 1969, 1988.

Nirbed Ray and Amitabha Ghosh, (Edited), Sedentary Games of India, The Asiatic Society, Calcutta, 1999.

Puri, B.N., India in the Time of Patañjali, Bharatiya Vidya Bhavan, Bombay, 1968.

Pusalkar, A.D., Bhāsa-A Study, Meharchand Lacchmandas, Sanskrit Book Depot, Lahore, 1940.

Raghavan, V., Festivals, Sports and Pastimes of India, B.L Institute of Learning and Research, Ahmedabad, 1979.

Ragozin, Z.A., Vedic India as Embodied Principally in the Ṛgveda, T. Fisher Unwin Ltd., London, 1895.

Ram Gopal, India / of Vedic Kalpasūtra, National Publishing House, Delhi, 1959.

Rangaswami Aiyangar, K.V, Rājadharma, Adyar, 1941.

Rapson, E.J., (Edited), The Cambridge History of India. Vol. I. Ancient India. Second Indian Reprint, Delhi [etc.] 1962.

Renou, Louis, Bibliographe Vedique, Paris, 1931.

Rhys-Davids, T.W., Buddhist India, Indological Book House, Delhi, 1970.

Saletore. R.N. Life in the Gupta Age, The Popular Book Depot, Bombay, 1943.

Sen, Chitrabhanu, A Dictionary of the Vedic Rituals, Concept Publishing Co., Delhi, 1978.

Sen Gupta, N.C., Evolution of Ancient Indian Law, Eastern Law House, Calcutta, 1953.

Sharma, Ramashraya, A Socio-Political Study of the Rāmāyaṇa, Motilal Banarsidass, 1971.

Sharma, R.N., Culture and Civilization as Revealed in the Śrautasūtras, Nag Publishers, Delhi, 1977.

Sharma, S.N., A History of Vedic Literature, Chowkhamba Sanskrit Series, Varanasi, 1973.

Shastri, Ajay Mitra, India As Seen in the Bṛhat -Saṁhitā of Varāhamihira, Motilal Banarsidass, 1969.

India as Seen in the Kuṭṭanīmata of Dāmodaragupta, Motilal Banarsidass, 1975.

Swami Vishveshvarananda & Swami Nityananda, A Complete Alphabetical Index of All the Words in the Ṛgveda, N.S. Press, Bombay, 1908.

Tawney, C.H., The Kathākośa, Oriental Translation Fund, New Series, Il, London, 1895.

Thadani, N.V., Thy Mystery of the Mahābhārata, Bharat Publishing House, Karachi, 1934.

Thime, P Indological Studies, American Oriental Society, 1962.

Upadhyaya, B.S., India in Kālidāsa, Kitabistan, Allahabad, 1947.

Vaidya, C.V., History of Sanskrit Literature, Vol. I Śruti (Vedic) Period, Poona, 1930.

...........The Mahābhārata — Criticism, A.J. Cambridge & Co., Bombay, 1905.

Varma, Satyakama, Studies in Indology, Bharatiya Prakashan, Delhi, 1976.

Varma, Siddheshwar, The Etymologies of Yāska, V.V. R. Institute, Hoshiarpur, 1953.

Voogt, Alexander J. de, Indian Archaeology- IIAS, 1995, Leiden.

Voogt, Alexander J. de (Edited), New Approaches to Board Games Research, Asian Origins and Future Perspectives, International Institute for Asian Studies, Leiden, 1995.

Vyas, S.N., India in the Rāmāyaṇa Age, Atma Ram & Sons, 1967.

Wheeler, Mortimer, The Indus Civilization, The Cambridge History of India, Cambridge University Press, 1953.

Winternitz, M., History of Indian Literature, Vol. I, part I, Translated into English by Mrs. S. Kelkar, University of Calcutta, 1959; Vol. III, part Il, Translated by Subhadra Jha, Motilal Banarsidass, Delhi, 1967.

Articles in Journals

Agrawala, V.S. "Terracotta Figurines of Ahichhatra, District Bareilly, U.P." in Ancient India, Bulletin of the Archaeological Survey of India, Number-4, Double Number: July 1947-January 1948, p. 104-179, Calcutta.

Altekar, A.S, "Report on Kumrahar Excavations 1951-1955", Patna p. 119.

Basak, R., Indian Society as Pictured in Mṛcchakaṭika, Indian Historical Quarterly, Vol. I, Calcutta, June 1929, pp. 299-325.

Bidev Pavle, "New investigations about chess origin", Mail Chess, Beograd, vol. 5, 1951/52, No 7, November 1951, 9-15; No 9 (January 1952).

Bidev Pavle, "How Old is Chess", British Chess Magazine, St. Leonards on Sea, 107, 1987.

Bhatt, G.H., The Draupadīvastrāpaharaṇa Episode an Interpolation in the Mahābhārata, Journal Oriental Research, Madras, vol. XVIII, part 11, pp. 170-178.

Bhatta, Panduranga C., "A Note on Rules and Conventions connected with Dice-Play', Vishveshvarananda Indological Journal, Hoshiarpur, 1985, Vol. XXIII, Pts i-ii.

..........."Antiquity of Indian Board Games" in Alexander J. de. Voogt (Ed.), *New Approaches to Board Games Research: Asian Origins and Future Perspectives,* International Institute for Asian Studies, Leiden, 1995.

..........."References to Astapada and Caturanga in Select Sanskrit Works: An Observation', The Adyar Library Bulletin, Madras, 1995.

..........."Analysis of the Game of Dice", *Sedentary Games of India,* (Ed.) Nirbed Ray and Amitabha Ghosh, The Asiatic Society, Calcutta, 1999.

..........."Indian Origin of Chess: An Overview", The Annals of BORI, LXXXIV, Poona, 2004.

..........."Dice- play related stories from India: Some general observations" in *Festschrift in Honour of Alessandro Sanvito,* (Ed.) Luca D' Ambrosio, Antonio Rosino, Published by Vindobona, Refordis Verlag, Austria, 2010.

..........."Origin of Chess in Relation to War and Piece as Gleaned from Sanskrit Literature" in: Indian Views, November 2001, p. 15-18, Forderkreis Schach-Geschichtsforschung e.V., Kelkheim/Ts (First presented at the 4th Symposium Initiativ-Gruppe Konigstein, entitled 'Searching for Facts, August 1997, Wiesbaden).

Bhattacarya, D.M, The Palm-Leaf Manuscripts of the Paippalādasaṁhitā, Textual Importance of the New Finds, Adyar Library Bulletin, XXV, 1961.

Bock-Raming, A, "The Varieties of Indian Chess Through the Ages", The Chess Collector, London, vol. IV, 1993/94, April 1994.

..........."The literary Sources of Indian Chess and Related Board Games", in A.J. de Voogt (ed.). New Approaches to Board Games Research: Asian Origins and Future Perspectives, International Institute of Asian Studies Working Papers Series 3, Leiden, 1995.

..........."The Game Board in Indian Chess and Other Board Games", Abstracts, International Symposium on Approaching the Roots of Chess, Pondicherry University, 1996.

.... "Analytical Assessment of the Contribution for the symposium on 'Approaching the Roots of Chess', Pondicherry University, 26th-29th November 1996 together with a report on the game pieces and chessmen exhibited in the museums of Madras and Hyderabad", Antique Indian Chessmen, Manfred A.J. Eder und Franz Josef Lang. Forderkreis Schach-Geschichtsforschung e.V. Kelkheim/Ts. Germany. 1997.

..........."The literary Sources of Indian Chess and Related Board Games", in A.J. de Voogt (ed.). New Approaches to Board Games Research: Asian Origins and Future Perspectives, International Institute of Asian Studies Working Papers Series 3, Leiden, 1995, pp. 112-124.

..........."The Gambling Scenes of Bharhut and Bodh-Gaya-A Critical Assessment of Their Previous Interpretations and Some New Suggestions" in Asiatische Studien-Etudes Aisatiques, Peter Lang, Bern,2000.

Brown, W.N., "Ṛgveda, 10.34 as an Act of Truth", Bharatiya Vidya, Vols. XX-XXI, Bombay, 1960-61.

Brown W.N., "The Indian Games of Pachisi, Chaupar and Chausar" in Chakravarti Chintaharan, "Sanskrit Works on the Game of Chess", The Indian Historical Quarterly, Calcutta, 14, 1938.

De Vreese, K., The Game of Dice in Ancient India, Orientalia Neerlandica, The Netherlands Oriental Society, Leiden, 1948.

Eder, Manfred, A.J, "Terracotta-Figures from Kanauj: Chessmen?"-Chapter II- Half an Answer and more Questions", Paper presented at the 19th International Congress of South Asian Archaeology, University of Bologna in Ravenna, July 2007.

Finkel, I.L. "Board Games and Fortune Telling: A Case from Antiquity," in A.J. de Voogt (ed.), New Approaches to Board Games Research: Asian Origins and Future Perspectives, International Institute of Asian Studies Working Papers Series 3, Leiden, 1995.

Greenberg, H.J, "An Anti-Wargame? The Origin of Chess is in India's Golden Age" in Chess-Life, London, June 1986, p. 38.

Grierson, George, Guessing the Number of Vibhītaka Seeds, Journal Royal Asiatic Society, 1904, pp. 356ff.

Hellmut Rosenfeld, "On the Morphogenesis of Games, especially of Chess and Playing Cards", The Playing Card Journal of the International vol. IX, No 3, 1981.

Hiram Cox, "On the Burmha Game of Chess: Compared with the Indian, Chinese, and Persian Game of the same Denomination", Sedentary Games of India, Nirbed Ray and Amitabha Ghosh, The Asiatic Society, 1999.

Indra, Ideologies of War and Peace in Ancient India, Vedic Research Institute, Hoshiarpur, 1957.

Irving L. Finkel, "The Sedentary Games of India: An Introduction", Sedentary Games of India, Edited by Nirbed Roy and Amitabha Ghosh, The Asiatic Society Calcutta, 1999.

Issak Linder, "My Personal Opinion on the Origin of Chess", Approaching the Roots of Chess, Abstract and Papers dedicated and presented to the Organisers and Participants of the Symposium at Pondicherry University, 1996.

Keith, A.B., The Game of Dice, J.R.A.S., July 1908, pp. 823-828.

Krishnamurti, "The Indian Games of Pachisi, Chaupar, and Chausar, India and Indology", Ed. by Rosane Rocher, American Institute of Indian Studies, U.S.A., 1978. pp. 297-302.

Krishnamurti. B, (ed.) Studies in Indian Linguistics. M.B. Emeneau Ṣaṣṭipūrti Volume, Poona, 1968.

Krishna Murthy, K. "Dice Play and its Archaeological Coroboration at Nāgārjunakoṇḍa - Andhra Pradesh," The Orissa Historical Research Journal, 1961, Vol. X.

Kunjunni Raja, K., Games, Sports and Amusements in the Vedic Age, Veda Samīkṣā, Ed. by E.R. Sreekrishna Sarma, S.V. University, Tirupati, 1967.

Leander A. Feiler, Searching For Traces of the Origin of Chess In India Chapter III: Visits to Archaeological Museums, The Former Eastern Core Territories of the Guptas, Working Papers: Mission Kannauj 2020, FSG, Edited by Manfred A.J. Eder, Kelkhem/Taunus, Germany, 2020.

Lohuizen de Leuuw, J. E, "What was the Purpose of the Terracotta Animal Figurines Discovered at Kondapur"? Kusumāñjali, New Interpretation of

Indian Art & Culture. Sh. C. Sivaramamurti Commemoration Volume, Vol. II. Delhi 1987.

Macdonell Arthur Anthony, "On the Origin and Early History of Chess", Journal of the Royal Asiatic Society of Great Britain and Ireland for 1898, London, NS 30, 1898.

Murray H.J.R, "How Old is Chess"? In British Chess Magazine, Leeds, 56, 1936.

Manfred AJ Eder, "Approaching the Roots of Chess by trying a definition in Historic Context" presented at the International Symposium on "Approaching the Roots of Chess" held at Pondicherry University, India, 26th-29th November 1996.

Manfred AJ. Eder, "Proto-Chess: No! Proto Chessmen: Yes!" New Considerations and Conclusions on the Origin of Chess", Working Papers: Mission Kannauj 2020, FSG, Edited by Manfred A.J. Eder, Kelkhem/Taunus, Germany, 2020.

Patkar, M.M., The Role of Gambling in Ancient Indian Society, VIJ, vol. 1, No. 1. March 1963.

Raghavan, V., Presidential Address of the 21st Conference of All India Oriental Conference, 1961.

Rath, Tridibnath, The Indoor and Outdoor Games in Ancient India, PIHC, 1939.

Rajendran C, "A New Look into the Caturanga Passages in Harsacarita", p.51. Working Papers: Mission Kannauj 2020, FSG, Edited by Manfred A.J. Eder, Kelkhem/Taunus, Germany, 2020.

Raman KV (Ed) 'Archaeological Excavations in Kanchipuram', Tamil Civilization, Tamil University, Thanjavur, 1987.

Sanito, Alexandro Sanito, "Some Remarks upon the Origin of Chess", Abstracts and papers dedicated and presented to the organisers and participants of the first ever international symposium organized at Pondicherry University, India in 1996 on 'Approaching the Roots of Chess', 1996.

Siddharth Y. Wakankar, "A Survey of Sanskrit Works on the Game of Chess", Journal of the Oriental Institute, University Baroda, Baroda, vol. 34, 1985/86, Numbers 3-4, March-June 1986.

..........."Chaturanga, Buddhibala and Their Literary Description", Abstracts, International Symposium on Approaching the Roots of Chess, Pondicherry University, 1996.

Syed Renate, "Śarvavarman Maukhari of Kanauj and the Way of Chess, *Caturanga,* from India to Persia: Facts and Theories," Working Papers: Mission Kannauj 2020, FSG, Edited by Manfred A.J. Eder, Kelkhem/Taunus, Germany, 2020.

Syed Renate, "War, Peace and Chess, Bana's References to "Terracotta Chessmen" and "Discourses on War", in the Harsacarita," Working Papers: Mission Kannauj 2020, FSG, Edited by Manfred A.J. Eder, Kelkhem/Taunus, Germany, 2020.

Thieme, Paul "Chess and Backgammon (tric-trac) in Sanskrit Literature", Indological Studies in Honour of W. Norman Brown, ed. Ernest Bender, New Haven 1962.

Tridibnath Ray, "The indoor and outdoor games in Ancient India," Proceedings of Indian Historical Congress, 1939.

Voogt, Alexander J. de. "Antiquity of Indian Board Games: A New Approach", New Approaches to Board Research (Ed.), Asian Origins and Future Perspectives (Ed) by, IIAS, Leiden, 1995.

Vreese, K. de: The Game of Dice in Ancient India in Orientalia Neerlandica, Leiden 1948.

William Jones, "On the Indian Game of Chess", The Asiatick Researches, Vol. II. 1790 under the title On the Indian Game of Chess By the President. This was the seventh annual deliberation of Sir William Jones as the President of the Asiatic Society of Bengal. Reprinted in Sendentary Games of India, Nirbed Ray and Amitabha Ghosh (Ed.) The Asiatic Society Calcutta, 1999.

Whyld, K. "The Birthplace of Chess-Some Reflections" in Abstracts and Papers Symposium 'Approaching the Roots of Chess' in Pondicherry 1996, edited by E. Meissenburg, Seevetal, November 1996.

Encyclopedias

Encyclopedia Britannica, Vols. 7 & 9, Published by William Benton.

Encyclopedia of Religion and Ethics, Vols. 4 & 6, Ed. James Hastings.

Encyclopedia of Social Sciences, Vol. 6, Ed. Edwin R.A. Seligman, New York.

Kannada Viśvakośa, Vol. 8, Ed. Kannada Adhyayana Samste, University of Mysore, 1975.

Purāṇanāma Cūḍāmaṇi (Kannada), Ed. Benegal Ram Rao, Prasaranga. University of Mysore, 1977.

Purāṇic Encyclopedia, Ed. Vettam Mani, Motilal Banarsidass, Delhi, 1975.

Lexicons

Amarakośa of Amarasiṁha, Ed. Pt. Sivadatta, N.S. Press, Bombay, 1929.

Anekārthasaṁgraha of Hemacandra, Ed. Chowkhamba Sanskrit Series, 1969.

Ekārthanāmamālā-Dvyakṣaranāmamālā of Saubhari, Ed. Deccan College, Poona, 1955.

Kalpadrukośa of Kesava, Ed. Ramavatara Sarma, Oriental Institute, Baroda, 1928.

Sanskrit Worterbuch, Petersburg, 1858.

Vaijayantī of Yādavaprakāśa, Ed. Haragovinda Sastri, Chowkhamba Sanskrit Series, Varanasi, 1971.

Reports

Archaeological Survey of India, Annual Report, 1908-09.

Archaeological Survey of India, New Imperial Series, No. 22, 1914.

Archaeological Survey (Western), India Reports, 1923-24.

Hindu, The (English Daily), Madras, 14 January 1978.

Northern India Patrika, Allahabad, 3 November, 1959.

APPENDIX

Appendix I: Association of Dice-Play with Religion

The connection between gambling and religion has; drawn the attention of scholars like Prof. Held G.J. As noted earlier the word deva (God) is derived from the root div, meaning, "sport". *Devana* and *dyūta* refer to gambling. A study of the references to dice-play found both in Vedic and Classical literature suggests the link between gambling and religion. The role assigned to dice-play in sacrifices like *agnyādheya* and *rājasūya* is already noted. One God who is, always found associated with dice-paly is Śiva. According to the Brāhmaṇas and the Śrautasūtras the wood for making the altar for Rudra in the *rājasūya* had to be fetched from the house of an *akṣāvāpa* (superintendent of dice-play).

Śiva is described as playing dice with Pārvatī in some Purāṇas and classical literary works. In the Skāndapurāṇa there are three references to Śiva playing the game of dice with Pārvatī. The Matsyapurāṇa also refers to such an event.[2] The Brahmapurāṇa contains another reference to the game played by this divine couple on a Dīpāvalī day. In one of the references found in the Mahābhārata, Śiva is represented as playing dice with his spouse being seated on a mountain. It is stated there that Śiva did not care even for a god like Indra as he was enraptured by the akṣas.[3]

An interesting incident recorded in the Great Epic is that before commencing the *rājasūya* sacrifice, Yudhiṣṭhira had a dream in which Rudra (i.e., Śiva) appeared with his face southwards, which was a bad omen indicating his imminent downfall.[4]

In the Kathāsaritsāgara, the story of Naravāhanadatta refers to Śiva's dice-play with Pārvatī.[5] Bhartṛhari's Vairāgyaśataka figuratively describes a dice-play between the god of death and his wife. Śiva is considered as the destroyer of the Universe and Bhartṛhari's reference may be taken as applying to Śiva also. To prove the association of Śiva with this game, Prof. Held G.J., points out that the Bower manuscript of Pāśakakevalī (a work which uses the throws of dice-play for assessing the astrological data) contains salutations to Nandi-Rudreśvara, Īśvara, Śiva and Rudra.[6]

Kapardas (cowries) are used in this game and *Kapardin* is a by-name of Rudra-Śiva. According to Prof. Held G.J., Rudra-Śiva is especially the "god of initiation" and the special function of a gambling-demon was assigned to Kali.

He argues that Kali resembles Kālī the spouse of Śiva. In the Mahābhārata one verse 'personifies the six *ṛtus* (periods into which the year is divided) playing the game of dice.' Prof. Held observes in this context: "One should not think of all this in the spirit of a game as a pastime, but as a ritual due to a god. World order is maintained by means of the ritual. The gods assist in this by sacrifice. Rudra-Śiva also contributes his part by means of a heavenly gaming-ceremony."[8]

Gambling also plays a prominent role on two festivals called *yakṣarātri* and *kaumudījāgara*. *Yakṣarātri* corresponds to the *dīpāvalī* festival of the present day. According to the Caturvargacintāmaṇi gambling is one of the important items of this festival.[9] There is an unpublished manuscript named Kārtīka-śuklapratipad dyūtakrīḍāvidhiḥ which deals with the significance of dice-play on the *dīpāvalī* day.[10] *Kaumudījāgara* or *kojāgara* is done on the full-moon night of *Āśvina*. The Kṛtyakaumudī of Raghunandana refers to *dyūta* that is to be played on this day. According to him those desirous of fortune should remain sleepless playing the game of dice during this night and worshipping the goddess of fortune.[11] The Liṅgapurāṇa quoted in Kṛtyasāgara also contains a similar reference.[12] The Nilamatapurāṇa prescribes gambling on *dīpāvalī* day to know the prospects of the players in the new year.[13]

Reference is already made to the Gṛhyasūtras prescribing gambling as part of an expiatory ceremony for curing a boy attacked by dog-demon.

According to Prof. Majumdar R.C., dice-play was elevated to the rank of religious ceremonies only to restrict indiscriminate gambling since its evil effect on men in society was quite well-known.[14]

References

1. TB, 1-7-3; KS, XV-4; TS 1-8-9.
2. Matsyapurāṇa, 154-520.
3. M.Bh., Ādi, 197.14.
4. Ibid., Sabhā, 46.13.
5. KSS, CX.155.
6. ASI, NIS, No. 22, part V, plates XLIII-XVIII, 1914.
7. M.Bh., X11L.43.5.
8. M.Bh., An Ethno. study, p. 243f.
9. Caturvargacintāmaṇi, Kālanirṇaya, p. 616.
10. Paper manuscripts preserved in Oriental Research Institute, Mysore, Ms. No. C. 696/12.
11. Kṛtyakaumudī on *dīpāvalī* festival.
12. Kṛtyasāgara, p. 33.
13. Nīlamatapurāṇa, verses 416 & 417. For further details

see Gode P.K's article entitled "Studies in the History of Hindu Festivals-Some Notes on the History of Dīvālī Festival" in the Annals of Bhandarkar Oriental Research Institute, Poona, Vol. XXVI, pp. 216-262, 1946.

14. The Vedic Age, p. 431.

Appendix II: A Glossary of Technical Terms Used

akṣa	die used in gambling.
akṣakitava	a gambler
akṣakuśala	one skilled in dice
dakṣaglaha	gambling
akṣatattva	the science of dice.
akṣadevana	gambling.
akṣadevin	a gambler.
akṣadyūta	gambling with dice.
akṣadhūrta	a gambler.
akṣapari	short of one die.
akṣapāta or akṣapātana	throw of dice.
akṣabhūmi	ground on which dice are cast.
akṣamālā	garland of dice
akṣarāja	king of dice (another name for *kali*).
akṣavṛtta	anything that happens in gambling
akṣaśauṇḍa	one skilled in gambling.
akṣasūkta	Gambler's Hymn.
akṣahṛdaya	the 'heart' or secret of gambling.
akṣāvāpa	superintendent of a gambling house.

akṣāvapana	box for keeping dice.
adhidevana	place for gambling.
adhikalpin	a gambler.
aṣṭāpada	a board with 64 squares.
ākṣika	a gambler.
adinavādarśa	a gambler.
āyānaya	a safety square on the dice-board.
ākanda	a gambler.
iriṇa	a place for throwing dice.
kaparda or *kapardikā*	cowrie shell.
kali	name of a die or the side of a die marked with one dot. Indicates a losing throw.
kitava	a gambler.
kūṭadevin	a fraudulent player.
kūṭākṣa	a false or fake die.
kūṭākṣadevin	one who plays with fake dice.
kṛta	name of a die or a side of a die marked with four dots: a lucky throw.
gardabhī	an unlucky throw.
graha (also *grābha*)	a throw of dice.
glaha	game of dice; a stake.
tretā	name of a die or the side of a die marked with 3 dots.
durodarāḥ	a dice player; a heap of dice.
durodaram	gambling.
devana	gambling.
dyūta	gambling.
dyūtakara	a gambler.

dyūtakāraka	the keeper of a gambling house.
dyūtakiṅkarī	a female slave won at dice-play.
dyūtakrīḍā	play with dice.
dyūtadharma	rule(s) of gambling.
dyūtapalāyita	one who has run away from the game of dice.
dyūtapūrṇimā	the full-moon day of *āśvina* spent in games of chance, to honour goddess Laksmi.
dyūtapratipad	the first day of the bright fortnight in the month of *kārttika*, celebrated with gambling.
dyūtaphalaka	gambling board
dyūtabhūmi	gambling place (see also *akṣabhūmi*).
dyūtamaṇḍala or dyūtamaṇḍalī	*circle* of gamblers
dyūtavṛtti	a professional gambler; keeper of a gambling house.
dyūta-vyavahāra	judicial proceedings regarding gambling.
dyūtaśālā or dyūtasabhā	a gambling house.
dyūtādyakṣa	superintendent of gambling.
dyūtābhiyoga	suit regarding gambling.
dvāpara	a die or the side of a die marked with 2 dots.
dūrta-kitava	a gambler; a winning gambler.
dūrtamaṇḍala	assembly of gamesters.
nardita	a kind of dice; a throw of dice.
pañcakadyūta	name of a game played with five dice.
paṇa	a wager.

paṇakrīḍā	gambling.
pāśa or pāśaka	a die.
pāśā krīḍā	dice play.
pāśakapīṭha	a gambling table.
bradhna	a die.
vibhītaka	nuts of the *vibhītaka* tree (Terminalia Belerica).
sabhā	gambling house.
sabhāvin	keeper of the gambling house.
sabhāsthaṇu	one who is skilled at dice.
sabhika	keeper of a gambling house.
sādhudevin	one who is skilled at dice.
salāka	a die.
śāra or śāri	a piece used on draught.
śāri-phalaka	a board for playing draught.
śvaghnin	a gambler

INDEX

A

B

C

D

T

V

W

Y